*Inferno Programming
with Limbo*

Inferno Programming with Limbo

Phillip Stanley-Marbell
Carnegie Mellon University

WILEY

Library of Congress Cataloging-in-Publication Data

(to follow)

British Library Cataloguing in Publication Data

A catalogue record for this book is available from the British Library

ISBN 0 470 84352 7

Typeset in 10/12 pt Palatino by T&T Productions Ltd, London.

Printed and bound by CPI Group (UK) Ltd, Croydon, CR0 4YY

This book is printed on acid-free paper responsibly manufactured from sustainable forestry in which at least two trees are planted for each one used for paper production.

C9780470843529_290623

To my friend Nebahat Noyan
Benim kuçuk mavi çiçeğim

Contents

Preface

The subject matter of the text is the development of software for the Inferno operating system, using the Limbo programming language.

Inferno is an operating system for building distributed applications in networked environments. It is targeted at resource-constrained computing systems such as set-top boxes, PDAs and point-of-sale terminals, which usually have limited computing resources, are networked and often need to handle multimedia such as streaming audio or video. It was designed from the ground up to address these issues.

Inferno derives its heritage from the creators of the Unix and Plan 9 operating systems and the C and C++ programming languages, Lucent Technologies' Bell Labs. Inferno has recently been made freely available to the general public in binary form, and source code is available for a small fee under an open-source-like licence. Limbo is the programming language in which applications for Inferno are written.

Purpose

This book is intended as a comprehensive guide for programmers who wish to develop applications for the Inferno operating system, with an emphasis on taking advantage of its unique capabilities. The text provides a brief introduction to the installation and use of Inferno, and an in-depth exposition and solid reference for developing Inferno applications in Limbo.

A reader with no prior experience of Inferno, or of related technologies, should be able to use the text both as an introduction to Inferno and as a reference on developing Inferno applications in Limbo.

Target Audience

The text is targeted primarily at professionals who will be developing applications in the Limbo language for Inferno and is therefore structured as a self-study text. It is also suitable for use as a college-level text, providing end-of-chapter exercises to further develop the concepts introduced in each chapter. For both the professional audience and the college student, a familiarity with programming languages such as Pascal, C/C++ or Java is assumed. It is not meant to be an introductory programming text.

Every attempt has been made to keep the book as self-contained as possible, making it an ideal introduction as well as a handy reference. Readers will appreciate the practical approach of the text. Each chapter concludes with an analysis of a complete representative application that uses concepts introduced in the chapter, which may be used as a starting point for developing the reader's own applications. The example discussion further serves to point out common pitfalls when programming with concepts introduced in that chapter. The tone of the book is intended to be refreshing, and every attempt is made to keep the presentation and discussions lively.

Material Covered

1 Introduction
   An introduction to the Inferno Operating System, its origin, design and use. A description of the heritage of the Limbo language, its origins and how it compares to other contemporary programming languages. Resources as files and per-process name spaces. Installing Inferno and setting up user accounts. The Inferno application development environment.

2 An Overview of Limbo
   An introduction to Limbo programming. The basic structure of Limbo programs. Operators. Flow control.

3 Data Types
   An overview of the basic data types in Limbo.

4 Using Modules
   Using modules to structure applications. Developing Inferno built-in modules.

5 System Input and Output
   Performing program input and output in Limbo. The Inferno built-in system module.

6 Programming with Threads

Writing multi-threaded applications in Limbo. Thread creation and control. Thread name spaces. The Inferno `/prog` interface.

7 Channels

Channels as communication paths. Simple fileservers—Files connected to channels.

8 Styx Servers

Introduction to the Styx protocol and its use in Inferno. Styx message formats. Intercepting Styx messages. Developing Limbo Styx servers.

9 Networking

Introduction to inter-networking in Inferno. Inferno's `/net` filesystem and network protocol stacks. Writing networking applications using the `/net` filesystem interface. Writing networking applications using Sys module calls. Developing applications that access the WWW. Dealing with HTML.

10 Cryptographic Facilities

The Inferno security model. Configuring Certificate Authorities. Mutual authentication.

11 Graphics

Introduction to graphics in Inferno. The `/dev/draw` interface. The Inferno Draw built-in module. The Inferno Tk and Wmlib modules.

Appendices Limbo language grammar. Some useful module interface definitions. Selected manual pages.

The source code for the examples included in the book, together with additional material such as more Limbo applications, updates to the text to reflect changes in Inferno and Limbo, and corrections, are available from the book's Web page at `http://www.gemusehaken.org/ipwl/`.

Conventions

Throughout the text, a handful of conventions are used to distinguish between different types of material.

Path names are listed relative to the root of the Inferno distribution and are displayed in a `teletype` font, in-line in the text. For example, `/appl/cmd/sort.b`. IP addresses and host names are also displayed in a `teletype` font.

Code fragments and command shell transcripts are listed in shaded boxes such as the following:

```
#
# Limbo source or command shell transcript
#
```

Variable names and Limbo module names appear in `teletype` font when they are being discussed; for example, one may refer to a variable `variablename`.

Inferno command-line utilities and other services are displayed in italics, with the section number of their respective manual pages in parenthesis. For example, the manual page for the application for displaying manual pages is referred to as *man(1)*, as its page is in Section 1 of the Inferno manual. Other applications, such as those developed in this text, are referred to by their name in italics.

Acknowledgments

Thanks to all those who provided encouragement at various stages of this work, spread over almost five years. I could not possibly mention by name all those who, either by their encouraging remarks or outright derision, have helped keep me motivated. Truman Boyes, Russ Cox, Vasilios Daskalopoulos, Ben Lui, Nebahat Noyan, Matthew Riben, Seth Rubenstein and Simon Wong all read early versions of the manuscript and provided valuable feedback. Truman Boyes, Ben Brewer, Jon Oberton, Andrew Sylvia and the collective energies of suspicious.org helped refine the final versions of the manuscript.

Bengt Kleberg, Vasilios Daskalopoulos and Vincent Matossian deserve special mention for their detailed reviews of many of the chapters of this book. Their feedback was invaluable. The artwork preceding each chapter was created (all in one night!) by Nebahat Noyan.

Last, but most importantly, I would like to thank the fine folk at Wiley and elsewhere who helped make this happen: Karen Mosman and Gaynor Redvers-Mutton (my editors in succession at Wiley), Jill Jeffries, Robert Hambrook (my production editor at Wiley), Jonathan Wainwright (my copy-editor at T&T Productions), whom I drove crazy with PDF sticky notes (almost 400 in one revision!)—Thanks Jon!—and countless others whom I will probably never know.

This document was typeset using free software. The typesetting was done in LaTeX, primarily on computers running derivatives of the 4.4BSD operating system.

Phillip Stanley-Marbell
Pittsburgh, PA

1

Introduction

This chapter provides an introduction to Inferno, its history, underlying concepts and construction. Also described in this chapter are the procedures for installing and configuring an Inferno system, and the basic tools provided for editing, compiling and debugging Limbo programs.

1.1 What is Inferno?

Inferno is an operating system well suited for building networked applications which run in heterogeneous environments. It runs on a variety of hardware architectures, such as the Intel x86 family, various flavors of the MIPS architecture, different variants of the ARM architecture such as the ARM Thumb and Intel StrongARM, the SPARC architecture and many more. Inferno was designed to be easily ported to a wide variety of architectures, and support for new microprocessor and system architectures is easily added. It is unique in being available to run directly over bare hardware, as traditional operating systems such as Unix do, as well as being available as an emulator. The Inferno emulator virtualizes the entire operating system, and Inferno applications and end users are presented with an identical interface on the native platform or on the emulator running over another host operating system.

The supported host platforms for the Inferno emulator include Sun Solaris for SPARC processors, Solaris for Intel x86 processors, Windows 95/98/ME/NT/2000, HP-UX, IRIX, OpenBSD, FreeBSD, Linux and Plan 9. Applications written for the emulator, or for the native platform, can be run on any Inferno system without recompilation. This is made possible by Inferno's use of a virtual machine to shield applications from the details of the underlying hardware. Having versions of Inferno that run both on bare hardware and in emulated environments lends a degree of flexibility in application development that is rare among operating systems. A developer, in order to develop applications for Inferno, therefore need not have access to hardware that will run Inferno natively.

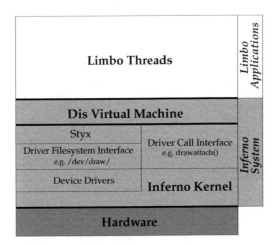

Figure 1.1 Organization of components in Inferno running directly over hardware (i.e. *native* Inferno).

Figures 1.1 and 1.2 illustrate the organization of components in the native and emulated versions of Inferno, respectively. The emulated and native environments are identical above the Dis virtual machine (Dis VM). Native Inferno, which runs over bare hardware, provides the necessary OS support to the Dis VM, whereas the emulated version of Inferno relies on the facilities of the host operating system. The facilities required of the host operating system include performing I/O and scheduling Dis VM threads. These Dis VM threads are threads (or processes, depending on the host platform) of the Dis VM itself. The Dis VM contains an *internal scheduler* for scheduling Limbo threads running over the VM. This is separate from the host platform's thread or process scheduling in the emulator, and from the process scheduling in native Inferno (which schedules Dis VM processes and the like, *not* Limbo threads).

1.2 History and Overview of Inferno

Inferno was created by the Computing Sciences Research Center (CSRC) at Lucent Technologies' Bell-Labs, Murray Hill, NJ, the creators of C, C++, Alef, Acid, Unix and Plan 9 to name but a few. In the mid 1980s, after their child Unix had reached pubescence, the creators of Unix created 'Plan 9' (named after Ed Wood's film 'Plan 9 from Outer Space'). In 1995, at about the same time as Sun's Java programming language was beginning to cause a stir, the developers of Plan 9 started work on a

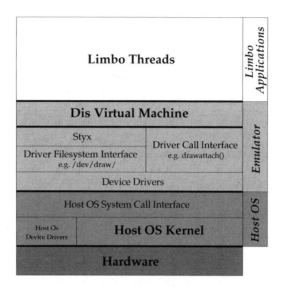

Figure 1.2   Organization of components in emulated version of Inferno.

decidedly commercial project that would later on be named 'Inferno' (after *The Inferno*, vol. I of Dante Alighieri's *Divine Comedy*)[1].

Several of the features of Plan 9 saw their way into Inferno. Unlike Plan 9, however, Inferno comes with a virtual machine, the Dis VM, to enable portability of Inferno applications across different hardware platforms. Dis has a memory-to-memory architecture as opposed to a stack architecture as in the Java virtual machine. A memory-to-memory architecture is essentially an infinite-register machine, with as many registers as there are words of memory. This simplifies on-the-fly compilation on most modern target architectures. At the time of the development of Inferno, the developers realized they needed a secure, type-safe, garbage-collected language. The developers considered using Java, but Java was in a state of flux and they decided they would rather deal with their own language that would be changing as it evolved rather than someone else's moving target [64]. Unlike Java, Limbo is not object oriented; however, it does support code reuse via modular programming.

1.3   Limbo

Limbo was designed by Sean Dorward, Rob Pike and Phil Winterbottom. It has certain features of other programming languages like Pascal (declarations), Alef (channels, ADTs), Occam (channels), Hoare's Communicating Sequential Processes (CSP) (channels, alternating on channels), Newsqueak, ML (module system, compile-time

---

[1]This naming decision was made because a member of the team (Rob Pike) had been reading the *Divine Comedy* at the time and noted that it would provide a rich source of names.

type checking, garbage collection), and introduces ideas of its own. Limbo employs strong type checking both at compile- and runtime, automatic garbage collection, and inter-thread communication over typed channels. Limbo was designed for the development of distributed applications. Its implementation makes it suitable for use on machines that do not have memory protection hardware such as a hardware memory management unit (MMU). There are no pointers in Limbo, and the language prevents direct access to machine memory—the virtual machine and the Limbo compiler cooperate to provide the functionality of memory protection. Limbo is compiled to machine-independent byte-code for execution on the Dis VM.

1.4   Resources as Filesystems and Per-Process Name Spaces

Representation of resources as files is a fundamental idea in Inferno. Computer users and programmers are familiar with files and their semantics, so make every resource behave like a file, subject to the well-known and understood file operators (open, read, write, etc.). If this hierarchy of files representing resources (referred to as a *name space*) is then made available over a network, it facilitates the easy distribution of resources in a network.

Entries in a name space may be ordinary disk files, interfaces to services, peripherals, programs or networks. There are operations provided for the management of the name space, and applications may be restricted by constraining their name spaces. For example, an application may be restricted from performing network communication by restricting its name space to exclude the network protocol stack, which is represented as a filesystem in the application's name space. The facilities which applications may use to perform operations on their name space are discussed in detail in Chapter 6.

Besides being able to restrict the entries in the name space of an application, entries in the name space are subject to file-access restrictions, similar to those in operating systems such as Unix.

1.5   Networks

Inferno (and to a lesser extent the Inferno emulator) supports a wide variety of internetworking protocols, such as IP, TCP/IP, UDP/IP, ICMP, GRE and ESP to name a few. Communication between Inferno devices is typically in the form of messages in a protocol called *Styx*, usually running over TCP/IP. Styx is a remote procedure call protocol similar to the NFS RPC protocol [69] (though significantly simpler in both design and implementation). Unlike NFS RPC, Styx is stateful, and a Styx server maintains information on connected clients.

1.6 Installing the Inferno Emulator

This section describes installing the Inferno emulator over a host operating system. Installing Inferno directly over the hardware of your computer, as you would for Linux or OpenBSD, is beyond the scope of this book.

1.6.1 Microsoft Windows

To install from an Inferno distribution CD, run the setup program in the `install` directory of the CD. If installing from the Web download, first download the necessary archive files. You should then uncompress them into a temporary installation directory. You can then run the setup program, which can be found in the `install` subdirectory. The setup program will attempt to install into the directory `C:\Users\Inferno` by default. You might want to add the emulator executables directory (`C:\Users\Inferno\NT\386\bin\`) to your PATH environment variable, but this is not absolutely necessary. If you installed the emulator in the default directory, you should now be able to start the emulator by running the `emu.exe` program in `NT/386/bin` relative to the installation root directory.

If the emulator was installed into a directory other than the default `C:\Users \Inferno`, you will need to supply the full path of the installation root directory when invoking the emulator executable. For example, if you installed into the directory `C:\Program Files\Inferno`, you would have to invoke the emulator in the following manner:

```
emu -rC:\Program Files\Inferno
```

The `-r` flag specifies the location of the Inferno root. Be careful that there is no whitespace between the `-r` flag and the path name. Further options accepted by the emulator command are detailed in the manual page for the emulator, which can be viewed by typing `man emu` from within the emulator. The manual page for emu (and other useful ones) are included in the appendices to this book.

There is nothing more in the setup that is specific to Windows platforms, and everything else is a matter of configuring your Inferno system correctly, from *within* the emulator.

1.6.2 Unix Platforms (Linux, FreeBSD, etc.)

The default installation location is `/usr/local/inferno`. You can override the root directory that the Inferno emulator knows of by using the `-r/<path>/` flag when starting up `emu`. It is advisable to create a startup script that will launch Inferno with the appropriate parameters. You will also need to create a user called 'inferno' on the host system, or whatever name you want the administrative user *within* Inferno to be called.

1.6.3   Plan 9

The default installation location of Inferno on Plan 9 is in /usr/inferno. You can override the root directory that the emulator knows of by using the -r/<path>/ flag when starting up the emulator. To be able to cleanly run Inferno services, you need to add the contents of the file /services/cs/services from your Inferno root to /lib/ndb/local. You will also need to create a user called 'inferno' on the host system, or whatever name you want the administrative user *within* Inferno to be called.

1.7   Getting Started with Inferno

The rest of the configuration is performed through the use of the configuration programs provided with the emulator. These run within the emulator to perform such functions as creating new users and setting up your machine as a server of some sort. Throughout the remainder of the book, all path names are relative to the Inferno installation root.

Figure 1.3   The initial console login prompt after starting the emulator.

1.7.1   Overview

After launching the emulator executable, you will be presented with the Inferno console, shown in Figure 1.3.

The Inferno graphical environment can be started by launching either the login window manager interface shown in Figure 1.4, by typing wm/logon at the initial

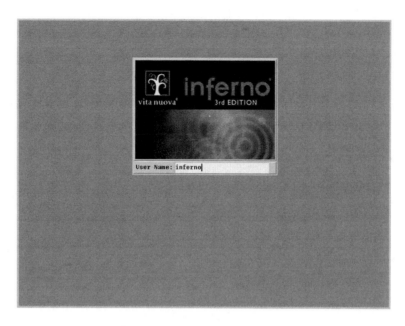

Figure 1.4 Logging in to Inferno.

Inferno console, or launching directly into the window manager by typing wm/wm. Once logged in, command consoles or *shells* can be opened via the button on the lower left of the screen, as illustrated in Figure 1.5.

For those familiar with operating systems such as Unix and its derivatives, a few of the familiar commands are also available in Inferno; *ls(1)* provides a listing of files in the current directory, and accepts many of the command-line flags available in Unix-like systems: *cd(1)* changes the current working directory; *ps(1)* provides a list of launched threads; *du(1)* provides a listing of disk usage statistics, etc. There are some new commands and variants of old commands: *lc(1)* provides a columnized output of the contents of the current working directory. These commands and a few more are illustrated below. Each line of the output of the ps command shows the thread ID, thread group ID, user executing the thread, state of the thread, memory size and module name, respectively:

```
;  ps
         1        1     pip    release    73K Sh[$Sys]
         6        6     pip        alt    32K Wm
         7        6     pip    release    25K Wm[$Sys]
         8        6     pip    release    25K Wm[$Sys]
         9        6     pip        alt    25K Wm
        10        6     pip        alt    25K Wm
        13        6     pip    release    36K Wmlib[$Sys]
        17       16     pip       recv    19K Plumber
        18       16     pip        alt    19K Plumber
```

Figure 1.5 The default window manager.

```
        20        20       pip        alt        88K WmEdit
        21         1       pip       ready       72K Ps[$Sys]

;  kill -g 6
;  ps

         1         1       pip      release      73K Sh[$Sys]
        17        16       pip        recv       19K Plumber
        18        16       pip        alt        19K Plumber
        20        20       pip        alt        88K WmEdit
        23         1       pip       ready       72K Ps[$Sys]

;  kill Plumber

17 18

;  ps

         1         1       pip      release      73K Sh[$Sys]
        20        20       pip        alt        88K WmEdit
        25         1       pip       ready       72K Ps[$Sys]

;  cd /dev
;  ls -l d*

dr-xr-xr-x d 0 pip pip 0 Jul 09 00:09 draw/2
-rw-rw-rw- d 0 pip pip 0 Jul 09 00:09 draw/new
-rw-r--r-- c 0 pip pip 0 Jul 09 00:09 drivers
```

```
;  cd

;  pwd

/usr/pip
```

The command *kill(1)* takes as argument a thread ID or Limbo module name, and terminates the corresponding thread or the threads executing the specified module, respectively. More information is available from the Inferno command line or shell by typing 'man' followed by a command, utility or application name.

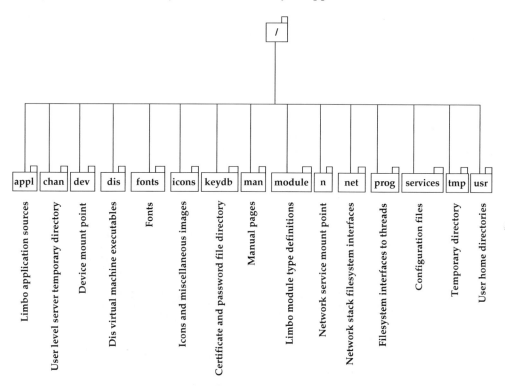

Figure 1.6   The general layout of an Inferno system.

1.7.2   Adding New Users and Passwords

There are no 'super users' and all users have equal privileges. However, on each system, most services are owned by an administrative user, usually the user 'inferno', but this need not necessarily be so. It is usually prudent to set up the filesystem so that all system-related configuration files are owned by the user 'inferno'. If using the Inferno emulator, this user must have an account on the host system, i.e. on Unix platforms there must be a user 'inferno' if your administrative user *within* Inferno is going to be 'inferno'. This is because the Inferno emulator exports the file ownership and permissions from the host system to the emulator level. Thus, for each user that has an account to login to the emulator, there should be a corresponding user with the same name on the host system (hopefully the same user!), but not necessarily the same password.

Users are added to the system by creating home directories with their user names under the /usr/ directory of the Inferno root. The directory lib/ in a user's home directory conventionally contains per-user configuration files, such as rule sets for the *plumber(8)* inter-application message router. The directory keyring/ is used for holding certificates obtained from a certifying authority. The directory charon/ is used to hold user configuration information and bookmarks for the Charon Web browser. These directories have to be created for each user added to the system with the *mkdir(1)* command. The creation of these directories is a separate process from the creation of user passwords, to be described next. Figure 1.6 shows the top-level hierarchy of a typical Inferno filesystem.

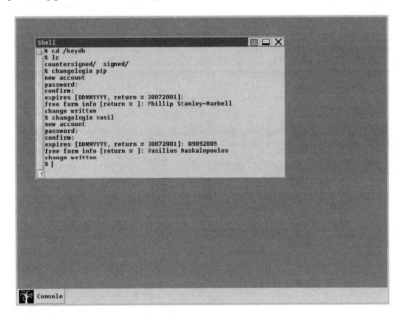

Figure 1.7 Adding a new user with the changelogin command.

Unless the machine is going to be used as an authentication server, there is no need to set user passwords. In an Inferno network, one machine, the *Authentication Server*, also known as the *Certificate Authority* (CA) or *Signer*, usually maintains the password database for users on all nodes in the network. For a machine that is going to be the sole Inferno entity on a network, one would set it up to be its own authentication server.

User passwords are set on an authentication server via the *changelogin(8)* utility. Passwords are stored in the file /keydb/password. The changelogin command changes the password of a user with a current password entry or creates a new entry in the /keydb/password file for a new user. To run changelogin, you need to have write permission on /keydb/password, so this can only be done by the administrative user. Figure 1.7 shows a typical session of the changelogin program.

1.7.3 Setting Up Services

You may define which machines in your network are going to provide services such as your certifying authorities, mail servers, HTTP proxy servers, etc. If you are running Inferno as a stand-alone system and not in a network, you might use your machine to provide these services to itself, or you might employ other non-Inferno machines to perform tasks such as acting as mail or file servers. The default servers for different services of interest are listed in the connection server database, /services/cs/db. The connection server, *cs(8)*, is an Inferno server that resolves symbolic names to host names and network addresses.

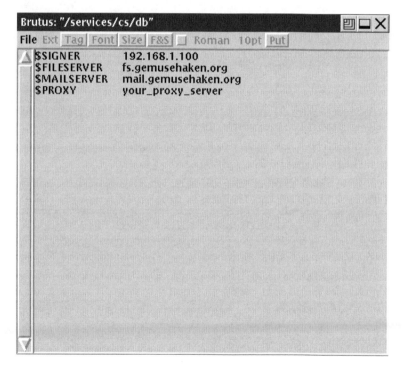

Figure 1.8 Editing the connection server database in the Brutus editor. The connection server database file has the name of the service in the first column and the name or IP address of the machine providing that service in the second.

The connection server database file, /services/cs/db, is read when *cs* is requested to resolve a name beginning with '$'. All other names are resolved by the external name servers, which are specified in the /services/dns/db configuration file. You may specify your DNS servers by creating entries in the /services/dns/db configuration file, with the IP address of each of your DNS servers in order of preference, one per line. Conventionally, names of well-known services are placed in the connection server database, and referred to by their entries, such as $MAILSERVER. For example, for the system whose connection server database file is shown in Figure 1.8, applications and users may use the symbolic name $MAILSERVER whenever they wish to refer to the system's designated mail server, mail.gemusehaken.org. Edit your connection server database file to reflect your local setup.

There is no means of explicitly specifying your machine's IP address in the emulator. The IP address for your machine is exported from the underlying host machine. The name of your machine, from within the emulator, can be read from /dev/sysname, which is a synthetic file, synthesized by the emulator kernel. Writing /dev/sysname sets the machine name, but since this is not a file on disk but rather a file synthesized by the system, the string written to /dev/sysname does not go into any persistent storage medium such as a disk, but rather is routed into the emulator. Thus, any changes written to /dev/sysname will be lost when you restart. You can set up your environment so that an appropriate string is written into /dev/sysname whenever you login by placing commands you want executed in the lib/wmsetup shell script in your user directory.

1.8   Name Spaces and Basic Name Space Configurations

An important Inferno concept is that of *per-process name spaces*. In simple terms, the name space is the hierarchy of files accessible to a thread.

Resources in Inferno—be they network protocol stacks, interfaces to devices, interfaces to local or remote servers or what have you—usually present simple file or filesystem interfaces to applications. The entries out of these resources (and also the more mundane disk files) that are visible to an application or thread make up its name space. The hierarchy of files visible to two threads from different applications might be entirely different, as might even be the hierarchy visible to two threads that are part of the same application.

Modifications to a name space are only seen by the thread making those changes. Changes made to the name space by a thread also affect the thread's parent, unless a thread explicitly detaches its name space from that of its parent's. Since name spaces are per-thread, modifications made to a thread's name space die with it. Modifications to the name space are made with *bind(2)*, *mount(2)*, *unmount(2)* and *pctl(2)* system calls. The *bind* system call causes the attachment of one part of an already existing portion of the file name space to another. The *mount* system call, on the other hand, causes the attachment of a new local or remote filesystem into the local name space. The *unmount* system call is used to undo the effect of either a *bind* or a *mount* operation.

The *pctl* system call is used to modify properties of a thread's name space, such as detaching its name space from its parent's.

A default name space is constructed upon login, based on the contents of the `namespace` file in the user's home directory. This is achieved through the *nsbuild(1)* Inferno utility. In most scenarios, this is either invoked by the *wm/logon* login program or *wm/wm*, the default window manager. The layout of the name space file is described in detail in the manual page for *namespace (6)*. In brief, it contains strings which are interpreted as commands to perform operations on the name space through *bind*, *mount*, *unmount* and *pctl*.

Figure 1.9 illustrates the operation of *bind* and *mount* system calls, using the equivalent Inferno utilities from the command shell. In the figure, a host, `nonetstack.gemusehaken.org`, has no network protocol stack implementation, but has an implementation of Styx over a serial RS-232 line. It attaches the interface to the network protocol stack of the host `gw.gemusehaken.org` into its local name space through a *mount* operation, and subsequently positions it into the default network protocol stack filesystem interface location through a *bind* operation. Subsequent to these steps, the network protocol stack of `gw.gemusehaken.org` will appear local to `nonetstack.gemusehaken.org`.

Applications which engage in network communication via TCP/IP will be using the network protocol stack of the `gw.gemusehaken.org` host. Each network access will cause the generation of Styx messages over the serial line to `gw.gemusehaken.org`, where they will be received by the network protocol stack driver. Note that it is only the *interface* to the protocol stack that is made local to `nonetstack.gemusehaken.org`. All the network traffic to the outside world is being handled by `gw.gemusehaken.org`, and `nonetstack.gemusehaken.org` only receives data that it explicitly requests, through the protocol stack interface. Network communication and the structure of the filesystem presented by the network protocol implementations is described further in Chapter 9.

1.9 The Inferno Application Development Environment

Inferno provides several facilities for writing and debugging applications. Figure 1.10 illustrates the general flow of application development in Inferno using Limbo.

There are two text editors distributed with the system (*wm/edit* and *wm/brutus*), and an integrated shell, window system and editor called *Acme* that literally does everything! There is a debugger (*wm/deb*) for debugging applications and, of course, a Limbo compiler, Dis assembler, as well as a Dis disassembler.

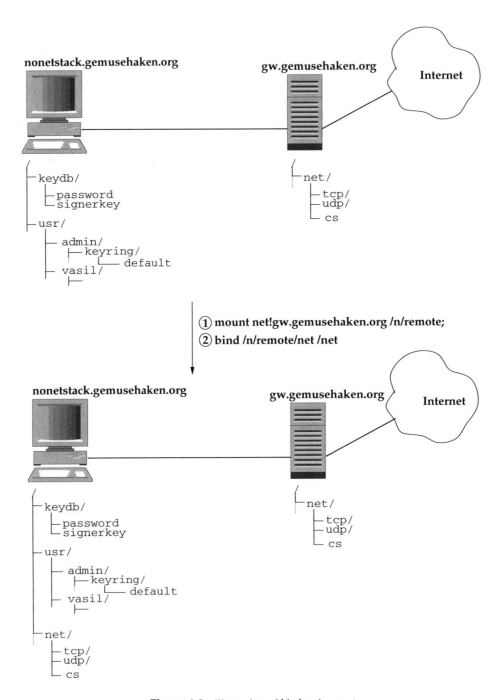

Figure 1.9 Illustration of *bind* and *mount*.

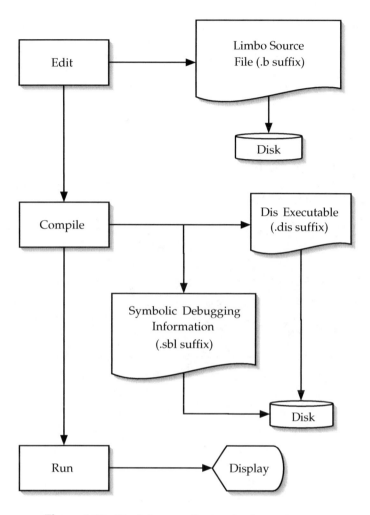

Figure 1.10 The Inferno application development process.

1.9.1 The Limbo Compiler

The Limbo compiler is available in the distribution in two forms: a version that runs directly on the host system and compiles Limbo source files to Dis byte-code, and a version that runs from within the emulator and also generates Dis byte-code.

Having a version that runs natively on the host platforms enables the use of your favorite editor to edit your Limbo programs, and you may even make use of facilities like makefiles on your host system to build your applications. However, once these applications are built, you can only debug, run and crash them from within the Inferno emulator (or native Inferno).

The Limbo compiler takes Limbo source files, ending with the extension '.b' by convention, and produces executables for the Dis VM, with the conventional extension '.dis'. The compiler will also generate a separate file containing symbolic debugging information to be used by a debugger. In addition to its use in developing Limbo programs, the Limbo compiler also provides facilities to ease the development of C language modules that interact with Limbo applications, so-called *built-in modules*. This use is discussed in detail in the appendix to Chapter 4. The following examples illustrate some modes of use of the Limbo compiler.

Calling the Limbo compiler without any arguments prints a brief summary of its usage. In the following example, the source file name is webdict.b and the resulting executable is webdict.dis. The executable can then be run by either giving its full file name or its file name without the '.dis' extension:

```
; lc
webdict.b
; limbo
usage: limbo [-GSagwe] [-I incdir] [-o outfile] [-{T|t|d} module]
 [-D debug] file ...
; limbo webdict.b
; lc
webdict.b    webdict.dis
; webdict pip
Retrieving http://www.gemusehaken.org/cgi-bin/dict.pl?term=pip


...


;
```

Symbolic debugging information to be used by debugging applications such as wm/deb and stack is generated with the -g flag to the Limbo compiler. It is placed in a separate file with the extension '.sbl'. In the example below, we cannot initially obtain any useful information from the stack utility, which prints the stack trace for a thread, because that utility cannot locate a symbolic debugging information file for the Cs thread[2]. Such debugging information can be generated by recompiling the source for the application (in this case, located in /appl/lib/cs.b) with the -g flag, and we can retry printing the stack trace. This is particularly useful when debugging a moribund thread that was not originally compiled with the -g flag:

```
; ps
        1        1       pip     release    74K Sh[$Sys]
       79        1       pip         alt    9K Cs
       83        1       pip       ready    73K Ps[$Sys]
; stack -v 79
unknown fn() Module ./cs.dis PC 160
```

---

[2]The mechanism by which .sbl files are located by stack and other debugging programs is described in their respective manual pages.

```
; cd /appl/lib
; limbo -g cs.b
; stack -v 79
cs(file=@501c34) cs.b:135.2, 8
        r=nil
        rc=nil
        pidc=@502bd4
        donec=@501e14
        fid=5002744
        wc=nil
        r=nil
        now=5250452
        buf=nil
        off=193779
        nbytes=1006363993
        fid=493
        r=nil
;
```

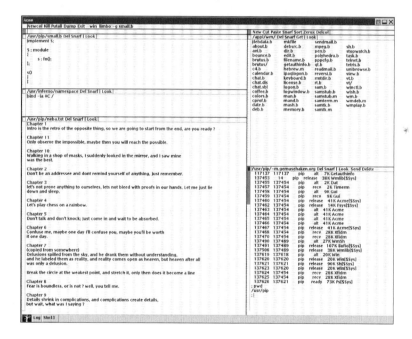

Figure 1.11 The Acme text window manager.

The Limbo compiler can generate warnings on potentially erroneous (but syntactically correct) statements and expressions in Limbo programs with the -w flag. Supplying more w's in the flag enables more verbosity:

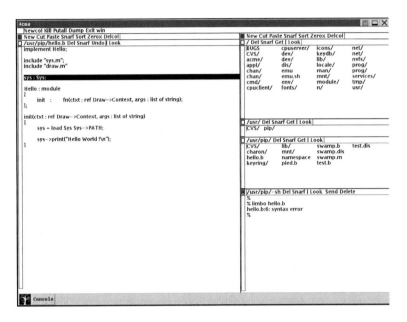

Figure 1.12 Using Acme as an integrated development environment.

```
; limbo webdict.b
; limbo -w webdict.b
webdict.b:36: warning: argument ctxt not referenced
; limbo -ww webdict.b
webdict.b:36: warning: argument ctxt not referenced
/module/sys.m:2: webdict.b:3: warning: con SELF not referenced
```

More options to the Limbo compiler—such as marking executables to be always interpreted (versus just-in-time compiled) and vice versa, generating Dis assembly code, etc.—are described in the manual page *limbo(1E)*, included in the appendices to this book.

1.9.2 The Acme User Interface

Acme is a user interface for programmers. It is a combined text window manager, text editor and file manager. It is also bundled with and serves as the interface for a few utility programs such as a mail reader and a command shell. To use Acme, you will need a three-button mouse.

An example Acme session is shown in Figure 1.11. In the figure, there is an active Acme session with five text windows open. In the figure, all the windows on the left-hand portion are being used to edit text files. The window on the upper right-hand

Table 1.1 Some useful Acme commands.

Action/Command	Description
Mouse *button-1*	Hold and drag to highlight text. Single words can be highlighted by double clicking on them.
Mouse *button-2*	Execute highlighted phrase. Single words may also be executed in this manner.
Mouse *button-3*	Clicking on a word with button-3 will move the cursor to the next occurrence of the word.
Delcol	Delete a sub-window (column).
Exit	Exit from Acme.
Get	Refresh the contents of a window.
Newcol	Create a new column.
New	Create a new window/file. This window may either be used as a scratch space or as a file. To save as a file, edit the tag of the window with the name you wish to assign to the file, then use the Put command to save.
Paste	Paste the contents of the snarf buffer.
Put	Write the contents of the window to disk.
Snarf	Copy the selected text.

side shows a directory listing of the path /usr/pip, and the window on the lower right is a command shell. The top row of each text window is an editable menu bar, often referred to as the *tag* of the window. In the case of the text window containing all five text windows previously mentioned, the menu bar contains the text strings Newcol Kill Putall Dump Exit and the phrase limbo -g small.b.

Each of these items, which can be edited, can be executed by highlighting and clicking with the middle mouse button (button-2). In the figure, the phrase limbo -g small.b has been highlighted, and clicking on it with the middle mouse button will cause the compilation of the program (small.b) being edited in the Acme window on the left. For single-word commands, highlighting is not necessary. For example, clicking on Exit with mouse button-2 will exit from Acme. Some of the more commonly used commands in Acme are listed in Table 1.1. Any new commands may be typed into the menu bar and executed at convenience in this manner. More details on Acme are provided in its manual pages, *acme(1)* and *acme(4)*.

Acme is the environment of choice for writing and debugging Inferno applications. A sample Acme session is shown in Figure 1.12, illustrating some of Acme's capabilities. In the figure, a text file, /usr/pip/hello.b, is open for editing in the left half of Acme. In the right half, there are four sections. The three uppermost window sections show the contents of three directories, the last being the directory containing the file hello.b. The last section of the right-hand side is a window running the program *win*, which is an interface to the shell.

In the shell window at the lower right of Figure 1.12, an attempt has been made to compile `hello.b`. It has resulted in an error message of the form `hello.b:6:syntax error`. Right clicking on this string automatically moves the mouse into the window containing `hello.b` (or opens it in a new window for editing if it is currently not being edited), and the faulting line (line 6) is highlighted. A more detailed description of Acme can be found in its manual pages.

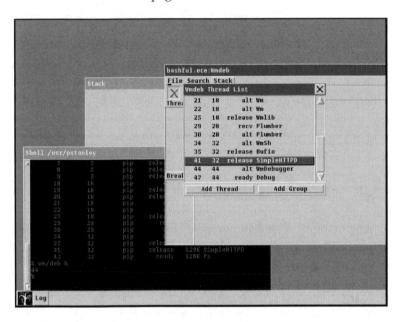

Figure 1.13 Attaching the debugger to an already existent thread—selecting the thread from the list of running threads in the system.

1.9.3 Debugging Programs

The *stack(1)* utility is used to examine a stack trace of a running or broken Limbo thread. The output of the stack is formatted so that it can be utilized by Acme and also by Inferno's *plumbing(6)*. Section 1.9.1 showed an example of the use of the stack utility.

There is also a graphical debugger, *wm/deb(1)*, which can be used to debug multi-threaded applications. Figures 1.13–1.15 illustrate the use of Inferno's graphical debugger.

The series of figures illustrate the use of the debugger to debug an application, `SimpleHTTPD`, which has previously been launched. The debugger is started by typing `wm/deb` from a command shell inside the window manager. It is then attached to the `SimpleHTTPD` thread by choosing *Thread* from the *File* menu of the debugger and

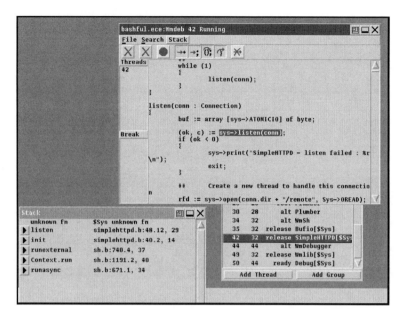

Figure 1.14 The graphical debugger after attaching it to the `SimpleHTTPD` thread. The highlighted source statement is the currently executing statement in the application.

selecting the `SimpleHTTPD` thread from the list of threads in the window that pops up, as illustrated in Figure 1.13.

Once the debugger has been attached to a thread, the main debugger window displays the source of the running application, with the currently running statement highlighted, as illustrated in Figure 1.14.

The values of variables and other module information may now be probed from the *stack* window of the debugger, as illustrated in Figure 1.15. The running program may be stepped through, stopped, breakpoints inserted, etc., using the buttons on the top row of the main debugger window.

1.10   Summary

This introductory section has provided a brief overview of Inferno and a walk-through of how to perform an installation, and we have touched upon how to edit, compile and debug Limbo applications. The next chapter provides an introduction to the Limbo language.

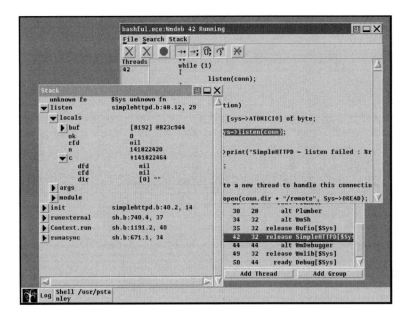

Figure 1.15 Probing the values of variables and module data.

Bibliographic Notes

More detailed histories of Unix can be found in [34, 68]. The Plan 9 operating system is described in [53, 54] and further in the accompanying system documentation available from [55]. Overviews of the Inferno operating system and Limbo language are provided in [15, 61, 75]. Brian Kernighan's *A Descent into Limbo* [27] was the earliest tutorial on programming Inferno in Limbo. The use of Inferno for developing distributed applications is discussed in [72]. Developing and debugging under Inferno are also described in [60]. Inferno's Styx protocol is described in [65]. The Dis virtual machine is described further in [31, 82], and its garbage collection mechanism in [26]. Execution of Java programs under Inferno, by translating Java byte-code to Dis instructions is described in [85]. The installation process for Inferno is described further in the Inferno system manuals [80]. The Acme programming environment, which originally appeared in the Plan 9 operating system is described in [51], and borrows some ideas from Wirth's Oberon system [84]. Commercial products which have employed Inferno to date include the Philips Consumer Communications *IS2630 Screen Phone*, Lucent Technologies' *PathStar Access Server*, which is described in [18], and Lucent Technologies' *VPN Firewall Brick* [19, 20, 43].

2

An Overview of Limbo

2.1 Introduction to Limbo

Limbo programs are made up of functions and data grouped into entities called *modules*. Modules consist of two parts: the interface definition and the implementation. The interface definition is the interface the module provides to other modules that wish to invoke it. It specifies functions the module implements and their function signatures, data constants the module provides and module variables. Interface declarations are typically placed in a separate source file with the extension '.m' by convention, while module implementations are placed in files with the extension '.b'. The interface definition may also be placed in the same file as the implementation. The interface declaration file may contain interface definitions for more than one module, and typically specifies the interface definitions for a closely related group of modules.

The module interface and module implementation can be thought of as types and values, respectively. Variables can be declared to be of the type of the module interface, and they must be initialized with a module implementation.

The module implementation consists of the actual Limbo program that performs the duties of a module. Module implementations are placed in source files with the extension '.b' by convention. Limbo '.b' files may only contain one module implementation definition. Putting the interface declaration and implementations in different files enables the programmer to write programs that interact with a specific module interface with an option to choose between different implementations of that interface at runtime. Module implementations are compiled by the Limbo compiler into programs for execution on the Dis VM. The compiled module implementation files have the extension '.dis' by convention. Figure 2.1 illustrates this organization of the

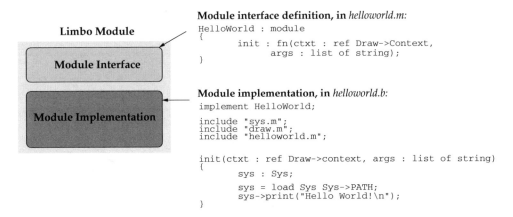

Module interface definition, in *helloworld.m:*
```
HelloWorld : module
{
        init : fn(ctxt : ref Draw->Context,
            args : list of string);
}
```

Module implementation, in *helloworld.b:*
```
implement HelloWorld;

include "sys.m";
include "draw.m";
include "helloworld.m";

init(ctxt : ref Draw->context, args : list of string)
{
        sys : Sys;

        sys = load Sys Sys->PATH;
        sys->print("Hello World!\n");
}
```

Figure 2.1   Parts of a Limbo module.

components of a module. We will now look at a concrete example which illustrates this further.

2.2   Hello World

Our first Limbo programming example implements a module that prints out the string 'Hello World!'. We organize this module into two parts: the interface definition and the implementation. We place the interface definition in the file `helloworld.m` and the implementation in the file `helloworld.b`.

The interface definition for the module, placed in `helloworld.m`:

```
# File : helloworld.m

HelloWorld : module
{
     init : fn(ctxt: ref Draw->Context, args : list of string);
};
```

The implementation of the `HelloWorld` Module, in `helloworld.b`:

```
# File : helloworld.b

implement HelloWorld;

include "sys.m";
include "draw.m";
include "helloworld.m";


init(ctxt : ref Draw->Context, args : list of string)
```

```
{
    sys : Sys;

    #    This is a comment
    sys = load Sys Sys->PATH;

    sys->print("Hello World !");
}
```

2.2.1 The HelloWorld Module Interface

The interface declaration for our example defines a module named `HelloWorld`, which contains one member item, `init`, of type `fn`, i.e. `init` is a function. The arguments to `init`, `ctxt` and `args` are of type `ref Draw->Context` and `list of string`, respectively. These arguments are not used by our program, but are required as part of the module's interface.

Our program will be launched from the Inferno shell, which is itself a Limbo program, implemented with several modules. To be able to execute our program, the shell must know which function in the module to invoke and what the number and types of parameters of the function are, i.e. its *signature*. The shell expects a module to be run to have a function named `init` and to have arguments equal in number and type to those we specified as the arguments for our `init` function. The `ctxt` argument is used to provide access to the graphics facilities, and the `args` argument provides a list of the command-line arguments supplied when the program was run.

2.2.2 The HelloWorld Module Implementation

All module implementations begin with the keyword `implement` followed by the name of the module implemented in that implementation file. Recall that a module implementation file may only implement a single module; thus there can only be a single `implement` statement in a Limbo '.b' file. It is almost always necessary to include the module interface definitions for other modules, and this is achieved with the keyword `include` followed by a string defining which file to include. The `include` statement is not solely for including module interface definitions, but rather simply causes the contents of any file specified in the argument to be included at that point. Unlike `#include` preprocessor directives in the C and C++ programming languages, the `include` statement in Limbo is part of the language and not a command for a preprocessor.

The implementation file defines one function, `init`. An implementation file may define functions not specified in the module interface definition, which will not be accessible from other modules, but the implementation's '.b' file must at the very least define implementations for all the functions defined in its module interface.

The first statement in the implementation of init defines a variable sys of type Sys. The type Sys is the type or *interface* of a module named 'Sys', whose interface declaration was included from the file sys.m. All module interface definitions are of a unique type, and a variable may be defined to be of the type of a particular module. Variables with the type of a module are used to hold references to an instance of the module.

When a Limbo program (module implementation) is compiled, the final compiled image placed in a '.dis' file only contains Dis VM instructions generated from the single module defined in the source file. Other modules which are invoked to perform tasks (in this case, we needed to invoke the print function from the Sys module) are not linked into the binary image. For example, even though the HelloWorld implementation in hello.b contains a call to sys->print, the compiled hello.dis executable does not contain the code to perform the sys->print operation.

At runtime, before using functions or accessing variables defined in a module, the module to be accessed must be loaded from a '.dis' file on disk or elsewhere. By convention, the location from which to load an implementation of a module is specified in a constant named PATH in the module's interface declaration. Module instances are created with the load expression. The load expression has the form:

```
module_variable = load   module_type   file_name;
```

Loading a module implementation should not be confused with including the module's interface defined in a '.m' file with an include statement.

In the above, the load expression causes an implementation of a module with type module_type to be loaded from the file file_name and a reference to this implementation to be placed in the variable module_variable.

At any point during the program's lifetime when this instantiation is no longer needed, it may be discarded by setting the variable module_variable to nil.

In the second line of the implementation of init, we create an instance of the module Sys, placing a reference to this instance in the variable sys[1]. Subsequent to this, we are able to access the function print in module Sys to print 'Hello World!' to the standard output.

The Sys module contains facilities for Limbo programs to interact with the Inferno system, providing facilities for I/O, networking and name space manipulation, to name a few.

2.3   Discourse on include and load

The basic unit of execution, or program, is a Limbo module. Each executable ('.dis') contains the code for just one module. The module interface definition (in a '.m' file)

---

[1]The Sys module is a special 'built-in' module, and we do not create an instance of it in the same way as for ordinary Limbo modules. More on this later in this chapter and in Chapter 4.

says what the 'type' of the module is. This module 'type' is a type just like 'int' or 'string', and it denotes the functions and data that are accessible in a module. An executable should be thought of as a value of the type of the module, e.g. for the type 'int', 5 is a value of type 'int'. Similarly, for the module type that was defined in the file 'hello-world.m', the code in 'hello-world.dis' is a value of that type.

An include statement is used to include a module type definition from another file at compile time. It simply causes the compiler to insert the contents of the specified file at the point of the include statement. It is not specific for use only in including module type definitions.

The module interface definition, from the '.m' file, just gives us the 'type' of the module we want to use; it says nothing of the 'value', i.e. the implementation of the module. To associate a module 'type' with a module 'implementation' or 'value' (so to speak), we must perform a 'load' operation to associate the type with a specific implementation, somewhere on the disk. The 'load' statement is evaluated at runtime.

A Limbo executable ('.dis') contains the code for only one module. To call functions in another module (e.g. a library of some sort), it must somehow get hold of another such module and then call the necessary functions within it. There is no equivalent static linking of binaries that exists in languages such as C. To use a module, it must be explicitly loaded at runtime from a '.dis' file.

The type of the implementation on disk must match the type of the variable being assigned the result of the load expression. This is analogous to the case of assigning a value to a variable of type 'int'; the value to be assigned must be an 'int' value, and, for example, we cannot assign a string to an int.

Just as there are several values that have the type 'int', there can be several implementations that have the type defined by a module definition. A module may choose between several implementations of another module that it wishes to load, and these different implementations may provide very different 'behaviors', though they must conform to the same interface: the same 'type'. The functions they define and implement must match the module interface definition. Chapter 4 delves into modules in a little more depth.

2.4   Some Details

Limbo, like C/C++, is case sensitive, thus `HelloWorld`, `Helloworld` and `helloworld` are distinct identifiers. Identifiers can be any sequence of letters and numbers, provided the first character is a letter from 'a' through 'z' and 'A' through 'Z', the underscore, '_', or any Unicode character with value greater than 160. Identifiers are restricted in length, and only the first 256 characters of an identifier are meaningful.

Comments are introduced with a '#' and continue to the end of the line. Identifiers may not contain whitespace, thus `Hello World` would not be a valid name for the example module.

If you try to run a module implementation without an `init` function from the command shell, you will get an error message similar to

```
myprog: link failed fn init() not implemented
```

If on the other hand you do have an `init` function with a different signature, you will receive an error similar to the following when you try to execute it from the shell:

```
myprog: link typecheck init() 9cd71c5e/f7549f0a
```

Chapter 4 contains more information on modules, their interfaces and functions and module types and type checking.

2.5 Reserved Identifiers, Operators and Associativity

The following identifiers are reserved for use as keywords. They cannot be used for any other purposes:

```
adt        alt       array      big        break       byte
chan       con       continue   cyclic     do          else
fn         for       hd         if         implement   import
include    int       len        list       load        module
of         or        pick       real       ref         return
self       string    tagof      tl         to          type
while      case      exit       nil        spawn
```

Valid operators in the Limbo language are shown in Table 2.1 in decreasing order of precedence or decreasing 'tightness' of binding, with the lowest-precedence operators shown separately in Table 2.2.

2.6 Scope

Blocks are statements enclosed within braces. Blocks start a new scope, and variables declared within a block are salvaged by the garbage collector as control passes out of the block, and thus out of the current scope. Thus, for example, if you want to declare a few variables and/or data structures, use them for a few computations, then immediately have the resources they occupy freed, you could enclose them within braces:

Table 2.1 Limbo language operators, their precedence and associativity. The operators are listed in decreasing order of precedence or 'tightness' of binding.

Operator	Description	Associativity
.	ADT member function access	left
->	Module member access	left
f()	Function call	left
a[]	Array or string subscript	left
!	Logical not	left
~	Bitwise not	left
++	Increment	left
--	Decrement	left
-	Unary minus	left
+	Unary plus	left
*	Dereference of ref ADT	left
hd	List head value	neither
tl	List tail value	neither
ref	ADT reference	left
load	Module load	left
tagof	Tag, for `pick` ADT	neither
len	Length	neither
type	Type cast	left
* / %	Multiplication, Division, Modulo	left
+ -	Addition, Subtraction	left
<<	Logical left shift	left
>>	Logical right shift	left
<	Less than	left
>	Greater than	left
< =	Less than or equal to	left
> =	Greater than or equal to	left
= =	Equals	left
! =	Not equals	left
&	Bitwise AND	left
^	Bitwise XOR	left
|	Bitwise OR	left
: :	List append	right
&&	Logical AND	left
||	Logical OR	left
Lowest-precedence operators	Shown in Table 2.2	

Table 2.2 Lowest-precedence Limbo language operators.

Operator	Description	Associativity
=	Assignment	right
: =	Declaration and assignment	left
+ =	Addition and assignment	right
– =	Subtraction and assignment	right
* =	Multiplication and assignment	right
/ =	Division and assignment	right
% =	Modulo and assignment	right
& =	Bitwise AND and assignment	right
| =	Bitwise OR and assignment	right
^ =	Bitwise XOR and assignment	right
<< =	Logical left shift and assignment	right
>> =	Logical right shift and assignment	right
<-	Assignment to/from channel	right

```
#   ...
{
    c : Compress;
    c = load Compress Compress->PATH;

    #   Access data and functions of the module Compress
    c->ID = "ZIP";
    c->compress(data);
}

#   Resources occupied by the instance of Compress are freed
#   at this point. Thus, the following statement is illegal,
#   since c is undefined in the current scope:
sys->print("%s\n", c->ID);
```

The above is one way of creating and using variables that are only going to be used for a limited period of time and must then be explicitly freed. The variable c goes out of scope and the resources consumed by the loaded module, Compress, are freed by the Dis VM's garbage collector. This effect could also have been achieved by explicitly setting c to nil in an assignment operation.

Consider the following example. What happens when this code segment is run. Is there any output printed out? What is printed?

```
n := 10;

sys->print("Hello Bengt!\n");
while (n > 0)
```

```
    {
        n := n - 1;
        sys->print("n = %d\n", n);
    }
    sys->print("Bye Bengt!\n");
```

2.7 Import Statements

In the 'Hello World!' example, to access the print function of the Sys module, the syntax was sys->print. Similarly, to access any function within a module, we use the arrow separator (->). As you might imagine, this can become cumbersome if we frequently access member functions of a module in a Limbo program.

To ease this burden, we can make member functions of another module visible as though they were functions defined within the current module with the import statement. The syntax of the import statement is:

```
    module_member : import module_variable;
```

So in the 'Hello World!' example, we would have written:

```
    print : import sys;
```

after including 'sys.m' and declaring the variable sys of type Sys. Note that the identifier after the keyword import must be a variable with type of a module interface, and must not itself be a module interface, i.e. it would be wrong to write:

```
    print : import Sys;
```

since Sys is a module interface, and sys is a variable with the type of the module interface Sys.

2.8 Flow Control

The constructs provided for flow control are similar to those provided in other programming languages like Pascal, C, C++ and Java.

2.8.1 The if Conditional Statement

The `if` conditional in Limbo is identical to that in C/C++ and Java. The syntax is:

```
if (expression) statement;
if (expression) statement1 else statement2;
```

The expression *expression* must be of type `int` and *statement* denotes one or more Limbo statements. In the first case, if the expression *does not* evaluate to zero, then the statement list *statement* is executed. In the second case, the statement list *statement1* is executed if the expression *expression* evaluates to a non-zero value; otherwise, the statement list *statement2* is executed. In both cases, the statement lists may consist of one or more statements.

In situations with nested `if` clauses and an `else` clause, the `else` clause is bound to the innermost `if` without an accompanying `else`:

```
if (a < 1)
     if (b > 1)
          if (c < 1)
               print("a < 1, b > 1 and c < 1");

#     This else belongs to the if (c < 1) statement
else
          print("a < 1, b > 1 but c >= 1");
```

2.8.2 The do Looping Construct

The do construct is used to create loops that will always be executed at least once. The syntax is:

```
do statement while (expression);
```

The statement *statement* may be just one statement or several statements enclosed in braces. The expression *expression* is optional, and if present must evaluate to an integer value. If an expression is specified, the body of the do loop will be executed repeatedly until the expression *expression* evaluates to zero. If no expression is specified, the body will be executed infinitely many times, or until a `break` statement is encountered. The break construct is discussed later in this chapter. Like other looping constructs, do loops may have an optional label. In cases where there are multiple nested loops, this permits a program to break out of a specific labeled loop:

```
n = 0;

fast: do
```

```
{
    glass: do
    {
        if (n >= 5)
            break fast;
        else
            print("wooo hooooo!\n");

        n++;
    } while ();

    print("m = %d\n", m++);
} while ();

print("Done\n");
```

In the above example, 'wooo hooooo!' is printed 5 times, after which 'Done' is printed to the output. The statement to print the variable m is never reached, since the break statement specifies to break out of the loop with the label fast, which is the outer containing loop.

2.8.3 The while Looping Construct

The while construct differs from the do construct only in the fact that the loop termination test is performed before the loop is entered, so the body of the loop may never execute. The syntax for while loops is:

> while (*expression*) *statement*

The body of the while loop (*statement*) is executed repeatedly as long as the expression *expression*, which should evaluate to an integer, evaluates to a non-zero value. Like do loops, while loops may have an optional loop label, as discussed for do loops above. For example:

```
while (!tired)
{
    run();
}
```

2.8.4 The case Statement

Of all the Limbo language flow-control constructs, the case statement differs the most from its counterparts in languages such as C. Like the switch statement in C/C++ and the case statement in Pascal, the case statement in Limbo is a multi-way branch. The syntax for Limbo case statements is shown below:

```
case expr
{
    expr1 => stmt;
    expr1 to expr2 => stmt;
    expr1 or expr2 => stmt;
    * => stmt;
}
```

The expression *expr* may evaluate to either an integer or a string, and based on its value, one of the expression-qualified statements within the body will be executed. The statements within the body of the case are qualified by either individual expressions, expression ranges specified as '*expr1 to expr2*', or the logical 'or' of two expressions specified as '*expr1 or expr2*'. The type to which the qualifiers must evaluate is determined by *expr* at the head of the case statement.

If the expression *expr* evaluates to an integer, then the expressions qualifying statements within the body must evaluate to integer constants. Similarly, if *expr* evaluates to a string, the expressions qualifying statements within the body must evaluate to string constants. If none of the qualifier expressions match the expression *expr*, the statement qualified by '*' is executed. The use of the '*' statement is optional:

```
n : int = 34;
case (n)
{
    0 to 9 => print("Numeric digit");

    'a' to 'z' or 'A' to 'Z' => print("Alpha character");

    * => print("Is not an alphanumeric character");
}

name : string = "Jane";
case (name)
{
    "jane" or "JANE" => print("Hello Jane!");
    * => print("Hi there.\n");
}
```

Duplicate qualifier expressions and overlapping qualifier expression ranges are not permitted. In the case of string qualifiers, the expression range may not take the form '*expr1 to expr2*'; thus in the above example, it would be illegal to write the qualifier expression as "jane" to "JANE". Unlike *switch* statements in C, control within a Limbo case statement does not automatically continue to the following statement; hence there is no need for break statements after each choice.

2.8.5 The for Looping Construct

The for looping construct is similar to do, while and its counterparts in languages such as C. The syntax is:

> for (*expr1*; *expr2*; *expr3*) *stmt*

The expression *expr1* is evaluated first, and this is typically used to initialize the loop induction variable. The statement *stmt* is then repeatedly executed while the expression *expr2*, which must evaluate to an integer, is non-zero. On each iteration, the expression *expr3* is also evaluated, and it is typically used to increment the loop induction variable. Any or all three of *expr1*, *expr2* and *expr3* may be omitted. The for statement may be labeled with an optional label, just as described for the while and do loops above. For example:

```
for (i = 1; i <= 10; i++)
{
    print("i = %d\n", i);
}
```

The above example prints out the integers 1 to 10 inclusive.

2.8.6 The break, continue, exit and return Statements

The break, continue, exit and return statements are used to alter the flow of control in a program. A break statement without a specified label transfers control out of the most immediate containing while, do, for or case statement (also used in alt and pick constructs discussed in later chapters). A break statement with a label specifier on the other hand transfers control to the first statement after the labeled loop, as discussed previously for do, while and for loops.

A continue statement causes the execution of a loop to proceed to the loop test condition (at the head of the loop for while and for loops and at the tail for do loops). If a label is specified in the continue statement, then control transfers to the loop head of the labeled containing loop. For for statements with an initialization of the loop induction variable, the initialization is *not* re-performed when control returns to the loop head due to a continue statement:

```
while (n < 100)
{
    if (n % 5)
    {
        n++;
        continue;
    }
```

```
        print("%d\n", n++);
    }
```

The above example prints out all numbers between 0 and less than 100 that are integer multiples of 5.

The `exit` statement terminates the execution of a thread. At this point, all resources of the thread are recovered by the Dis VM's garbage collector.

A `return` statement transfers control to the caller of a function. If the called function is defined to return a value, then the return statement must include a return expression of the same type as the function's defined return type. If the function returns no value, then the return statement may be omitted, or a return statement with no return expression may be used.

One peculiarity of the return statement is that if the function is defined as having no return value, but the last statement before the function returns to its caller is another function call, the language permits using that function call as the return expression of the function that has no return value. This enables compilers for the language to take advantage of tail recursion optimizations that can be performed for such a situation:

```
tr : module
{
    first : fn (arg : int);
    second : fn (arg : int);
}

first (arg : int)
{
    print("Nothing to see here, move along...");

    return second(arg);
}
```

In the above, even though the function `first` is defined as having no return value, it is valid to use the call to function `second` as its return expression.

2.9 Summary

In this chapter, the structure of Limbo programs was introduced. Limbo programs are made up of functions and data objects, grouped into modules. Modules consist of a module interface and a module implementation. The module implementation is compiled by a Limbo compiler into a sequence of instructions for execution on the Dis VM. Modules may dynamically load other modules from disk and access their data and function members. Limbo provides constructs for flow control similar to those in languages such as Pascal, C/C++ and Java.

Bibliographic Notes

Brian Kernighan's *A Descent into Limbo* [27] is a good whirlwind tour of programming the Inferno system with Limbo. The Limbo language reference, *The Limbo Programming Language* [66], by Dennis Ritchie, provides a complete description of the language syntax and semantics. An overview of the design of the Inferno system and programming in Limbo is provided in [15]. Other overviews of the Inferno system and programming in Limbo can be found in [61, 75]. A comparison of the performance of Limbo programs against other languages (C, Awk, Perl, Tcl, Java, Visual Basic and Scheme) is detailed in [28].

2.10   Chapter Examples

2.10.1   A Tiny Limbo Program

The example for this chapter is a very small Limbo program. It does not conform to the specifications that must be met for a program that wants to be run from the shell, so we write another Limbo program to load our tiny program and run it. The tiny Limbo program is shown below:

```
# File : tiny.b

implement S;

S : module
{
    s : fn();
};

s()
{
}
```

And the program needed to load and run it is:

```
# File : pump.b

implement Loader;

include "sys.m";
include "draw.m";

sys : Sys;

Loader : module
{
    init : fn (nil : ref Draw->Context, args : list of string);
};

S : module
{
    s : fn();
};

init (nil : ref Draw->Context, args : list of string)
{
    sys = load Sys Sys->PATH;

    if (len args != 2)
    {
        sys->print("Usage :: pump <file.dis>\n");
        exit;
    }
    path := hd tl args;
```

```
    pump := load S path;

    if (pump == nil)
    {
        sys->print("Loader :: %r\n");
        sys->print("Usage -- pump <file.dis>\n");

        exit;
    }

    sys->print("Loading %s...\n", path);
    pump->s();
}
```

Discussion   The tiny program demands little explanation, other than to point out that you can write syntactically correct programs that cannot be run from the Inferno shell. Try running the compiled S module from the shell and see what happens.

As you will observe, this small program cannot be run as is from the shell and needs a special program to load it and run it. Programs that wish to be run from the shell must define a function, init, in their module interface, with a specific signature (i.e. number and type of arguments). Since the tiny module does not adhere to this interface specification, it cannot be loaded by the shell.

The loader for the tiny module (the module Loader) includes the module interface definition for the module S implemented by the tiny program. It declares a variable pump to be of the type of the included module interface. It loads an implementation of the tiny module from disk, and then invokes its sole member function, s().

The loader module gives you a glimpse of what we are going to see in the next chapter—Limbo data types such as lists, and the operations the language provides for their manipulation. It also illustrates a module that loads and runs another. Just as the Loader module is loaded and run from the shell, so also does it load and run the module S.

The loader module also illustrates the method of printing out system error messages:

```
    sys->print("Pump :: %r\n");
```

The most recent system error message is printed out when the %r format specifier is used in a print message. The formatted output routines provided by the Limbo runtime system are described in more detail in Chapter 5 and the manual page *sys-print(2)* included in the appendices, in Section C.3.

2.10.2 Fibonacci Numbers

The second example for this chapter generates Fibonacci numbers using a recursive algorithm:

```
# File : fibonacci.b

implement Fibonacci;

include "sys.m";
include "draw.m";

sys : Sys;
MAX : con 50;

Fibonacci : module
{
     init : fn(nil : ref Draw->Context, nil : list of string);
};

init(nil : ref Draw->Context, nil : list of string)
{
     sys = load Sys Sys->PATH;

     sys->print("0  .\n1  ..\n");
     f(0, 1);
}

f(a, b : int)
{
     sys->print("%-3d", a + b);
     for (i := 0; i <= a+b; i++)
     {
          sys->print(".");
     }
     sys->print("\n");

     if (a+b < MAX)
     {
          f(b, a+b);
     }
}
```

Discussion   The program prints out the Fibonacci numbers from 0 until just beyond the constant MAX, and provides a simple representation of the trend in the values by printing out dots to depict the values of the numbers pictorially.

The init function initializes the variable sys, which holds a reference to the Sys module. Since sys is in global scope, all the functions within the module will be able to access the facilities of the Sys module subsequent to this initialization. The function which does all the work, imaginatively named f(), is an example of a *recursive function* in Limbo—not at all different from what you would see in a language like C. It calls itself recursively with the last two Fibonacci numbers printed out, and those are used to calculate the next number, and so forth.

Problems

2.1 Compile the example program with the -S flag (i.e. `limbo -S a.b`) and take a look at `a.S`. Do not worry if it does not yet make sense. What is the byte count?

2.2 Write the smallest possible program that can be run from the shell. What is the byte count for the Limbo source? The Dis assembler (compile with -S)? The Dis executable? Note that this program does not have to do anything useful.

2.3 When you compile the program you wrote in problem 2.2 with the -S flag, is it much bigger than the `.S` file from problem 2.1? Explain why there are differences, if there are any.

2.4 Rewrite the 'Hello World!' program using `import`, so that there are no ->'s in the program.

2.5 Repeat problem 2.4 for the loader in the chapter example.

2.6 Rewrite the loader with the line `draw = load draw Draw->PATH;` inserted but commented out. Compile the program with the line commented out and with the line uncommented. Is there a large difference in executable size? Explain what you observe.

2.7 Rewrite the loader with an additional print statement after the last print statement in the program. Insert the statement `sys = nil;` between these last two print statements. Compile and execute. What happens? Why?

2.8 Look at the file `/module/sys.m`. Implement your own sys module, using dummy functions to replace all the functions defined in `sys.m`. The functions do not have to do anything. You will have problems compiling it.

3

Data Types

Limbo is a strongly typed language. The compiler will not accept a program for which an unchecked type error can occur at runtime. Type checking is enforced at both compile- and runtime. Runtime type checking is necessary for situations like module loading, in which the function signatures of the module loaded from disk must match those of the module interface.

3.1 Primitive Data Types

The sizes of the primitive types in Limbo—`big`, `byte`, `int`, `real` and `string`—are defined to be independent of the architecture of the machine running the Limbo program. The basic Limbo types are illustrated in Table 3.1.

The three integral types are `byte`, `int` and `big`. An expression of type `byte` can take on values in the range 0 to 255. An `int` expression can take on values in the range -2^{31} to $2^{31} - 1$. An expression of type `big` takes on values in the range -2^{63} to $2^{63} - 1$.

Integer constants such as 7 or 'a' and constant expressions such as (1 << 10 + 50), have the type `int` if they evaluate to a value within the range of values that can be held in an `int`. If they exceed this size, they have type `big`. Values larger than the representable range in an integral type lead to overflow, so assigning the value 2^{63} to a variable of type `big` will leave it with the value -2^{63}.

The initial value of variables of type `int`, `big`, `real` and `byte` is undefined if they are declared local to a function. If they are declared in global scope, however, they will be initialized to zero.

Table 3.1 Primitive types in Limbo.

Type	Description
int	32-bit signed, in two's complement notation
big	64-bit signed, in two's complement notation
real	64-bit, represented in IEEE long floating notation
byte	8 bits, unsigned
string	Sequence of 16-bit Unicode characters

Implicit coercion between types is not permitted, but there is the provision for explicit type casting. Integer constants and expressions of type byte, int or big must be explicitly cast when assigning them to variables not of the same integral type. For example the assignment of the constant 7 to a variable of type byte requires an explicit cast, since 7 has type int. Likewise, the assignment of the constant 0 to a variable of type big requires an explicit type cast. The following code fragment illustrates some of these ideas:

```
b : byte;
i : int;
r : real;


#   This is legal, the expression on the right-hand
#   side has type int:
i = (1 << 10) + 2334;

#   The following statement is illegal:
#b = 1;

#   We must explicitly cast 255 to type byte to assign it
#   to variable b:
b = byte 255;

#   Given the previous assignment to variable b, the following
#   leads to overflow, and b ends up with value 9
b = b + (byte 10);

#   This is valid, r ends up with the value 2.866242:
r = real b / 3.14;
```

Implicit type declaration is permitted and is achieved using the ':=' operator. The ':=' operator permits the declaration of a variable whose type is the type of the expression being assigned to it. In the example below, the type of variable p is int, since the constant 1 has type int. Likewise, the variable q is of type real since the constant 1.0 is of type real:

```
p := 1;
q := 1.0;
```

3.2　The string Data Type

Strings are sequences of Unicode characters. The `string` data type is notably different from character constants such as `'Y'`, enclosed in single quotes, which are of type `int` (characters are represented with their 16-bit Unicode encoding). A one-character string such as `"Y"`, enclosed in double quotes, is *not* a character (i.e. not an `int`). The length of a string is obtained by applying the `len` operator, and yields the number of Unicode characters in the string. The length of an empty string, `""`, or equivalently the constant `nil`, is zero. The number of Unicode characters in a string can be different from the number of bytes needed to encode the constituent characters. Inferno uses the UTF-8 encoding to encode Unicode characters. The UTF-8 encoding of a Unicode character may be 1, 2 or 3 bytes; thus the number of bytes needed to encode a Unicode string may be greater than its length as reported by `len`. Section 3.5.3 and Chapter 5 provide further discussion on conversion between Unicode strings and arrays of bytes.

The indices of the elements of a string are zero-based, and individual Unicode characters in a string can be accessed. The first Unicode character in a string s is s[0], and the last character in the string is s[len s - 1]:

```
c : string;

#   This is illegal. Character constants have type int:
#c = '?';

#   This is a correct implicit type declaration of string d:
d := "yes";
d[1] = 'E';

#   "yEs" printed to the standard output stream:
sys->print("%s",d);

#   This prints out the letter "p"
s : string;
s[0] = 112;
sys->print("%s\n", s);
```

It is generally only permitted to index within the allocated size of a string. The only exception to this rule is indexing one position beyond the end of a string, which can be used to grow a string, but only a single character at a time. In the last group of statements in the above example, the string variable s is declared and has length zero. The statement s[0] = 112 grows the length of the string s by one character. This may be repeated to grow the length of a string, a single character at a time:

```
s : string;

s[len s] = 'h';
s[len s] = 'e';
s[len s] = 'l';
s[len s] = 'l';
s[len s] = 'o';
```

It is possible to cast character constants and other integer expressions of type int to strings. This results in the string representation of the integer value being stored in the string variable. For example, the character 'A' has ASCII value 65. If we cast the character constant 'A' to type string, it becomes the string "65". Similarly, if we cast the constant 45279 to a string, it becomes the string "45279".

Strings can be converted to integers with a cast. In the following, the initial value of variable x is the integral value 32. The leading numeric substring (if any) in the argument to the cast is converted to an integer. Casts of all other strings evaluate to zero. Thus, for example, a cast to integer of the string "34y" evaluates to the value 34, as does "34   92". The string "e34" evaluates to zero on a cast to int, as does the string "hello":

```
x := int "32";
```

Strings can be concatenated with the + operator; thus, after the following, the string greeting contains "Hello World!":

```
h := "Hello";
w := "World";

greeting := h + " " + w + "!";
```

3.3 Reference Versus Value Types

The basic types in Limbo—string, int, big, real and byte—are *value types*. They are always passed by value when passed as parameters to functions, and assignments *from* them yield the values they hold. There are no pointers in Limbo, and it is not possible to obtain references or pointers to the primitive types.

Some of the structured data types in Limbo to be discussed in later sections of this chapter are *reference types*. This means they are always passed by reference, and assignments *from* them yield a reference to them.

The initial value of reference types is always nil, or the *undefined reference*. Before use, storage must be allocated for reference types. Table 3.2 summarizes the declaration and use of variables of the basic Limbo types.

Table 3.2 Summary of the properties of the basic Limbo data types.

Type	Example declaration	Notes
int	a : int; b := 5;	Initial value is zero *only* if declared to be global.
big	a : big; b := big 5;	Values inside the range of -2^{31} to $2^{31} - 1$ have type int and must explicitly be cast when assigning to a variable of type big. Initial value undefined unless global.
real	a : real; b := 4.2;	Initial value is zero *only* if global.
byte	a : byte; b := byte 'A';	Single characters such as 'A' or 'ψ' are 16-bit Unicode characters, and have the type int. Assignment of such values to bytes is therefore not always meaningful, and requires a cast regardless. Initial value is zero only if global.
string	a : string; b := "Vincent";	Strings are value types, though the empty string is equivalent to nil.

3.4 Lists

Limbo provides a list data type, a list of elements of the same type.

A list may be constructed out of elements of any of the primitive or aggregate data types, including lists. The Limbo language provides operators for retrieving the head item of a list (hd), retrieving the tail of a list (tl), and concatenating an item to a list (::).

The hd operator returns the first item in a list. The tl operator returns the remaining items in the list[1]. The :: or 'cons' operator is used to concatenate an item to the head of a list. This construction of lists and behavior of the list operators is illustrated in

---

[1]The semantics of the hd and tl operators are similar to those of the *car* and *cdr* operators of LISP.

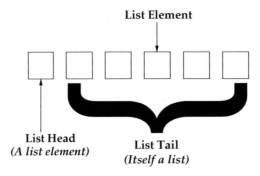

Figure 3.1   Lists in Limbo.

Figure 3.1. An example of a list variable declaration, declaring a list of items of type `string` is shown below:

```
menu : list of string;
```

It is possible to specify initializers for the elements of a list in its declaration. For example, our list of strings, `menu`, could have been declared and initialized in one fell swoop in the following manner:

```
menu := list of {"Quinoa", "Soy"};
```

Lists in Limbo are *reference types*. A list variable contains a reference to a list, and not to the actual storage for items of the list. The list operators that will be described next operate on these references, and do not modify the actual elements of the list.

3.4.1 The :: Operator

The `::` operator, or 'cons' operator, is the list constructor. It is an infix operator, which always takes two arguments: an item to be appended to the head of a list, and a list. The item to be appended to the list must have the same type as the items on the list it is being appended to. The behavior of the `::` operator is shown below:

```
#   Initial value of a list variable is nil : no storage allocated
menu : list of string;

#   Add one item to the empty list
menu = "Soy"::menu;
```

```
#   After this, the head of the list of 2 items is "Quinoa"
menu = "Quinoa"::menu;
```

In the above example, when the variable menu is initially created, its value is set to nil, and it has length 0. The first assignment appends the string "Soy" to the head of the list. The list now has length 1, with its head being the string "Soy", and its tail being a reference to an empty list, nil.

After the concatenation of the second item, "Quinoa", to the list, the head of the list is now the string "Quinoa". The tail of the list is now a reference to a list whose head item is the string "Soy" and whose tail is nil.

3.4.2   The hd Operator

The hd or 'head' operator returns the first element of the list to which it is applied. The *value* of the head of the list is returned, and not a reference to it; thus any changes made to the returned value do not affect the original list.

The operator does not have any side effects; you can take the hd of a list as many times as you want, and do all sorts of mean things to it, leaving the original list (and its head) unperturbed.

A hd expression has the type of the list's elements, so applying the hd operator to a expression of type list of string yields an expression of type string. The following example illustrates:

```
#   This declares q to be of type string and initializes
#   it to the value of the head of the list of string 'menu'
q := hd menu;
```

3.4.3   The tl Operator

The tl or 'tail' operator returns all the items in a list after the head. A tl expression has the same type as the list on which it operates. Like the hd operator, applying the tl operator to a list is non-destructive.

The result of a tl expression is a reference to a *copy* of the tail of the original list. For example:

```
#   Declare a variable sub_menu of type list of string and
#   initialize it with a copy of the tail of the list menu
sub_menu := tl menu;
```

Applying the len operator to a list yields the number of elements in the list. Given the previous declaration of the list menu, the following declares a variable and initializes it to the length of menu:

```
#   The list menu now has two items, so this declares a
#   variable of type int and initializes it with the value 2
num := len menu;
```

3.5 Arrays

Like lists in Limbo, arrays are reference types. An array expression such as a[i] (denoting the *i*th element of array variable a) or b[27] (the 28th element of array variable b) is a *reference* to an item in memory, and does not hold the value itself. Arrays in Limbo are indexed from 0, and an array of n elements will have its elements indexed from 0 to $n - 1$.

In a declaration such as the following, which declares a variable jimbox to be an array with elements of type int, no storage is initially allocated for the variable jimbox. It is initialized to the value nil:

```
jimbox : array of int;
```

Since arrays are reference types, the above declaration has not associated any storage with the variable jimbox, and the variable contains the value nil. The length of a nil array, such as the one above, is zero.

Before using the variable jimbox, it is necessary to allocate storage for it:

```
jimbox = array [64] of int;
```

Alternatively, the actions of declaration and allocation can be performed in a single step:

```
jimbox := array [64] of int;
```

It is possible to specify initializers for the elements of an array in its declaration:

```
people := array [] of {"jimbox","matter","pip","vasil","sbourne"};
```

The above example declares an array of strings, `people`. The array has length 5, and its elements are initialized to the strings "jimbox", "matter", "pip", "vasil" and "sbourne".

It is possible to initialize all the members of an array to a specific constant, or to initialize ranges of array indices to constants. The syntax for this closely follows that for the case statements discussed in Chapter 2:

```
#   An array with all 4 elements initialized to the value 3.14
#   The variable p thus has type array of real, and length 4:
p := array [4] of {* => 3.14};

#   The following array, however, has length 0. The initialization
#   is ignored:
q := array [] of {* => 3.14};

#   Initialize all odd indices to zero, even indices to 1
#   The array has length 10:
w := array [] of {0 or 2 or 4 or 6 or 8 => 1,
            1 or 3 or 5 or 7 or 9 => 0};

#   The following is illegal : the range '0 to 10' overlaps
#   with the specifier '1 or 3 or 5 or 7 or 9':
#x := array [] of {0 to 10 => 1, 1 or 3 or 5 or 7 or 9 => 0};

#   Same as the array w : the '*' specifier has no effect since
#   the size and initial values of the array are determined by
#   the explicit range specifiers. The array length is 10:
y := array [] of {
            0 or 2 or 4 or 6 or 8 => 1,
            1 or 3 or 5 or 7 or 9 => 0,
            * => -1
        };


#   This array has length 20. The last 10 elements are
#   initialized to -1, and the first 10 identical to
#   the arrays w and y above:
z := array [20] of {
            0 or 2 or 4 or 6 or 8 => 1,
            1 or 3 or 5 or 7 or 9 => 0,
            * => -1
        };
```

3.5.1 Multi-Dimensional Arrays

Multi-dimensional arrays in Limbo can be created by creating arrays of arrays, as shown below:

An array, a, with 7 elements

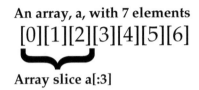

Array slice a[:3]

Figure 3.2 Array slices.

```
#   No storage allocated yet
m1 : array of array of big;

#   This is insufficient, can you tell why?
m1 = array[10] of {array[100] of big};

#   Alternatively, we could have done this (also insufficient):
m2 := array[10] of {array [100] of big};
```

In the above, we only allocate one dimension of the array. The correct way to initialize a two-dimensional array, so that all its members have storage allocated for them, is as follows:

```
#   No storage allocated yet
m1 : array of array of big;

#   This allocates storage for both dimensions
m1 = array[10] of {* => array[100] of big};

#   Alternatively, we could have done
m2 := array[10] of {* => array [100] of big};
```

In the above example, the curly braces around the type of the second dimension of the array for m1 and m2 are necessary. You could create a 12×8 matrix with all members initialized to the string "hello" by:

```
m2d := array [12] of {* => array [8] of {* => "hello"}};
```

3.5.2 Array and String Slices

Limbo supports slicing of arrays and strings. Slices are subset ranges of an array or string, starting with an integral *start* index and continuing up to, but not inclusive of, an integral *end* index. The syntax of array and string slicing is identical, although slices of arrays are references, whereas slices of strings are values:

varname [*start* : *end*]

Figure 3.2 and the example below illustrate the use of array slices:

```
story := array [] of {"I","should","get","a","life"};

#   This sets task to {"get", "a", "life"};
#   It is permitted to leave out the upper index
#   in a slice expression:
task := story[2:];

#   Declares a string dream and initializes it to "got a life"
dream := task[0][:1]+"o"+task[0][2:]+" "+task[1]+" "+task[2];
```

The example above illustrates two shorthand notations for slices, when either the start of the slice is the first item (as in `task[0][:1]`), or when the end of the slice is the last item (as in `story[2:]`).

For arrays only, it is possible to use a slice as an *lvalue*, i.e. it is possible to perform an assignment to a slice (due to the fact that array slices are references, not values like string slices). In an assignment to an array slice, the ending index of the slice cannot be specified. The starting index may also optionally be omitted:

```
a := array [10] of int;
b := array [20] of int;

#   Assign reference to array a, to array b starting
#   at index 10. It is illegal to specify the end index
#   for the destination (variable b):
b[10:] = a;

#   Assign reference to array a, to array b starting
#   at index 0. The starting index is implicit (index 0):
b[:] = a;

#   Assign reference slice of array a, starting at index
#   5 (implicit end at length of a), to variable b,
#   starting at index 15:
b[15:] = a[5:];
```

3.5.3 Conversion Between Strings and Arrays of Bytes

A cast expression from a string to an array of bytes converts the string (recall a string is a vector of Unicode characters) to the UTF-8 byte sequence representing the string. UTF-8 is an encoding scheme which represents 16-bit Unicode characters as one-, two- or three-byte sequences, depending on their value.

If the string contains only ASCII characters (ASCII is a subset of Unicode), then the resulting UTF-8 byte array would be as you would intuitively expect, with each character of the string represented by a byte. Thus the resulting byte array will have the same number of elements as the initial string. Applying the `len` operator to both will yield the same result.

If, however, the string contains Unicode characters outside of the ASCII subset, the resulting UTF-8 byte array may contain multi-byte representations for some of the constituent Unicode characters. As a result, the number of elements in the byte array may be greater than the number of Unicode characters in the original string.

The following example illustrates this behavior. The variables `english` and `greek` hold strings meaning 'ant' in English and Greek, respectively:

```
english := "ant";
greek := "μυρμιγκι";

sys->print("Length of variable english is [\%d] Unicode chars",
    len english);
sys->print("Length of variable greek is [\%d] Unicode chars",
    len greek);

englishbytes := array of byte english;
greekbytes := array of byte greek;

sys->print("Length of variable englishbytes is [%d] Unicode chars",
    len englishbytes);

sys->print("Length of variable greekbytes is [%d] Unicode chars",
    len greekbytes);
```

The variable `english` has a length (as would be reported by `len`) of 3. The variable `greek` has a length of 8. These lengths signify the number of Unicode characters in the respective strings. When the variable `greek` is cast to an array of bytes, the number of bytes resulting from the cast differs from the number of Unicode characters. This is because the Unicode characters making up the string in this case are each represented by 2 bytes in their UTF-8 encoding. Thus, in the example above, the length of the array `greekbytes` is 16, twice the length of the variable `greek`. The variables `english` and `englishbytes`, however, have identical lengths of 3.

The behavior of casts from strings to arrays of bytes is fairly straightforward. Casts from arrays of bytes to strings, however, are much more subtle.

In a cast from an array of bytes to a string, the Limbo runtime interprets the array of bytes as a sequence of UTF-8 bytes, and attempts to construct a Unicode string from these bytes. If the array of bytes being cast is indeed a valid UTF-8 stream, then all is well, and the reverse operation can be performed to retrieve the original byte array. If the array of bytes in the cast is, however, not a valid UTF-8 sequence, then the official behavior of the Limbo runtime in the cast operation is undefined. The reverse of the cast (from string back to array of bytes) is therefore not guaranteed to yield the original byte array.

Consider the following snippet of code. The variable `buf` is an array of bytes containing arbitrary data. Does the following really do what it seems to be attempting to do (adding a stream of bytes representing two strings to either end of an existing stream of bytes)? What happens when `qitem.buf` is converted to a string in the first line? When it is converted back to an array of bytes, are the data originally represented by buf guaranteed to be unchanged?

```
clientfmt(qitem : ref Qitem) : (int, array of byte)
{
    body  := "<HTML><!"+string qitem.buf+"></HTML>\r\n";
    bytes := array of byte body;

    return (len bytes, bytes);
}
```

The following shows a more appropriate method for inserting the bytes. The moral of this example is resist the temptation to use string operations as shortcuts, as this may lead you down the path to madness:

```
clientfmt(qitem : ref Qitem) : (int, array of byte)
{
    headlen := len "<HTML><!";
    taillen := len "></HTML>\r\n";
    bytes := array [qitem.size + headlen + taillen] of byte;

    bytes[0:] = array of byte "<HTML><!";
    bytes[headlen:] = qitem.buf;
    bytes[headlen+qitem.size:] = array of byte "></HTML>\r\n";

    return (len bytes, bytes);
}
```

3.6 Tuples

The Limbo `tuple` type is an unnamed collection of data items. Tuples in Limbo are represented as a list of data items, enclosed in parentheses, such as:

```
a := ("Jane", "Doe", 22, 3.8);
```

which is a tuple consisting of two `strings`, an `int` and a `real`. Tuples provide a simple means of grouping data of different types into a single entity and may be passed as arguments to functions, may be the return type of functions, and may essentially be used in every way that a non-conglomerative data type is used.

Tuples may be used as either the source or destination in assignment statements. When used as the destination of an assignment, the elements of the tuple are variables to which values are assigned. It is permitted to use the value `nil` as any of the elements in a tuple. If the tuple is receiving a value, this signifies that the value that would be bound to the variable at that position in the tuple should be discarded, as illustrated below:

```
major : string;
gpa : real;

personalinfo := ("R. James", "engineering", "tree", 10.0, "art", "music");

#   Extract 2nd and 4th fields, discard the rest
(nil, major, nil, gpa, nil, nil) = personalinfo;
```

In the above example, the second and fourth elements of the tuple `personalinfo` are extracted and assigned to the variables `major` and `gpa`, and the other fields of the tuple are discarded.

3.7 ADTs

Limbo aggregate data types or ADTs are an extension of its tuple type. They are named structures and permit direct access to their individual members by name. ADTs may also have member functions. Unlike arrays and lists, ADTs are value types.

The following illustrates the definition of an ADT with two members. The ADT members have type `int` and type `string`:

```
Person : adt
{
    age : int;
    name : string;
};
```

Items are declared to be ADTs with the `adt` keyword. Subsequent to the declaration of an ADT, it may be used just as though it were a regular built-in type. For example, having defined the ADT type `Person` above, one may declare a variable that is an instance of the `Person` ADT:

```
patient : Person;
```

Uninitialized ADT instances have the value `nil`. An ADT's members are accessed with the dot separator, '.'. For example, `patient.name` refers to the member `name` of the ADT instance `patient`.

Because of the close relation between ADTs and tuples, the Limbo language permits direct assignments between an ADT and a tuple with the same number and types of elements. If the ADT contains a function, it is ignored. The following example illustrates the use of ADTs:

```
# File : bday.b

implement Bday;

include "sys.m";
include "draw.m";

#    ADT type definition. This cannot be placed
#    inside a function definition:
B: adt
{
    year: int;
    month: string;
    day: int;
    age : fn(me : B) : int;
};
Bday : module
{
    init : fn(nil : ref Draw->Context, nil : list of string);
};

init (nil: ref Draw->Context, nil : list of string)
{
    #    ADT instance declaration:
    bdate : B;

    #    Assigning to the ADT instance members:
    bdate.year = 1928;
    bdate.month = "August";
    bdate.day = 6;

    #    The variable date is a tuple that can be
    #    assigned to the B ADT, as it has type
    #    (int, string, int) which matches data members
    #    of the ADT B:
    date := (0,"", 0);

    #    Thus the following assignment is valid; The
    #    age() member of bdate is ignored in the assignment:
    date = bdate;

    #    The age function takes its instance as an explicit argument:
    age := bdate.age(bdate);
}

#    The definition of the ADT function age for ADT type B:
B.age(me : B) : int
{
    #    Body of ADT function implementation

    return 0;
}
```

The definition of the ADT must not be placed inside the body of a function, and in the example above the definition of the ADT B is placed outside the definition of the function `init`.

In the example above, the ADT instance `bdate` of the ADT type `B` is created and initialized and subsequently assigned to a tuple `date`. In the above, the function `age` takes as argument a copy of itself, which must be specified explicitly. We shall see in later sections how to improve on this construction with the use of the `self` keyword.

Data members of an ADT can only be accessed through an *instance* of the ADT. It is incorrect to access data members of an ADT *type*. For example, if the variable `bdate` is an instance of ADT type B, `bdate.year` is valid but `B.year` is incorrect, since that would be accessing the data member of a type.

ADT member functions may, however, be accessed through the ADT type. Unlike datum members, an ADT member function has its implementation pre-specified: it must be specified in the implementation of the module that defines the ADT type.

When using ADTs defined within one module's interface in another module, it is often necessary to import the ADT definition from the module instance[2]. ADTs are always associated with a module and this module provides the implementation of any ADT member functions. Importing the ADT definition from a module instance associates variables of the ADTs type with a particular module implementation instance, and therefore invoked module functions are unambiguously tied to a particular implementation.

Along the same lines of reasoning, you cannot define an ADT inside a function. This is because the ADT definition would be limited to the scope of the function, and it would not be possible to define any ADT member functions, since one cannot define functions inside other functions.

3.7.1   Reference ADTs

Limbo restricts direct access to memory by not having pointer types as in C and C++. ADTs are value types, but it is possible to create a restricted form of pointers to this value type.

Applying the `ref` operator to an existing ADT instance makes a *copy* of that ADT (a value) and yields a *reference to this new copy* and *not a reference to the already existing ADT value*. This reference can be used in much the same manner as ordinary value ADTs—accessing datum and function members of reference ADTs is still done with the '.' separator. During assignments and when passed as arguments to functions, however, reference ADTs behave differently from value ADTs. Assignments from reference ADTs yield references to the same object.

The example below illustrates the use of reference ADTs. What do you expect the output of the print statements to be, and why?

---

[2]As discussed in Chapter 2, imports are always performed from a module *instance* rather than a module *type*.

```
# File : clinic.b

implement Clinic;

include "sys.m";
include "draw.m";

sys : Sys;
print : import sys;

PatientRecord : adt
{
    name : string;
    age : int;
};

Clinic : module
{
    init : fn(nil : ref Draw->Context, nil : list of string);
};

init (nil : ref Draw->Context, nil : list of string)
{
    np, p, newpatient : ref PatientRecord;
    patient : PatientRecord;

    sys = load Sys Sys->PATH;

    newpatient = ref patient;
    patient.name = "John Doe";
    patient.age = 46;

    print("Patient Name = %s\n", newpatient.name);
    print("Patient Age = %d\n", newpatient.age);

    np = p = ref PatientRecord("John Doe", 46);
    print("Patient Name = %s\n", p.name);
    print("Patient Age = %d\n", p.age);
    np.age = 120;
    print("Patient Name = %s\n", p.name);
    print("Patient Age = %d\n", p.age);
}
```

The output of the first set of print statements is:

```
Patient Name =
Patient Age = 0
```

You were probably expecting to see the contents of the instance patient printed out, right?

In the statement newpatient = ref patient;, a copy of the patient ADT instance is made and a reference to that copy is what gets assigned to newpatient.

The variables np and p are, however, both references to the same instance of PatientRecord. Thus the last pair of print statements print out the following:

```
Patient Name = John Doe
Patient Age = 120
```

It is not possible to copy data directly between ADTs and reference ADTs; however, values may be extracted from reference ADTs using the '*' operator, as shown below:

```
a, d : ExpData;
b : ref ExpData;
c := ref a;

#   We might want to do this to initialize b, but it's illegal:
#b = a;

#   Can obtain the value that c references:
d = *c;

#   The following is also legal:
*b = a;
```

Note that you can only initialize a reference ADT within a function, even though it might be defined in global scope.

3.7.2 Functions Defined within ADTs and the self Keyword

Functions defined within an ADT are identical to functions defined elsewhere in a module except for one addition: functions in ADTs often have to refer to data in the ADT instance of which they are part, and the Limbo language provides a facility to make this straightforward—the self keyword.

The self keyword may be used in the first argument to an ADT function to signify that the argument is a reference to the function's own ADT instance:

```
YourData : adt
{
    pkt_no : int;
    nmpkts : int;

    filter : fn (x : self ref YourData, method : string);
    handler : fn (x : self  ref YourData) : int;
};

YourData.filter(x : self YourData, method : string)
{
```

```
    }

    YourData.handler(x : self ref YourData) : int
    {
        return 0;
    }
```

Subsequent to this definition, the function handler is called without any arguments, even though its type definition defines one argument. Similarly, the ADT member function filter is called with only its method argument:

```
    yourdata : YourData;

    #   The following demonstrate calls of the two ADT
    #   methods:
    yourdata.filter("default");
    yourdata.handler();
```

The following example ties together some of the ideas on ADTs presented thus far.

3.7.3   Example: CacheLib

The module CacheLib is a simple associative memory module that can be used to store integers. The module interface definition for CacheLib is shown below:

```
# File : cachelib.m

CacheLib : module
{
    PATH : con "cachelib.dis";

    Cache : adt
    {
        cachesize : int;
        cache          : array of list of int;

        isincache : fn(cache : self ref Cache, fid : int) : int;
        addtocache     : fn(cache : self ref Cache, fid : int);
        delfromcache   : fn(cache : self ref Cache, fid : int);
        hash        : fn(cache : self ref Cache, fid : int) : int;

        allocate   : fn(cachesize : int) : ref Cache;
    };
};
```

The module implementation for CacheLib:

```
# File : cachelib.b
implement CacheLib;
include "cachelib.m";

Cache.hash(c : self ref Cache, n : int) : int
{
    return n % c.cachesize;
}

Cache.isincache(c : self ref Cache, id : int) : int
{
    bucket := c.hash(id);

    tmp := c.cache[bucket];
    while (tmp != nil)
    {
        if (hd tmp == id)
        {
            return 1;
        }

        tmp = tl tmp;
    }

    return 0;
}

Cache.addtocache(c : self ref Cache, id : int)
{
    if (!c.isincache(id))
    {
        bucket := c.hash(id);
        c.cache[bucket] = id :: c.cache[bucket];
    }
}

Cache.delfromcache(c : self ref Cache, id : int)
{
    newbucket : list of int;

    bucket := c.hash(id);
    tmp := c.cache[bucket];

    while (tmp != nil)
    {
        if (hd tmp != id)
        {
            newbucket = (hd tmp) :: newbucket;
        }

        tmp = tl tmp;
    }

    c.cache[bucket] = newbucket;
```

```
}
Cache.allocate(cachesize : int) : ref Cache
{
    cache := ref Cache (cachesize, array [cachesize] of list of int);

    return cache;
}
```

The Cachelib module provides a simple associative memory. Items in the cache are of type int.

The Cache ADT defines the data elements and methods for creating a new cache, inserting items into the cache, deleting items from the cache and querying the cache.

Queries may be made for the existence of items in the cache by presenting their value with the Cache.isincache method. Similarly, new items can be added to the cache or existing entries deleted using Cache.addtocache and Cache.delfromcache.

The allocate ADT member function creates a new instance of the Cache ADT and returns a reference to it to the caller. The remaining ADT member functions all take as an implicit argument this instance of the cache, and thus all have the first argument c : self ref Cache.

To use the Cache ADT, a module would first have to declare an instance of the CacheLib module. It would then have to import the Cache ADT type from the declared CacheLib module instance, and load an implementation of CacheLib. It can then call Cache.allocate() to obtain an instance of the Cache ADT. With the Cache ADT instance, it would then be able to call the ADT member functions from the instance to add and delete entries form the cache. The following example illustrates this:

```
include "cachelib.m";
cachelib : CacheLib;
Cache : import cachelib;

# ...
init (nil : ref Draw->Context, nil : list of string)
{
    cachelib = load CacheLib CacheLibPATH;

    #   Create a Cache instance with 1024 entries:
    numcache := Cache.allocate(1024);

    #   Add an entry to the cache:
    numcache.addtocache(12);
}
```

3.7.4 The cyclic Keyword

The `cyclic` keyword is a flag to the compiler to prevent it from complaining about cyclic data *structures*.

It is possible to define cyclic data *types* such as the following:

```
Tree : adt
{
    child : ref Leaf;
};

Leaf : adt
{
    parent : ref Tree;
};
```

There is a cycle in the above ADT definitions, with a `Tree` containing a reference to a `Leaf` and vice versa. We can go ahead and create instances of both the `Tree` and `Leaf` ADTs defined above:

```
tree : Tree;
leaf : Leaf;
```

The above defines two variables whose types could lead to a cycle, but we do not have a cyclic structure, and the above code fragment would be accepted by the compiler.

If we tried to assign to, say, the `child` field of `tree`, then the compiler would complain that this could lead to a cycle, with an error message such as the following:

```
cyclic.b:28: cannot assign to 'tree.child' because field 'child' of 'tree'
could complete a cycle to 'tree'
```

If we expressly wanted to create a structure with a cycle, we could make these intentions known to the compiler to make it stop complaining. The following will create a cyclic structure and will suppress the complaints from the compiler:

```
# File : cyclic.b

implement Cyclic;

include "sys.m";
include "draw.m";

Cyclic : module
{
    init : fn (nil : ref Draw->Context, nil : list of string);
```

```
};

Tree : adt
{
    child : cyclic ref Leaf;
};

Leaf : adt
{
    parent : ref Tree;
};

init (nil : ref Draw->Context, nil : list of string)
{
    tree : Tree;
    leaf : Leaf;

    tree.child = ref leaf;
}
```

The restriction on creating cyclic data structures is in place purely to make sure that they are only created when the programmer expressly wishes them to be created. The Dis VMs garbage collection algorithms are able to detect when such cyclic structures have no other references and free them appropriately. However, the structure is no longer guaranteed to be freed immediately upon its reference count decrementing to zero.

The effect of such non-instantaneous freeing is most visible when such cyclic structures contain references to garbage-collected entities with which the user interacts, such as windows in the graphics system. The virtual machine's garbage-collection algorithms are described in [26].

3.7.5 Pick ADTs

Pick ADTs are a variation on ADTs, with the addition of named *union substructures*. They can be used in situations where many variations of some data structure with overlapping substructures is desired, and they provide a means of naming each of these substructures.

The pick ADT then enables a program to select the substructure which has been given a value at runtime without any *a priori* knowledge of which substructure has been set. The syntax for declaring a pick ADT is as follows:

> *adtname* :   adt
> {
>
>>   *variable declarations*
>>   or
>>   *function declarations*
>
>>   pick

```
            {
                        SubstructureName  =>   variable  :   type;
                        . . .
                        variable  :   type;
            }
                        function declarations only, or empty
      };
```

Note that the variables qualified by a substructure name are not enclosed in braces.

Pick ADTs may only contain one `pick` statement and this must appear after all data declarations. Function definitions may be placed before and after the definition of the `pick`. The definition of a single pick ADT makes several new types available for variable definitions. These types are the name of the ADT (as would happen for any ordinary ADT definition) and the name of the ADT qualified by a '.' followed by each of the pick's substructure names. In the following example, the definition of the pick ADT `AudioHeader` makes the types `AudioHeader`, `AudioHeader.DSTMtracker`, `AudioHeader.ATOMtracker` and `AudioHeader.SMASHERtracker` available, and variables may be defined to be any of these four types. For example:

```
    AudioHeader : adt
    {
        mod : string;
        version : int;
        pick
        {
            DSTMtracker => header : array of byte;
            ATOMtracker or SMASHERtracker  => header : string;
        }
        decode : fn ();
    };
    AudioHeader.decode()
    {
    }
```

Note that in the ADT definition above, the second clause in the pick statement associated two different identifiers with the variable of type `string` using an `or` statement.

Variables may only be defined as references to pick ADTs. It is illegal to declare a variable as an instance of a pick ADT. A violation of this rule will lead to a compiler error such as the following:

```
filterfs.b:94: cannot declare msg with type Filter->Filtermsg
```

Possible valid variable declarations using our previous `AudioHeader` ADT definition are:

```
#    The following statement is illegal (can only declare
#    variables to be a ref to a pick ADT:
#a : AudioHeader;

#    This is one valid variable definition:
ha : ref AudioHeader;

#    This is a second valid definition:
hb : ref AudioHeader.DSTMtracker;

#    This is a third valid definition:
hc : ref AudioHeader.ATOMtracker;

#    This is a fourth valid definition:
hd : ref AudioHeader.SMASHERtracker;

#    A definition with an initialization from a tuple:
he := ref AudioHeader.DSTMtracker("ambient01", 9, array of byte "$DSTM");
```

In the above example, the variables hb, hc, hd and he can be used like ordinary ref ADTs. The variable ha, however, is different. This variable may at runtime be of any of the three pick variations, i.e. it will always have the members mod and version of types string and int, respectively, but its header field may be either of type array of byte or of type string, and may be tagged with the identifiers DSTMtracker in the former case and SMASHERtracker or ATOMtracker in the latter.

A variable such as ha which is not defined to be a specific version of the pick ADT must be initialized with a reference to one of the specific versions of its pick ADT type. This is illustrated below:

```
myfunc ()
{
   ha : ref AudioHeader;
   hb := ref AudioHeader.DSTMtracker("ambient01", 9, array of byte "$DSTM");

   hb = ha;
}
```

Subsequent to initialization, the variation of the pick ADT that the variable is a reference to can be determined using the tagof operator, and the data members of the variable may be selected using a pick statement.

In the example below, the type of a reference to an instance of a pick ADT, ha, is determined using a pick statement. Based on the type, different sections of code in the pick statement are executed:

```
myfunc ()
{
```

```
sys = load Sys Sys->PATH;

ha : ref AudioHeader;
hb := ref AudioHeader.DSTMtracker("ambient01", 9, array of byte "$DSTM");
ha = hb;

sys->print("tagof ha = %d\n", tagof ha);

flabel : for (i := 0; i < 5; i++)
{
    plabel : pick h := ha
    {
        ATOMtracker =>
        {
            sys->print(
            "The variable ha is of pick variant ATOMtracker\n");

            #   Break out of pick, not out of loop
            break plabel;
        }

        DSTMtracker =>
        {
            sys->print(
            "The variable ha is of pick variant DSTMtracker\n");

            #   Break out of loop
            break flabel;
        }

        SMASHERtracker =>
        {
            sys->print(
            "The variable ha is of pick variant SMASHERtracker\n");
        }

        * =>
        {
            sys->print("The variable ha has an unknown tag type!\n");
        }
    }
}
```

As illustrated above, pick statements may have an optional label as in case statements and the looping constructs. This may be used to break out of the execution of a tag-qualified statement list within a pick statement.

Note that the head of the pick statement must contain an implicit declaration and initialization of a variable, i.e. we 'pick' on an expression of the form x := y.

The output of the above example is:

```
tagof ha = 0
```

```
The variable ha is of pick variant DSTMtracker
```

If none of the identifiers (tags) in the pick statement matches the tag of the expression at its head, the statement list qualified by '*' is executed.

3.8 Type Definitions

Limbo allows you to declare synonyms for a type, using the `type` keyword. The syntax for type synonym declarations is:

> *identifier-list* **:**   `type` *data-type***;**

For example:

```
long : type int;
uchar : type byte;

#   ...

#   We can declare variables using the type synonyms long and uchar:
a : long;
b : uchar;
```

Subsequent to these definitions, `uchar` and `long` may be used as synonyms for types `byte` and `int`, respectively, and variables declared to be of type `uchar` have type `byte`, etc.

3.9 Summary

Limbo is strongly typed. It enforces type checking both at compile time and at runtime. Coercion between types requires explicit type casting and is only permitted in a restricted number of situations.

Limbo provides a rich set of data types. The primitive data types are `big`, `byte`, `int`, `real` and `string`. It also provides structured data types in the form of arrays, lists, tuples and ADTs. Limbo arrays and strings support element indexing and slicing. Tuples are unnamed collections of types. ADTs are named collections of functions and data, and may be cast to tuples and vice versa. Lists in Limbo are lists of elements of the same type. The language provides operators for retrieving the head of a list, retrieving the tail of a list (which is a list consisting of the original list minus its head), and appending an element to the head of a list.

Most Limbo types are value types. Of the data types discussed thus far, the exceptions are arrays, lists and ref ADTs, which are reference types. Limbo provides a restricted form of pointers through reference ADTs. Modules and channels, which are discussed in more detail in Chapters 4 and 7, are also reference types.

Bibliographic Notes

An enjoyable (though dated) overview of the history of programming languages is [1]. The idea of abstract data types is often credited to the CLU language [30]. Pierce [49] provides a lucid description of the relation between ADTs and objects, and their relation to existential types in type theory. The concepts of channels and alternation on channels are from Hoare's *Communicating Sequential Processes (CSP)* [25] via Alef [81] and Newsqueak [50]. A thorough formalism for concurrent systems is Milner's π-calculus [41]. The language level lists and list operators, as well as the module system bear similarity to those of ML [42]. An overview of the floating point facilities in Inferno is provided in [23]. A good general overview of floating point arithmetic is [22]. The description of Inferno's Dis virtual machine in [31] provides a good exposition of how the types from the Limbo language are implemented in the underlying system.

3.10   Chapter Examples

3.10.1   Example: Liner

The following example is a file line numbering program. It reads in the contents of a text file, and prepends a line number to each line of the file.

```
# File : liner.b

implement Liner;

include "sys.m";
include "draw.m";
include "bufio.m";

sys : Sys;
bufio : Bufio;
Iobuf : import bufio;

Liner : module
{
    init : fn(ctxt : ref Draw->Context, argv : list of string);
};

init (nil : ref Draw->Context, argv : list of string)
{
    param := tl argv;
    while (param != nil)
    {
        liner(hd param);

        param = tl param;
    }
}

liner(filename : string)
{
    lines : list of string;
    temp_line : string;

    sys = load Sys Sys->PATH;
    bufio = load Bufio Bufio->PATH;

    file_buf := bufio->open(filename,sys->ORDWR);
    while ()
    {
        temp_line = file_buf.gets('\n');
        if (temp_line == "")
            break;
        else
            lines = temp_line::lines;
    }

    file_buf.seek(0,0);
    lines = reorder(lines);
```

```
    i := 1;
    while (lines != nil)
    {
        file_buf.puts(string i +"\t"+ hd lines);
        lines = tl lines;
        i++;
    }

    file_buf.flush();
}

reorder(flist : list of string) : list of string
{
    rlist : list of string;

    while (flist != nil)
    {
        rlist = hd flist::rlist;
        flist = tl flist;
    }

    return rlist;
}
```

Discussion   The file is read in line by line, and each line concatenated to the head of `lines`, which is of type `list of string`. Due to the fact that new lines are added to the head of the list `lines`, when the file has been read in, the most recently read line (the last line of the file) is at the list's head. To print out the items on the list, however, there is no way to index directly to the last item at the tail of the list, which holds the string representing the first line read from the file. We therefore reorder the items on the list to be able to print out the lines in correct order.

   For each line, the line number is concatenated by casting a counter to type `string`, then using the + operator to concatenate the string obtained from the cast to the string dequeued from the head of the list.

Problems

3.1   Limbo has the built-in data type list. Is it more efficient to implement lists using this built-in data type or using ADTs? Create a program to sort the list of numbers

   9 4 33 2 1 55 6 3 22 78 345 13 68 2465 7 8 5 5 3 45 6 78 8 90

in ascending order using the built-in list type. Record the average execution times.

3.2   Re-implement the program from Problem 3.1 using ADTs. Is it faster or slower? What do you think is the reason for the performance difference you observe (if there is any)?

3.3   Write a program to find the first 1024 prime numbers.

4

Using Modules

4.1 Review

Modules provide the basic structure in Limbo applications, permitting a clean functional decomposition of applications into disjoint, possibly reusable components. Modules were briefly introduced in Chapter 2 and the material presented there is assumed here. A quick perusal of the relevant sections in Chapter 2 would be a good idea before continuing with this chapter.

Throughout this chapter, the term *application* will be used to refer to a conglomeration of executables interacting to solve some problem, ranging from simple cases such as the 'Hello World' application in Chapter 2 to more complex applications such as the Inferno shell or a Web server. The individual executables (residing in '.dis' files) that make up these applications will be referred to as *modules*. The simplest application (for example, the tiny Limbo program at the end of Chapter 2) comprises a single module. For the most part, even trivial applications will use several modules. In other words, several compiled modules will be used to achieve the goals of the application.

For example, the 'Hello World' program in Chapter 2 comprises the module `HelloWorld` (the main module) and utilizes the `Sys` module (used for the `print` routine to print the greeting).

In Figure 4.1, the application, *Sh* (which happens to be the Inferno command shell), begins with the execution of the Sh module. This module, whose implementation resides in the file `/dis/sh.dis`, requires other modules to perform its task. In particular, it needs functionality provided by the Inferno system, as do most other modules, for performing I/O, etc. This is provided through the `Sys` module (shown as `$Sys` in the

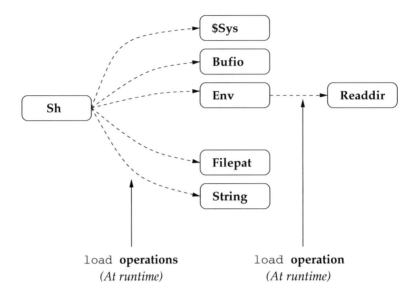

Figure 4.1 A Limbo application comprising many modules.

figure to hint at the fact that it is a built-in module). The Sh module thus *loads* the Sys, Bufio, Env, Filepat and String modules at runtime using Limbo load expressions. The loaded modules provide functionality that the shell uses, e.g. buffered I/O from the Bufio module and string manipulation facilities from the String module. One of the modules loaded by Sh, the Env module, further loads the Readdir module.

Even though applications typically comprise several modules, any Dis executable can only contain the implementation of (i.e. executable code for) a single module. Unlike in the case of C, C++ and other languages, there is no static linking performed when a Limbo program is compiled. A Limbo module that uses other modules as part of some application must therefore explicitly *load* the module of interest before references to functions and data elements in the module are made.

For example, if a Limbo program makes references to other modules, such as to the print routine of the Sys module, the compiled Limbo program will not contain any of the code for the Sys->print routine but rather only references to it. Before calling Sys->print at runtime, the module must load an implementation of the Sys module and place a reference to this implementation in a module variable. It can then invoke the print method of the module instance:

```
sys : Sys;

sys = load Sys Sys->PATH;
sys->print("Hello\n");
```

At load time, only the functions in a module that will be used have their function signatures checked. All the module's global data on the other hand are type checked if any module global datum is accessed.

In other words, you can load an implementation with a different type into a module variable, provided the signatures of its functions which you use match and you do not use any of the module's data elements. If you *do* use any of the module's data members, then *all* the data members in the module type and loaded implementation must type check.

Furthermore, if the Limbo runtime system determines that a reference to an implementation (through a module variable) will be used by *another* loaded module, then the signatures of all functions are checked, and not just those of the functions that are used within the module performing the original load operation. This is because the second module in question might access any of the loaded modules functions and global data through the module reference that is passed to it.

4.1.1   Example

The following module definition shows the interface of a module, Swamp. Subsequent to this definition, the identifier Swamp is a module *type*, and variables may be defined to be of this type. The module defines two constants PATH and DESCR, a function think, a string datum, mind and an ADT Monk.

Another module that wishes to use the Swamp module must include this module definition, either by explicitly spelling out the definition in its module implementation or by an include statement. An include statement causes the textual substitution of the contents of a named file at the location of its definition. Subsequent to the inclusion of the Swamp module's definition (e.g. from a '.m' file), the Swamp module must still be *loaded* at runtime (e.g. from a '.dis' file) before the think function can be accessed:

```
# File : swamp.m

Swamp : module
{
    PATH : con "swamp.dis";
    DESCR : con "Dismal Swamp Tech. Monastery monk module";

    think : fn(init : string);
    mind : string;

    Monk : adt
    {
        new : fn(drawcontext: ref Draw->Context): ref Monk;
        name : string;
        B, E, J, P: con 1 << iota;
    };
};
```

The other components of the Swamp module, besides think and mind (i.e. constants PATH and DESCR and the ADT definition Monk), may, however, be used without loading the module since they are not tied to the module's implementation: they are part of the interface. Thus, after including swamp.m and without loading the Swamp module from, say, 'swamp.dis', Swamp->PATH and Swamp->DESCR are valid uses. Similarly, a variable of type Swamp->Monk may be defined. Note that any module that implements the Swamp module must provide a definition for the function think as well as a definition for the new method of the Monk ADT:

```
# File : swamp.b

implement Swamp;

include "sys.m";
include "draw.m";
include "swamp.m";

think(init : string)
{
}

Monk.new(drawcontext: ref Draw->Context): ref Monk
{
    k : Monk;

    return ref k;
}
```

4.1.2 Instantiating Modules

The steps involved in instantiating a module are illustrated in Figure 4.2. Before the functions in a module are invoked, an implementation of the module must be *loaded*. This means the implementation (Dis executable) must be read off the disk or other such medium and loaded into the Dis VM.

A reference to this instance of the module is placed in a variable with type of the module interface. This variable acts as a handle to the loaded instance of the module, and is thereafter used to refer to the implementation's functions and data. A module may contain state, such as the mind variable of the Swamp module, and once a module is loaded this state may be modified per loaded instance of the module.

Loading the implementation of a module consumes system resources—the module in question is read off some storage medium (usually the local disk) and loaded into memory. The loaded implementation is unloaded from memory by the Dis VM when the last reference to it (via the module handle) is lost, ensuring that only in-use code remains in the memory of the host machine, a key consideration for the resource-constrained systems for which Inferno and Limbo were designed.

An application may explicitly request that the virtual machine unload a loaded implementation, by assigning the value nil to the corresponding module instance variable. If the module variable in question contained the only remaining reference

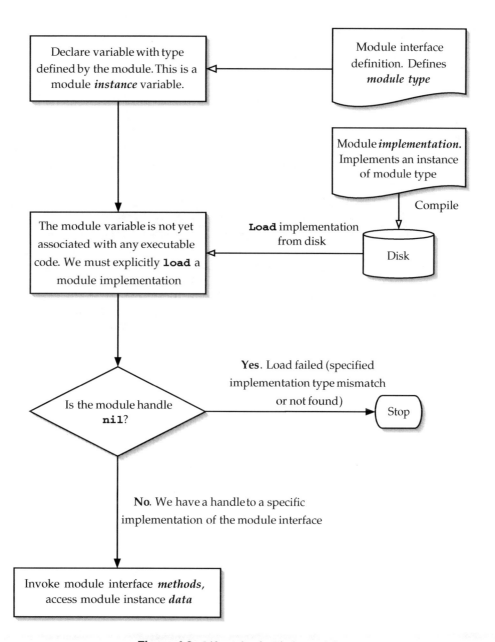

Figure 4.2 Life cycle of a Limbo module.

to the loaded module, storage for the module would be reclaimed by the Dis VM's reference-counting garbage collector.

4.1.3   Module Types and Variables

Subsequent to the definition of a module, the module name is a newly visible type and variables of its type may be declared. Such variables are usually referred to as handles for the module and are used to hold the result of a load expression. When the implementation of a module is loaded, by way of a load expression, a reference to the instantiated module is returned. This is stored in a variable with type of the loaded module.

The member constants of a module may either be accessed via the module type name (i.e. the module interface), e.g. Swamp->DESCR, or via a variable with type of the module, e.g. swamp->DESCR, subsequent to a declaration such as:

```
swamp : Swamp;
```

Member ADT definitions of a module may similarly be referenced through either the module type or through a variable with the module's type.

Member functions and data of a module may only be accessed through an instance of the module via a module handle. Even though such accesses will be syntactically valid, an implementation of the module must also be loaded before the accesses at runtime.

4.1.4   Importing Module Definitions

Thus far, whenever the member functions, variables, ADT definitions or constants of a module have been referred to, they have explicitly been qualified by either the module type or a variable with the module's type. The names of members of a module may be made visible in the current scope through an `import` statement. The example below illustrates the use of the `import` construct:

```
# File : testswamp.b

implement Test;

include "sys.m";
include "draw.m";
include "swamp.m";

sys : Sys;
swamp : Swamp;

#     This import statement is syntactically legal, but a subsequent
#     unqualified 'print' statement would be illegal, because it would
#     be equivalent to a Sys->print, which is illegal since Sys is a
#     module interface and not a module instance variable:
#print : import Sys;

#     The following are valid import statements:
```

```
print : import sys;
Monk : import swamp;

Test : module
{
        init : fn(nil : ref Draw->Context, nil : list of string);
};

init(nil : ref Draw->Context, nil : list of string)
{
    #     These are both valid definitions of ADTs of type Monk
    botis : ref Swamp->Monk;

    sys = load Sys Sys->PATH;
    swamp = load Swamp Swamp->PATH;

    swamp->mind = "Take Over The World";

    print("swamp->DESCR [%s]\n", swamp->DESCR);
    print("Swamp->DESCR [%s]\n", Swamp->DESCR);

    #     Illegal, because Swamp is a module interface (type),
    #     and not a module instance (value)
    #sys->print("Swamp->mind [%s]\n", Swamp->mind);

    #     This is valid, since we can call functions in the ADT type,
    #     provided we've previously loaded an implementation of Swamp
    #     and imported the ADT definition Monk from the Swamp module
    #     instance (i.e. from module variable swamp, not module
    #     type Swamp):
    botis = Monk.new(nil);
}
```

4.2   Taking Advantage of Dynamic Module Loading

As an example of a situation in which the features of Limbo modules might come in very handy, consider a real-time data-collection application. It is constantly sampling a device for data and performs basic processing on the data it receives. The processing is carried out by a module which is loaded at runtime. After many days of collecting data, a trend is observed in the data stream which forces a design change: the data processing must be done in a different way, but we do not want to terminate the data-collection application.

A new implementation could be compiled, and at the command prompt a directive issued which causes the data-processing code to be reloaded between calls to it. Thus we can interactively change the application while it is running without shutting it down. The application could even be designed to generate source code and compile it, based on its input data, or it could even directly generate Dis byte-code to be on-the-fly compiled. Other applications might also include a program that does not know beforehand what type of input it will receive, and to avoid an implementation that caters for all possible situations (and is thus overly complex and bug prone), several separate implementations are made and the appropriate one loaded at runtime. An example of such an application is the View module, implemented in /dis/wm/view.dis.

4.3   Module Resource Consumption and Built-in Modules

A loaded module remains in memory until the last reference to it goes out of scope. In general, a module implementation must be loaded from disk or some other persistent storage. This is true for modules that are written in Limbo.

There are a select number of built-in modules that are part of the Inferno Dis VM. These include the Draw, Keyring, Math, Prefab, Sys and Tk modules, and it is possible to write new built-in modules for inclusion in the virtual machine. The built-in modules are written in C and compiled with the Inferno system. The appendix to this chapter details how to write built-in modules. Since built-in modules are part of the system, they are usually always occupying memory of the machine on which they run.

In general, most Limbo applications declare a global variable with type Sys to be a handle to the Sys module. Thus Sys is usually loaded (a reference to it placed in this global variable) at the beginning of execution of a Limbo program. Even though defining local variables of type Sys and loading the Sys module in each function of a module where it is needed would not cause significant memory overhead (the Sys module is always memory resident; loading it does not lead to the allocation of more resources), there is a possible performance overhead that will be incurred for the creation of the new module variable and its garbage collection.

4.4   Self-Referential Modules

A module instance may obtain a reference to itself with a different module interface or type, provided that type is a subset of its interface.

This is achieved by loading the special module implementation path, $Self, and placing the module reference resulting from the load expression into the variable of the new module type (which should be a subset of the loading module's type).

For example, consider the following module interface definition, taken from /module/styxlib.m. The interface defines a single function, dirgen. In normal use, an instance of Dirgenmod is passed as an argument to functions[1]:

```
Dirgenmod: module
```

---

[1]You can use module instance variables just like any other variable, passing them as arguments to functions, as return values, etc.

```
{
    dirgen : fn(srv: ref Styxlib->Styxserver, c: ref Styxlib->Chan,
        tab: array of Styxlib->Dirtab, i: int): (int, Sys->Dir);
};
```

The obvious way to supply such an instance of the module is to load an implementation of Dirgenmod from a file. This is, however, cumbersome as it would mean we would need a separate source file, defining an implementation for Dirgenmod, and we would have to compile that implementation separately.

The Limbo language provides a shorter approach. A Limbo application may associate its own instance, at runtime, with a module variable of a different type, provided that second type is a subset. For example, any module defining a dirgen function identical to that in the Dirgenmod module will be able to associate its own instance with a module variable of type Dirgenmod.

As an example, consider the following module definition, which is a superset of the definition of Dirgenmod:

```
StyxServer : module
{
    init : fn(ctxt : ref Draw->Context, args : list of string);

    dirgen : fn(srv: ref Styxlib->Styxserver, c: ref Styxlib->Chan,
        tab: array of Styxlib->Dirtab, i: int): (int, Sys->Dir);
};
```

If in the implementation of the above module we required an instance of Dirgenmod, for example, to pass as an argument to a function, we could obtain a reference to the StyxServer module implementation (i.e. to ourselves), place this in a variable of type Dirgenmod and use it as needed. The following fragments of an application illustrate this:

```
implement StyxServer;

StyxServer : module
{
    init : fn(ctxt : ref Draw->Context, args : list of string);

    dirgen: fn(srv: ref Styxlib->Styxserver, c: ref Styxlib->Chan,
        tab: array of Styxlib->Dirtab, i: int): (int, Sys->Dir);
};

init(ctxt : ref Draw->Context, args : list of string)
{
    #   Load ourselves into a module variable of type
    #   Dirgenmod. This module variable (devgen) will
    #   be used in the function server() below, as though
    #   it had been loaded from an implementation of Dirgenmod:
```

```
   devgen = load Dirgenmod "$self";
}

server(tmsgchan : chan of ref Styxlib->Tmsg, srv : ref Styxserver,
   sync : chan of int)
{
   #  ...
   while ()
   {
       msg := <-tmsgchan;
       if (msg == nil)
       {
           exit;
       }

       pick m := msg
       {
           #   Pass our current instance loaded
           #   into a Dirgenmod type to srv.devopen()
           Open =>   srv.devopen(m, devgen, dirtab);
       }
   }
}
```

In the above, an instance of the currently running StyxServer module is loaded
into a module variable of type Dirgenmod at initialization and is later passed as an
argument to a function.

4.5 Summary

Modules provide a means of structuring Limbo programs into modular, reusable
components.

Limbo modules comprise two parts: a module *interface* which defines a *module type*,
and a module *implementation*. Limbo applications are typically implemented using
several modules. These modules are not statically linked into a binary image but
rather load each other from disk at runtime, as needed, and may further explicitly
unload these implementations to conserve memory. The Dis VM's garbage collector
also performs garbage collection on module types, and thus a loaded module whose
last reference goes out of scope will have the resources it occupies reclaimed. This
runtime loading/unloading permits Limbo applications to use a minimum of system
resources.

A Limbo module that will load the implementation of another must specify the
type of the module that is being loaded. Limbo module definitions are what define
these module types, and they are typically placed in a separate '.m' source file. Thus
most Limbo applications will first include the definition of a module with an include
statement, then subsequently load its implementation from disk with a load expression.

At load time, the type of the module being loaded from disk (or other storage medium) is checked against the type of module as defined in the load expression.

The separation of the interface of a module from its implementation permits several implementations to be provided for a given interface with the most appropriate implementation being determined ('computed' if you will) at runtime, and subsequently loaded.

Bibliographic Notes

Examples of languages with sophisticated module systems include ML [42], the Oberon language [62, 84] and Modula-2 [24, 83].

4.6   Chapter Example: Xsniff

An example of the use of the Limbo module system is in the Xsniff application. Xsniff is an extensible packet sniffer, which loads appropriate modules for decoding captured traffic based on the type of traffic detected. Without going into the details of networking (covered in Chapter 9), it is insightful to look at the relevant portions of Xsniff. The code for the entire Xsniff application without the per-packet type modules is shown below. The Xsniff module interface (xsniff.m):

```
# File : xsniff.m

Ether : adt
{
    rcvifc    : array of byte;
    dstifc    : array of byte;
    data : array of byte;
    pktlen    : int;
};

XFmt : module
{
    BASEPATH: con "";
    ID   : string;
    fmt  : fn(data : array of byte, args : list of string) : (int, string);
};
```

The Xsniff implementation (xsniff.b):

```
# File : xsniff.b

implement Xsniff;

include "sys.m";
include "draw.m";
include "arg.m";
include "xsniff.m";

Xsniff : module
{
    DUMPBYTES : con 32;

    init : fn(nil : ref Draw->Context, args : list of string);
};

sys       : Sys;
arg       : Arg;
verbose        := 0;
etherdump := 0;
dumpbytes := DUMPBYTES;

init(nil : ref Draw->Context, args : list of string)
{
    n    : int;
```

```
buf   := array [Sys->ATOMICIO] of byte;

sys = load Sys Sys->PATH;
arg = load Arg Arg->PATH;

dev := "/net/ether0";
arg->init(args);
while((c := arg->opt()) != 0)
{
    case c
    {
        'v' => verbose = 1;
        'e' => etherdump = 1;
        'b' => dumpbytes = int arg->arg();
        'd' => dev = arg->arg();
        *  =>   usage();
    }
}
args = arg->argv();

tmpfd := sys->open(dev+"/clone", sys->OREAD);
if ((n = sys->read(tmpfd, buf, len buf)) < 1)
{
    fatal("Could not read "+dev+"/clone : "+
        sys->sprint("[%r]"));
}

(nil, dirstr) := sys->tokenize(string buf[:n], " \t");
channel := int (hd dirstr);

infd := sys->open(dev+sys->sprint("/%d/data", channel),
        sys->ORDWR);
if (infd == nil)
{
    fatal(dev+sys->sprint("/%d/data : [%r]", channel));
}

sys->print("Sniffing on %s/%d...\n", dev, channel);
tmpfd = sys->open(dev+sys->sprint("/%d/ctl", channel),
    sys->ORDWR);
if (tmpfd == nil)
{
    fatal(dev+sys->sprint("/%d/ctl : [%r]", channel));
}

#   Get all packet types
if (sys->fprint(tmpfd, "connect -1") < 0)
{
    fatal("setting interface for all packet types : "+
        sys->sprint("%r"));
}

if (sys->fprint(tmpfd, "promiscuous") < 0)
{
    fatal("setting interface promiscuous failed : "+
        sys->sprint("%r"));
```

```
        }

    spawn reader(infd, args);
}

reader(infd : ref Sys->FD, args : list of string)
{
    n       : int;
    ethptr      : ref Ether;
    fmtmod      : XFmt;


    ethptr = ref Ether(array [6] of byte,
            array [6] of byte,
            array [Sys->ATOMICIO] of byte,
            0);

    while (1)
    {
        n   = sys->read(infd, ethptr.data, len ethptr.data);
        if (n < 0)
        {
            fatal("error reading from fd : "+sys->sprint("%r"));
        }

        ethptr.pktlen = n - len ethptr.rcvifc;
        ethptr.rcvifc = ethptr.data[0:6];
        ethptr.dstifc = ethptr.data[6:12];

        #   Construct a new module name based on payload type
        #   This 'computed' module name will then be used to
        #   load an appropriate formatting module:
        nextproto := "ether"+sys->sprint("%4.4X",
                (int ethptr.data[12] << 8) |
                (int ethptr.data[13]));

        #   We only load new format module if it is not already
        #   loaded. We use the module data item fmtmod->ID to
        #   keep state within the loaded instance
        if ((fmtmod == nil) || (fmtmod->ID != nextproto))
        {
            fmtmod = load XFmt XFmt->BASEPATH +
                    nextproto + ".dis";

            if (fmtmod == nil)
            {
                continue;
            }
        }

        #   Call the loaded format module's formatter:
        (err, nil) := fmtmod->fmt(ethptr.data[14:], args);
    }

    return;
}
```

```
b2s(a : array of byte, n : int) : string
{
    tmp, s : string;

    #    Convert an n-byte array to a 2n Hex character string
    for (i := 0; i < n; i++)
    {
        tmp = sys->sprint("%2.2X", int a[i]);

        #    Grow by pushing the ceiling
        s[len s] = tmp[0];
        s[len s] = tmp[1];
    }

    return s;
}

usage()
{
    sys->print(
        "sniff [-e][-v][-d device][-b <# of Ethernet bytes to dump>]\n");
}

fatal(s : string)
{
    sys->print("Sniff FATAL :: %s\n", s);

    kill(sys->pctl(0, nil));
}

kill(pid: int)
{
    fd := sys->open("#p/"+string pid+"/ctl", sys->OWRITE);

    if (fd != nil)
    {
        sys->fprint(fd, "kill");
    }
}
```

Discussion   The Xsniff application operates as follows. The core of the application (the function `reader`) continuously reads Ethernet frames off an interface. Based on the type of payload determined from the Ethernet header, the name of an appropriate formatter module is *computed*, and an attempt is made to load the module if it is not already loaded:

```
    #    Construct a new module name based on payload type
    #    This 'computed' module name will then be used to
    #    load an appropriate formatting module:
    nextproto := "ether"+sys->sprint("%4.4X",
            (int ethptr.data[12] << 8) |
            (int ethptr.data[13]));
```

```
#   We only load new format module if it is not already
#   loaded. We use the module data item fmtmod->ID to
#   keep state within the loaded instance

if ((fmtmod == nil) || (fmtmod->ID!= nextproto))
{
    fmtmod = load XFmt XFmt->BASEPATH +
            nextproto + ".dis";

    if (fmtmod == nil)
    {
        continue;
    }
}

#   Call the loaded format module's formatter:
(err, nil) := fmtmod->fmt(ethptr.data[14:], args);
```

If loading the appropriate formatter for a given Ethernet frame payload type fails, the frame is silently dropped on the floor and the reader continues scanning Ethernet frame headers.

The Xsniff module header file defines an additional module interface, XFmt. This is the module interface specification that formatter modules must implement. Each formatter module has two components of interest to this discussion: an ID and a method for decoding and formatting information for the given frame type. The fmt method decodes and prints out information on the supplied data. The ID field is initialized by a formatting module the first time its fmt method is called. Storing this state within a module enables the reader thread to check whether the currently loaded formatter is the appropriate one for each frame.

Problems

4.1 Look at the module interface definitions of the modules in /module. Are they all identical? If not, how does the shell still manage to run them, given that the shell could not possibly have an *a priori* knowledge of the types of all modules it might have to run?

4.2 Name some changes that can be made to the command shell that would force all applications it will run to have identical module interface definitions. Would you want these changes made to your system?

4.3 Implement a Limbo module that will replicate itself when run, i.e. the output of running the module is the source of the module.

Appendix: Developing Built-in Modules

A few modules in the Limbo runtime environment are implemented in the kernel in native versions of Inferno or as part of the emulator in emulated environments. This means that these modules are implemented in C and are most likely to provide better performance than modules written in Limbo, since they do not incur the overhead of interpretation or on-the-fly compilation by the Dis VM.

Built-in modules are also good for conserving memory. When a built-in module is loaded, it occupies no more extra space in the environment of the application; it is part of the kernel and the space it occupies is fixed. In an Inferno system where the system functionality is heavily dependent on a particular module, it makes sense to implement that module as a built-in module, providing better performance, and amortizing its memory cost across the entire system. The key modules in the Limbo runtime (Sys, Tk, Math, Crypt, Draw) are implemented in this manner.

Application-level modules written in Limbo have all the capabilities of built-in modules with one exception: variadic functions. Limbo applications may define interfaces for variable-argument methods in a module declaration and may call a method that takes a variable number of arguments. Such functions may, however, only be implemented as part of a built-in module, examples being the print, fprint and sprint methods of the Sys module.

Developing built-in modules is an interesting process that straddles the boundaries of application and kernel development. The process begins with defining the module interface, as one would do for any Limbo module. The Limbo compiler is then used to generate C header files and stub functions, which the application developer fleshes out and compiles into the kernel or emulator. This process is illustrated in Figure A.1. Applications that wish to use the new built-in module then include the module interface definition and can now access routines written in C and compiled into the system software.

A.1 Defining the Module Interface

The first step in developing a built-in module is defining the module interface, as one would do for any module written in Limbo. For the purpose of this discussion, say we wish to implement a module, named Demo, that defines two functions, demoget() and demoset(), an ADT called DemoData and a constant DEMOCONST as shown below:

```
Demo : module
{
    DEMOCONST : con 6.023E23;

    DemoData : adt
    {
        demoint : int;
        demostring : string;
```

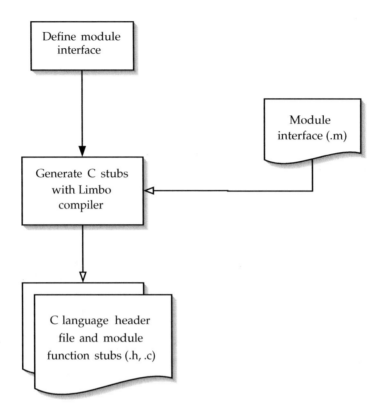

Figure A.1 Generating a C language implementation from a Limbo module interface definition.

```
    demochan : chan of (int, int);

    demofxn : fn(argc : int, argv : list of string);
};

demoset : fn(argc : int, argv : list of string);
demoget : fn() : (DemoData, int);
};
```

The next step is to implement functions in C which implement Demo. The Limbo compiler provides a lot of help in mapping this Limbo module interface to C functions.

A.2 Generating C Stubs with the Limbo Compiler

A C header file with the function and data definitions that will be needed for the implementation of our Demo module can be generated with the Limbo compiler from this module definition by executing `limbo -a demo.m`, assuming the module definition detailed above is placed in the file `demo.m`. The output generated by the Limbo compiler is sent to the standard input, and we may redirect it into a file, say demo.h. The result of such an operation is shown in Figure A.2, with cosmetic modifications to improve readability.

Stub functions for the functions defined in the above header file are also generated using the limbo compiler. The syntax is `limbo -T modname module.m`. The parameter `modname` must be the name of the required module defined in the file `module.m`. This is required since there may be several different modules defined within a single module declaration file, and we may wish to generate C function stub files for each of them independently. Thus, for our module Demo, the command is `limbo -T Demo demo.m` and the generated stub C file is shown in Figure A.3.

On the other hand, if we had specified the name of a module that was not defined in demo.m, say, by the command line `limbo -T Foo demo.m`, the operation would still succeed with the generated stub being:

```
#include <lib9.h>
#include <isa.h>
#include <interp.h>
#include "Foomod.h"

void Foomodinit(void){}
```

The final step for which we call on the Limbo compiler is the generation of the linkage table for the module. The command-line syntax is similar to that for the generation of the C function stubs and is `limbo -t modname module.m`. The parameter modname must be the name of the module of interest defined in the file `module.m`. Once again this is required since there may be several different modules defined in a particular module declaration file, and we may wish to generate the linkage tables for each of them separately. Thus, for our module Demo, the command is `limbo -t Demo demo.m` and the generated linkage table, cosmetically updated to improve readability, is shown in Figure A.4.

If the module name specified does not match that of any module defined in the file specified, the compiler proceeds and generates only the definition of the Runtab structure. If several module declarations existed in the file, the compiler would have to be called with the `-t` flag for each case, each case generating the appropriate Runtab instance.

A.3 Module Function Signatures

One interesting feature of the linkage table is the second entry, the signature. It is a 32-bit digital signature of the function type; thus, two functions with different names but the same types of arguments will have the same 32-bit `sig` field in the Runtab

```
typedef struct Demo_DemoData Demo_DemoData;

struct Demo_DemoData
{
    Channel*        demochan;
};

typedef struct{ WORD t0; WORD t1; } Demo_DemoData_demochan;

#define Demo_DemoData_demochan_size 8
#define Demo_DemoData_demochan_map {0}
#define Demo_DemoData_size 4
#define Demo_DemoData_map {0x80,}

void DemoData_demofxn(void*);
typedef struct F_DemoData_demofxn F_DemoData_demofxn;
struct F_DemoData_demofxn
{
    WORD      regs[NREG-1];
    WORD      noret;
    uchar     temps[12];
    WORD      argc;
    List*     argv;
};

void Demo_demoget(void*);
typedef struct F_Demo_demoget F_Demo_demoget;
struct F_Demo_demoget
{
    WORD      regs[NREG-1];
    struct{ Demo_DemoData t0; WORD t1; }*   ret;
    uchar     temps[12];
};

void Demo_demoset(void*);
typedef struct F_Demo_demoset F_Demo_demoset;
struct F_Demo_demoset
{
    WORD      regs[NREG-1];
    WORD      noret;
    uchar     temps[12];
    WORD      argc;
    List*     argv;
};

#define Demo_DEMOCONST 6.023e+23
```

Figure A.2 C structure definitions and function prototypes generated automatically by the Limbo compiler from the module's Limbo interface definition.

structure. The module defined below, a variation on our original Demo module, has five functions: foo and bar with the same types of arguments, and three more functions, bupkus, horrid and squish:

```
#include <lib9.h>
#include <isa.h>
#include <interp.h>
#include "Demomod.h"

Type*    T_DemoData;

void
Demomodinit(void)
{
    builtinmod("$Demo", Demomodtab);
    T_DemoData = dtype(freeheap, sizeof(DemoData), DemoDatamap,
            sizeof(DemoDatamap));
}

void
DemoData_demofxn(void *fp)
{
    F_DemoData_demofxn *f = fp;
}

void
Demo_demoget(void *fp)
{
    F_Demo_demoget *f = fp;
}

void
Demo_demoset(void *fp)
{
    F_Demo_demoset *f = fp;
}
```

Figure A.3   C function stubs generated automatically by the Limbo compiler from the example module's Limbo interface definition.

```
Demo : module
{
   DEMOCONST : con 6.023E23;

   DemoData : adt
   {
       demochan : chan of (int, int);
       demofxn : fn(argc : int, argv : list of string);
   };

   foo : fn() : (DemoData, int);
   bar : fn() : (DemoData, int);
   bupkus : fn() : (int, DemoData);
   horrid : fn(argc : int, argv : list of string);
   squish : fn(argc : int, argv : list of string) : int;
};
```

```
typedef struct
{
    char *name;
    long sig;
    void (*fn)(void*);
    int size;
    int np;
    uchar map[16];
} Runtab;

Runtab Demomodtab[]={
    "DemoData.demofxn",0x53d215b3,DemoData_demofxn,40,2,{0x0,0x40,},
    "demoget",0x572975e4,Demo_demoget,32,0,{0},
    "demoset",0x53d215b3,Demo_demoset,40,2,{0x0,0x40,},
    0
};
```

Figure A.4 Linkage table for the example Limbo module generated automatically from the module interface definition by the Limbo compiler.

and the generated function table:

```
typedef struct
{
    char *name;
    long sig;
    void (*fn)(void*);
    int size;
    int np;
    uchar map[16];
} Runtab;

Runtab Demomodtab[]={
    "bar",0x572975e4,Demo_bar,32,0,{0},
    "bupkus",0xf4045ae7,Demo_bupkus,32,0,{0},
    "DemoData.demofxn",0x53d215b3,DemoData_demofxn,40,2,{0x0,0x40,},
    "foo",0x572975e4,Demo_foo,32,0,{0},
    "horrid",0x53d215b3,Demo_horrid,40,2,{0x0,0x40,},
    "squish",0x5d8fa2f9,Demo_squish,40,2,{0x0,0x40,},
    0
};
```

Even though horrid and squish have the same argument type, they have different return types, and thus the compiler generates different function signatures for them. Similarly, bupkus has the same argument types as foo and bar but in a different order, and once again a different signature is generated. Foo and bar have the same signatures as they have identical function types, of fn():(DemoData,int);.

5

System I/O

This chapter covers the facilities provided by the Inferno system (specifically the Sys module) that are essential in the creation of most Limbo applications. The topics discussed in this chapter revolve around file and console input/output, string manipulation, filesystem manipulation and name space manipulation facilities provided by the Inferno system to Limbo applications.

5.1 The Sys Module

The functions provided in the Sys module are listed in Figure 5.1, with those functions not discussed in this chapter preceded by a '#'. The functions `dial`, `announce` and `listen` are not covered here since they are better discussed in the context of networking, covered in Chapter 9. Likewise, `pctl` will be discussed in Chapter 6, `file2chan` in Chapter 7 and `mount`, `unmount` and `export` in Chapter 8. The functions `dirread`, `sleep` `fprint`, `print`, `sprint`, `stat`, `pipe`, `stat`, `fstat`, `fwstat`, `wstat`, `millisec`, `tokenize` and `utfbytes` are best described by their respective manual pages, included in the appendices. The remaining functions defined in the Sys module's interface definition are described next.

5.2 aprint

Synopsis : `aprint:fn(s:string, *):array of byte;`

```
#announce:      fn(addr: string): (int, Connection);
aprint:         fn(s: string, *): array of byte;
bind:           fn(s, on: string, flags: int): int;
byte2char:      fn(buf: array of byte, n: int): (int, int, int);
char2byte:      fn(c: int, buf: array of byte, n: int): int;
chdir:          fn(path: string): int;
create:         fn(s: string, mode, perm: int): ref FD;
#dial:          fn(addr, local: string): (int, Connection);
#dirread:       fn(fd: ref FD, dir: array of Dir): int;
dup:            fn(old, new: int): int;
#export:        fn(c: ref FD, flag: int): int;
fildes:         fn(fd: int): ref FD;
#file2chan:     fn(dir, file: string): ref FileIO;
#fprint:        fn(fd: ref FD, s: string, *): int;
fstat:          fn(fd: ref FD): (int, Dir);
fwstat:         fn(fd: ref FD, d: Dir): int;
#listen:        fn(c: Connection): (int, Connection);
#millisec:      fn(): int;
#mount:         fn(fd: ref FD, on: string, flags: int, spec: string): int;
open:           fn(s: string, mode: int): ref FD;
#pctl:          fn(flags: int, movefd: list of int): int;
#pipe:          fn(fds: array of ref FD): int;
#print:         fn(s: string, *): int;
raise:          fn(s: string);
rescue:         fn(s: string, e: ref Exception): int;
rescued:        fn(flag: int, s: string): int;
read:           fn(fd: ref FD, buf: array of byte, n: int): int;
remove:         fn(s: string): int;
seek:           fn(fd: ref FD, off, start: int): int;
#sleep:         fn(period: int): int;
#sprint:        fn(s: string, *): string;
stat:           fn(s: string): (int, Dir);
stream:         fn(src, dst: ref FD, bufsiz: int): int;
tokenize:       fn(s, delim: string): (int, list of string);
#unmount:       fn(s1: string, s2: string): int;
unrescue:       fn();
utfbytes:       fn(buf: array of byte, n: int): int;
write:          fn(fd: ref FD, buf: array of byte, n: int): int;
wstat:          fn(s: string, d: Dir): int;
```

Figure 5.1 Functions defined in /module/sys.m for the Sys built-in module.

The aprint function takes as arguments a format string and a variable list of arguments, in the fashion of print. The format string is made up of Unicode characters, and the returned array of bytes is the UTF-8 encoding of the Unicode string. For example, the string $\mu\upsilon\rho\mu\iota\gamma\kappa\iota$, which is made up of eight Unicode characters, is converted to a UTF-8 stream, consisting of 16 bytes, illustrated by the following Limbo program:

```
# File : aprint.b

implement Aprint;
```

```
include "sys.m";
include "draw.m";

sys : Sys;

Aprint : module
{
    init : fn(nil : ref Draw->Context, nil : list of string);
};

init(nil : ref Draw->Context, nil : list of string)
{
    i : int;

    sys = load Sys Sys->PATH;

    myrmigki : string;
    myrmigki[len myrmigki] = 16r03bc;  #mu
    myrmigki[len myrmigki] = 16r03c5;  #upsilon
    myrmigki[len myrmigki] = 16r03c1;  #rho
    myrmigki[len myrmigki] = 16r03bc;  #mu
    myrmigki[len myrmigki] = 16r03b9;  #iota
    myrmigki[len myrmigki] = 16r03b3;  #gamma
    myrmigki[len myrmigki] = 16r03ba;  #kappa
    myrmigki[len myrmigki] = 16r03b9;  #iota

    sys->print("%s\n", myrmigki);

    ma := sys->aprint("%s", myrmigki);
    sys->print("Unicode string has %d UTF-8 bytes\n",
            len ma);

    sys->print("The UTF-8 bytes are -->\n");
    for (i = 0; i < len ma; i++)
    {
        sys->print("\t\t[%x]\n", int ma[i]);
    }

    sys->print("\nThat is, -->\n");
    for (i = 0; i < len ma; i++)
    {
        sys->print("\t\t[");
        bitprint(8, int ma[i]);
        sys->print("]\n");
    }
}

bitprint(nbits, number : int)
{
    for (i := nbits-1; i >= 0; i--)
    {
        sys->print("%d", (number >> i)&1);
    }
}
```

The corresponding output for the application above is:

```
Unicode string has 16 UTF-8 bytes
The UTF-8 bytes are -->
        [ce]
        [bc]
        [cf]
        [85]
        [cf]
        [81]
        [ce]
        [bc]
        [ce]
        [b9]
        [ce]
        [b3]
        [ce]
        [ba]
        [ce]
        [b9]

That is, -->
        [11001110]
        [10111100]
        [11001111]
        [10000101]
        [11001111]
        [10000001]
        [11001110]
        [10111100]
        [11001110]
        [10111001]
        [11001110]
        [10110011]
        [11001110]
        [10111010]
        [11001110]
        [10111001]
```

5.3 bind

Synopsis : `bind:fn(source, on:string, flags:int):int;`

The `bind` function operates on the name space of a thread and all threads within its name space group. It is used to modify the name space, to attach a portion of the name space at one location to another location. After a successful `bind` operation, the file or directory at path `on` is a synonym for the file or directory that used to be at path `source`. The path `on` must exist prior to the bind operation. The parameter `flags` determines the manner in which the bind operation is performed. Possible values of the flag, defined in the Sys module, are Sys->MREPL, Sys->MAFTER, Sys->MBEFORE and Sys->MCREATE.

The MREPL flag specifies to replace the path on, which may be either a file or directory, by the path source. The MBEFORE and MAFTER flags can only be used successfully with directories and not with files. The MBEFORE flag specifies to add the entries in the portion of the name space at path location source to the union directory at path location *on*, in such a manner that the added entries appear first in the name space at path location on. The MAFTER flag, similarly, causes the entries in the name space at path location source to appear at path location on; however, the entries appear after those originally present in the union.

Any of the above three flags may be OR'ed with the flag MCREATE. It is meaningless for files. For directories, when an attempt is made to create a file in a union directory (recall that unions are created with bind operations), the file is created in the first member of the union that permits creation.

The Inferno utility *bind(2)* is best used to illustrate the behavior of the bind system call. The *bind* application takes four flags, *r*, *a*, *b* and *c*, which are analogous to the four constants defined in /module/sys.m, listed above:

```
; mkdir x y z
; ls -ls
drwxr-xr-x U 0 pip pip 0 Jun 17 22:53 x
drwxr-xr-x U 0 pip pip 0 Jun 17 22:53 y
drwxr-xr-x U 0 pip pip 0 Jun 17 22:53 z

; chmod 555 x
; echo 'test' > x/newfile
sh: cannot open x/newfile: permission denied

; bind -r x y
; echo 'test' > y/newfile
sh: cannot open y/newfile: mounted directory forbids creation

; unmount y
; echo 'test' > y/newfile

; ls -l **
-rw-r--r-- U 0 pip pip 5 Jun 17 22:54 y/newfile

; rm y/newfile
; bind -a y x
; echo 'test' > x/newfile
sh: cannot open x/newfile: mounted directory forbids creation

; unmount x
; bind -ac y x
; echo 'test' > x/newfile
; ls -l *
-rw-r--r-- U 0 pip pip 5 Jun 17 22:55 x/newfile
-rw-r--r-- U 0 pip pip 5 Jun 17 22:55 y/newfile

; rm y/newfile
```

```
; ls -l *
; touch y/fruit z/fruit
; ls -l *
-rw-r--r-- U 0 pip pip 0 Jun 17 22:56 x/fruit
-rw-r--r-- U 0 pip pip 0 Jun 17 22:56 y/fruit
-rw-r--r-- U 0 pip pip 0 Jun 17 22:56 z/fruit

; unmount x
; ls -l *
-rw-r--r-- U 0 pip pip 0 Jun 17 22:56 y/fruit
-rw-r--r-- U 0 pip pip 0 Jun 17 22:56 z/fruit

; bind -a y x
; bind -a z x
; ls -l *
-rw-r--r-- U 0 pip pip 0 Jun 17 22:56 x/fruit
-rw-r--r-- U 0 pip pip 0 Jun 17 22:56 x/fruit
-rw-r--r-- U 0 pip pip 0 Jun 17 22:56 y/fruit
-rw-r--r-- U 0 pip pip 0 Jun 17 22:56 z/fruit
;
```

For binding of files onto files, the flags play a limited role: binding of files to files can only happen in one way—the file on becomes a synonym for the file source in the name space, as shown below:

```
; touch a b
; ls -ls a b
-rw-r--r-- U 0 pip pip 0 Jun 17 21:12 a
 -rw-r--r-- U 0 pip pip 0 Jun 17 21:12 b

; bind a b
; ls -ls a b
-rw-r--r-- U 0 pip pip 0 Jun 17 21:12 a
-rw-r--r-- U 0 pip pip 0 Jun 17 21:12 a

; unmount b
; ls -ls a b
-rw-r--r-- U 0 pip pip 0 Jun 17 21:12 a
-rw-r--r-- U 0 pip pip 0 Jun 17 21:12 b

; bind -r a b
; ls -ls a b
-rw-r--r-- U 0 pip pip 0 Jun 17 21:12 a
-rw-r--r-- U 0 pip pip 0 Jun 17 21:12 a

; unmount b
; ls -ls a b
-rw-r--r-- U 0 pip pip 0 Jun 17 21:12 a
-rw-r--r-- U 0 pip pip 0 Jun 17 21:12 b

; bind -a a b
bind: cannot bind a onto b: inconsistent mount
```

```
; bind -b a b
bind: cannot bind a onto b: inconsistent mount

#   The Sys->MCREATE flag is meaningless for files
; bind -c a b
; ls -ls a b
-rw-r--r-- U 0 pip pip 0 Jun 17 21:12 a
-rw-r--r-- U 0 pip pip 0 Jun 17 21:12 a
;
```

5.4   byte2char

Synopsis : `byte2char:fn(buf:array of byte, n:int):(int,int,int);`

The routine `byte2char` converts a UTF-8 encoded sequence of bytes into a Unicode character. It is used to convert a stream of bytes into a string of Unicode characters. It takes the sequence of bytes starting at the index n in buf and attempts to identify a valid UTF-8 byte sequence. The first element of the returned tuple is the recognized Unicode character (or `Sys->UTFerror`, a boxed question mark like ⸾?⸾ in most fonts, if no valid UTF-8 sequence was seen). The second element in the returned tuple is the number of UTF-8 bytes that were read out of the supplied buffer to create the Unicode character. Thus, as described above, the maximum value returned in the second tuple element is the value of `Sys->UTFmax`, 3. If the sequence of bytes encountered is too short to form a valid Unicode character, the second field of the returned tuple is set to zero. If on the other hand enough bytes were seen but these did not form any valid UTF-8 sequence, the value 1 would be returned for the second element of the tuple. The third element of the returned tuple is the status of the conversion, and would be zero if an invalid UTF-8 sequence were detected. The following illustrates the use of `byte2char` with an example:

```
# File : byte2char.b

implement Byte2char;

include "sys.m";
include "draw.m";

sys : Sys;

Byte2char : module
{
    init : fn(nil : ref Draw->Context, nil : list of string);
};

init(nil : ref Draw->Context, nil : list of string)
{
    unistring: string;
    sys = load Sys Sys->PATH;
```

```
    mu := array [] of {byte 16rce, byte 16rbc};
    (unichar, utflen, status) := sys->byte2char(mu, 0);
    unistring[len unistring] = unichar;

    if (status == 0)
    {
        sys->print("byte2char failed, invalid UTF-8 sequence\n");
    }
    else
    {
        sys->print("[%d] bytes used to create Unicode character [%s]\n",
                utflen, unistring);
    }
}
```

5.5   char2byte

Synopsis : char2byte:fn(c:int, buf:array of byte, n:int):int;

The routine char2byte performs the opposite function to byte2char: it converts
a Unicode character, c, into a UTF-8 sequence of bytes, placing the sequence in buf
starting at index n. The returned value indicates the number of bytes that were placed
in the buffer, and is zero if the supplied buffer was too small, in which case the buffer
is left unchanged. The following shows an application employing char2byte:

```
# File : char2byte.b

implement Char2bytes;

include "sys.m";
include "draw.m";

sys : Sys;

Char2bytes : module
{
    init : fn(nil : ref Draw->Context, nil : list of string);
};

init(nil : ref Draw->Context, nil : list of string)
{
    i, n : int;

    sys = load Sys Sys->PATH;

    mu := array [Sys->UTFmax] of byte;
    if ((n = sys->char2byte(16r3bc, mu, 0)) == 0)
    {
        sys->print("char2byte failed, buffer too small\n");
    }
```

```
    else
    {
        sys->print("UTF-8 sequence is:\n");
    }

    for (i = 0; i < n; i++)
    {
        sys->print("\t\t[%x]\n", int mu[i]);
    }

    sys->print("i.e. :\n");
    for (i = 0; i < n; i++)
    {
        sys->print("\t\t[");
        bitprint(8, int mu[i]);
        sys->print("]\n");
    }
}

bitprint(nbits, number : int)
{
    for (i := nbits-1; i >= 0; i--)
    {
        sys->print("%d", (number >> i)&1);
    }
}
```

The corresponding output is as follows:

```
UTF-8 sequence is:
                [ce]
                [bc]
i.e. :
                [11001110]
                [10111100]
```

5.6 chdir

Synopsis : `chdir:fn(path:string):int;`

The `chdir` Sys module routine changes the working directory of the calling thread and its name space group to the path `path`. The return value is zero if the operation is successful. This is illustrated in the following example:

```
sys = load Sys Sys->PATH;

#   Change current working directory to /n/remote
```

```
    if (sys->chdir("/n/remote") < 0)
    {
        sys->print("Chdir failed: %r\n");
    }
```

5.7 create

Synopsis : `create:fn(s:string, mode, perm:int):ref FD;`

The `create` routine creates a new file or directory, depending on whether the `Sys->CHDIR` bit is set in the `perm` field. The permissions specified are AND'ed with the access privileges of the user in the current working directory. If the user does not have write permissions in the current working directory, the call will fail. The `CHDIR` flag is defined in `/module/sys.m` as the constant 16r80000000.

Masks for various file permissions can be expressed in radix notation as *8rNNN*— the three octal digits NNN represents the *usr*, *group*, *all* privileges.

Each such privilege character is obtained by transforming flags for read, write and execute permissions, represented as bit positions in a three-bit binary word, into decimal. For example, to create a file with read and write permissions (no exec permission) by the owner, and no access by all else, the binary representation of the user, group and global permissions will be 110, 000 and 000, respectively. Thus we would use the mask 8r600, since 110 (binary) is 6 (decimal), as shown below:

```
    #   ...

    sys = load Sys Sys->PATH;

    if ((fd := sys->create("garbage", sys->ORDWR, 8r600)) == nil)
    {
        sys->print("Create failed: %r\n");
    }
```

The following example is a utility, *Adduser*, for creating the necessary files and directories when a new user is added to an Inferno system, and illustrates the use of `create` for both files and directories:

```
# File : adduser.b

implement Adduser;

include "sys.m";
include "draw.m";
include "arg.m";

sys : Sys;
```

```
arg : Arg;

Adduser : module
{
    init : fn(nil : ref Draw->Context, args : list of string);
};

init(nil : ref Draw->Context, args : list of string)
{
    sys = load Sys Sys->PATH;
    arg = load Arg Arg->PATH;
    arg->init(args);

    #    Defaults
    username  := "";
    homedir          := "/usr/";
    namespace := "";
    error            := "";

    while((c := arg->opt()) != 0)
    {
        case c
        {
            'u' => username = arg->arg();
            'h' => homedir = arg->arg();
            'n' => namespace = arg->arg();
            *   =>
            {
                usage();
                exit;
            }
        }
    }
    if (arg->argv() != nil)
    {
        usage();
        exit;
    }

    if (homedir[(len homedir) - 1] != '/')
    {
        homedir += "/";
    }

    if (username == nil)
    {
        (username, homedir, namespace) = prompt();
    }

    error = createdirs(username, homedir, namespace);
    if (error != nil)
    {
        sys->print("%s\n", error);
    }
}
```

```
createdirs(username, homedir, namespace : string) : string
{
    #    Create home directory. Omode for create must be OREAD:
    if (sys->create(homedir+username,
        Sys->OREAD, 8r755|Sys->CHDIR) == nil)
    {
        return sys->sprint(
            "Could not create user home directory (%s) : %r",
            homedir+username);
    }

    #    Create keyring/ directory. Omode for create must be OREAD:
    if (sys->create(homedir+username+"/keyring",
        Sys->OREAD, 8r755|Sys->CHDIR) == nil)
    {
        return sys->sprint(
            "Could not create user's keyring directory (%s) : %r",
            homedir+username+"/keyring");
    }

    #    Create lib/ directory. Omode for create must be OREAD:
    if (sys->create(homedir+username+"/lib",
        Sys->OREAD, 8r755|Sys->CHDIR) == nil)
    {
        return sys->sprint(
            "Could not create user's lib directory (%s) : %r",
            homedir+username+"/lib");
    }

    #    Create namespace file. Omode for create here is ORDWR
    #    since we'll write:
    if ((fd := sys->create(homedir+username+"/namespace",
            Sys->ORDWR, 8r644)) == nil)
    {
        return sys->sprint(
            "Could not create user's lib directory (%s) : %r",
            homedir+username+"/namespace");
    }

    sys->fprint(fd, "%s\n", namespace);
    fd = nil;

    return nil;
}

usage()
{
    sys->print("adduser -u <username> [-h homedir][-n namespace string]\n");
}

prompt() : (string, string, string)
{
    buf := array [Sys->ATOMICIO] of byte;
    stdin := sys->fildes(0);

    sys->print("User name: ");
```

```
        n := sys->read(stdin, buf, len buf);
        username := string buf[:n-1];

        sys->print("Home directory: ");
        n = sys->read(stdin, buf, len buf);
        homedir := string buf[:n-1];
        if (homedir[(len homedir) - 1] != '/')
        {
                homedir += "/";
        }

        sys->print("Namespace config string: ");
        n = sys->read(stdin, buf, len buf);
        namespace := string buf[:n-1];


        return (username, homedir, namespace);
}
```

5.8   dup, fildes

Synopsis : `dup:fn(old, new:int):int;`
Synopsis : `fildes:fn(fd:int):ref FD;`

File descriptors in Limbo are of the type `ref FD`. The FD ADT contains a solitary member, `fd`, of type `int`:

```
FD: adt
{
     fd: int;
};
```

The reason that this is encapsulated within an ADT is so that the Limbo runtime can track references to an open file descriptor, permitting activities like closing a file which is open for I/O when the file descriptor corresponding to it no longer has any references. There is no explicit 'close' system call, and this effect is achieved when a descriptor no longer has any references to it, such as when it goes out of scope or is explicitly assigned the value `nil`.

Within the underlying Inferno system, however, as is the case in systems such as Unix, file descriptors are handled as integers. Given such an integer, *fildes* returns a Limbo file descriptor, a reference to an FD ADT as above, or nil if it cannot convert the integer to a Limbo `ref FD`.

The `dup` method lets you refer to an open descriptor `old` by a new file descriptor, `new`. This operation affects all threads within the calling thread's file descriptor group. One common use of this is to provide a new standard input, standard output and standard error to a group of threads.

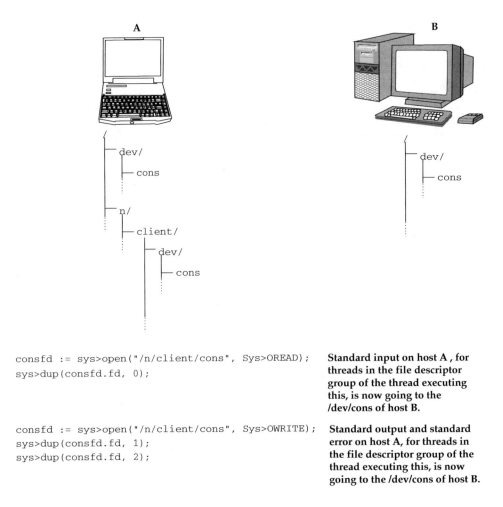

```
consfd := sys>open("/n/client/cons", Sys>OREAD);
sys>dup(consfd.fd, 0);
```

Standard input on host A , for threads in the file descriptor group of the thread executing this, is now going to the /dev/cons of host B.

```
consfd := sys>open("/n/client/cons", Sys>OWRITE);
sys>dup(consfd.fd, 1);
sys>dup(consfd.fd, 2);
```

Standard output and standard error on host A, for threads in the file descriptor group of the thread executing this, is now going to the /dev/cons of host B.

Figure 5.2   The *dup* system call.

Consider the following scenario. An application running on host machine A mounts the name space of machine B to, say, /n/client. Applications running on host A which perform I/O on the standard I/O stream have their messages printed on the local console or read from the local keyboard. If it was desired to run applications on host A, but rather use the keyboard of host B, and likewise have the output of commands, etc., appear on host B, it would be necessary to somehow 'reroute' all of the standard input, standard output and standard error of machine A, to use that of machine B. Figure 5.2 illustrates the scenario further.

The solution, given that the name space of B is already mounted into the name space of A at /n/client, would be to open /n/client/dev/cons, the console I/O device on B, mounted into the name space of A, and dup the file descriptors so that they become the standard input, output and error of the calling thread's file descriptor group. The fragment of code to achieve this is shown below:

```
#    Open /dev/cons which is that for machine B
#    for reading
consfd = sys->open("/dev/cons", sys->OREAD);

#    Dup the file descriptor we got for reading
#    to be our new standard input
sys->dup(consfd.fd, 0);

#    Open /dev/cons for writing
consfd = sys->open("/dev/cons", sys->OWRITE);

#    Dup the file descriptor to be both stdout
#    and stderr (both now go to B)
sys->dup(consfd.fd, 1);
sys->dup(consfd.fd, 2);
```

5.9   open

Synopsis : `open:fn(s:string, mode:int):ref FD;`

This opens a file for I/O. The return value, of type `ref Sys->FD`, is a file descriptor for the file opened. If the attempt to open the file was unsuccessful, open returns `nil`. The parameter mode is the mode in which the I/O is to be performed. For simplicity, there are constants defined in `/module/sys.m`.

These values may be OR'ed with two additional flags, `Sys->OTRUNC` and `Sys->ORCLOSE`, to define additional behavior of the file descriptor referencing a file. `Sys->OTRUNC` and `Sys->ORCLOSE` may be used only on descriptors referencing files and not on descriptors referencing directories. An example of opening a file named 'my_file' for reading only is as follows:

```
fd := sys->open("my_file", sys->OREAD);
```

5.10   read

Synopsis : `read:fn(fd:ref FD, buf:array of byte, n:int):int;`

This routine reads nbytes bytes from the file referenced by the file descriptor fd into the buffer buf starting at the current position of the file. This position may be altered by a seek call. A read() will not automatically give you data from the beginning of the file: the side effect of a read call is to alter the current position in the file referenced by fd.

    read returns the number of bytes read. If the read is successful, read returns an integer equal to nbytes. If the end of the file was reached before nbytes had been read, read returns the number of bytes read, which is then less than nbytes:

```
n := sys->read(fd, buf, len buf);

#   At this point, you most probably want to do the following
#   to get rid of any garbage at the end of buf:
buf = buf[:n];
```

5.11   remove

Synopsis : remove: fn(name:string):int;

The remove routine deletes a disk file. The call will fail if either the file does not exist or the user does not have write permission for the file specified by the string name. If remove succeeds, it returns 0, else it returns -1:

```
n := sys->remove("garbage");
```

5.12   seek

Synopsis : seek:fn(fd:ref FD, off, start:int):int;

This routine *seeks* to the position in the file referenced by fd, specified by start. If off is non-zero, then seek seeks off bytes past the position specified by start. There are three constants, SEEKSTART, SEEKRELA and SEEKEND defined in /module/sys.m for specifying seeks to the start, relative positions and ends of files. Thus if you wanted to seek to a point 16 bytes after the beginning of a file you may do something like:

```
n := sys->seek(my_fd, 16, sys->SEEKSTART);
```

5.13   stream

Synopsis : `stream:fn(src, dst:ref FD, bufsiz:int):int;`

The `stream` call copies `bufsiz` bytes between two open files, referenced by the descriptors specified in the `stream` call. The return value of `stream` is the same as `bufsiz` if the `stream` call is successful:

```
n := sys->stream(fd_src, fd_dst, 1024);
```

Why use `stream` rather than a loop of read/write? `stream` was designed for performing media copies, such as streaming video/audio. A thread that executes a `stream` system call is placed in the highest priority run queue of the Dis VM's scheduler. The scheduling of Limbo threads in the Dis VM is discussed further in Chapter 6.

5.14   write

Synopsis : `write:fn(fd:ref FD, buf:array of byte, n:int):int;`

The routine `write()` copies `nbytes` bytes from the buffer `buf` into the file referenced by the file descriptor `fd`. `write` returns the number of bytes written. If the write is successful, `write` returns an integer equal to `nbytes`. If the write encountered error conditions before `nbytes` had been written (e.g. out of disk space), the return value of the `write` call is then less than `nbytes`:

```
n := sys->write(fd, buf, len buf);
```

5.15   Unbuffered Character I/O

The `/dev/cons` device provides buffered I/O by default, i.e. reads from `/dev/cons`, and will return one line each time, being the last entry at the keyboard terminated by a newline. Unbuffered character I/O can be enabled by writing the string `"rawon"` to the console control file, `/dev/consctl`. It can be disabled by writing the string `"rawoff"`:

```
cctlfd = sys->open("/dev/consctl", Sys->OWRITE);
sys->write(cctlfd, array of byte "rawon", len "rawon");
```

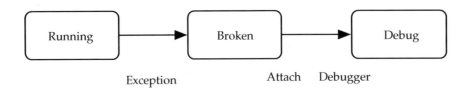

Figure 5.3   Limbo programs too may fail. On receiving an exception, the program transitions into the *broken* state.

If it is desired to have both raw and buffered I/O, then the console device and its control interface are useful. In situations where only the keystrokes as they happen are required or when the raw codes produced by the keyboard hardware are required[1], the /dev/keyboard might be of better use. The example *Pong* in Chapter 11 uses the /dev/keyboard interface, while the *Pled* application example for this chapter uses the /dev/cons interface in both the 'raw' and 'cooked' modes at different times. See the example at the end of the chapter for more.

5.16   Exception Handling

Sometimes in life, bad things happen, and we have to deal with them. Your pet eats your homework, you forget to 'save often', there is a power outage, and you lose several hours of inspired writing, the espresso machine breaks, and so on. In such situations you have to maintain poise, recover from the tragedy and move on. Likewise, as you are probably acutely aware, programs fail, and often right when you have to give an important demonstration. Some programmers are left staring at the screen in wide-eyed amazement. Others shriek, howl or pull out their hair. Some are able to recover from these exceptional conditions, make repairs and continue. Limbo programs too, may fail. A program may try to access a function in a module that has not been loaded, or it may attempt to index beyond the boundaries of an array. In such situations the system raises exceptions, and the default behavior of programs in the presence of these exceptions is to terminate execution and go into the 'broken' state, as illustrated in Figure 5.3.

Inferno provides a facility for application-based exception handling. This facility is provided through the Sys built-in module. Sys provides functions for installing exception handlers, raising exceptions and performing cleanup after the handling of exceptions. In all there are four methods defined in the Sys module for application-based exception generation and handling—raise, rescue, rescued and unrescue—with the following function signatures:

---

[1]In the emulated Inferno environment, the /dev/keyboard file behaves as a /dev/cons file that is always in 'raw' mode.

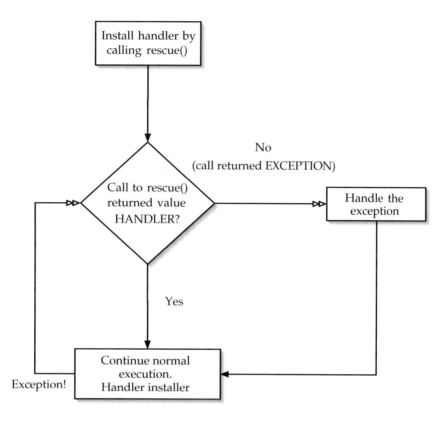

Figure 5.4   Installing exception handlers and catching exceptions.

```
raise : fn(s: string);
rescue : fn(s: string, e: ref Exception) : int;
rescued : fn(flag: int, s: string) : int;
unrescue : fn();
```

The flow of installing exception handlers and catching exceptions is illustrated in Figure 5.4. Exception handlers are installed by calling `rescue`. The call to `rescue` takes as parameters a string indicating what exception strings we wish the handler to be responsible for and a reference to an allocated `Exception` ADT. The string may contain a wildcard so that it matches a large number of exceptions, e.g. the string 'module*' will match any exception with the exception string beginning with 'module'. The `Exception` ADT, defined in the Sys module, is populated by the runtime system with information about the cause of the exception, when one occurs.

The runtime system saves the return address of the caller of `rescue`, along with the string for which the caller wishes to install a handler. The call to `rescue` returns with the value `Sys->HANDLER` defined in `/module/sys.m`. In the example below, when the code fragment is executed during normal program execution, the `else` branch will be taken, since the call to rescue returns `Sys->HANDLER` under normal program execution and not `Sys->EXCEPTION`:

```
e := ref sys->Exception;

if (sys->rescue("Espresso machine broken", e) == sys->EXCEPTION)
{
    # The code to handle the exception is placed here
}
else
{
    # This is the case where rescue() returns HANDLER
}
```

On an exception, the system tries to match the current exception string against all the registered exception strings, registered by calls to `rescue`. If a match is found, control is transferred to the return address associated with the match, with the return value `Sys->EXCEPTION`. In other words, even though only one call is made to `rescue`, *rescue returns a second time* if there is a matching exception. In this second return, the head of the `if` statement in the above example evaluates to true, since the return value of this second return is `Sys->EXCEPTION`. At this point, the variable e has been populated with the complete exception string of the exception, the responsible module, and the program counter at which the exception occurred. The `Exception` ADT defined in the Sys module is shown below:

```
Exception: adt
{
    name:   string;
    mod:    string;
    pc: int;
};
```

After performing any necessary cleanup, the code placed in the `if` branch should call `rescued`. This determines any action that should be performed on the installed exception handler. A program might wish to suspend execution so that the application developer can perform a detailed post-mortem analysis using a debugging tool. It may be desirable to uninstall the handler so a subsequent exception of the same kind is not handled at this level, or a program might re-raise the exception so that it is caught at a higher level in the call chain.

The first parameter to `rescued` determines which of these actions is taken. Specifying `Sys->ACTIVE` makes no changes to the installed handler and continues execution of the next statement in the program order. The argument `Sys->ONCE` specifies that the handler should be uninstalled and program execution continued. An argument of `Sys->RAISE` causes the exception to be raised again, hopefully to be caught at a higher level in the call chain. In this case, the second argument specifies the exception to be raised. If `nil`, the same exception is raised. Lastly, a first argument to `rescued` of Sys->EXIT causes program execution to be suspended, with the program placed in the *broken* state. A programmer may then use a debugger to debug the thread.

One point about `rescued` demands further attention. For the arguments Sys-> ACTIVE and Sys->ONCE, execution returns to the statement in the program after the call to `rescued`, in static program order. This statement may be anywhere in the program with respect to the dynamic execution stream, so it might very well be *before* the location of the raised exception, causing exceptions *ad infinitum*, as would be the situation below:

```
e := ref sys->Exception;
a := array [1] of int;

if (sys->rescue("array*", e) == sys->EXCEPTION)
{
    sys->print("Ignoring array bounds exception\n");
    sys->rescued(sys->ACTIVE, nil);
}
sys->print("a[50] = %d\n", a[50]);
```

It is therefore usually necessary to place the code that contains potentially excepting statements in the `else` clause of the `if` corresponding to the `rescue`, as shown below:

```
if (sys->rescue("array*", e) == sys->EXCEPTION)
{
    sys->print("Ignoring array bounds error\n");
    sys->rescued(sys->ACTIVE, nil)
}
else
{
    sys->print("a[50] = %d\n", a[50]);
}
```

Thus, after the exception is taken, the `if` branch of the `if` statement is taken and after `rescued` is called, the next statement to be executed in program order is the one right after the `else` branch.

5.17 Summary

This chapter provided an overview of some of the facilities provided to Limbo programs to interact with the Inferno system. The facilities discussed in this chapter excluded those which fall under topics covered in other chapters, such as networking (Chapter 9). More detailed coverage of the system facilities visible to Limbo programs is available in Section 2 of the Inferno manual pages.

Bibliographic Notes

The Inferno system manual pages [79] provide more detail on the routines discussed in this chapter, as well as those omitted. The `announce`, `dial`, `export` and `listen` routines are described in detail in the manual page *sys-dial(2)*. The `dirread` routine is described in the manual page *sys-dirread(2)*. The `file2chan` routine is described in *sys-file2chan(2)*. The formatted I/O routines—`fprint`, `print` and `sprint`—are described in detail in *sys-print(2)*. The manual pages detail the various formatting verbs that these routines take. The millisecond time routine, `millisec`, is described in *sys-millisec(2)*. The `bind`, `mount` and `unmount` routines are detailed in *sys-bind(2)*. The `pctl`, `pipe` and `sleep` routines are described in the manual pages *sys-pctl(2)*, *sys-pipe(2)* and *sys-sleep(2)* respectively.

5.18   Chapter Example: Pled, a Simple Line Editor

Pled is a simple *line editor* that permits a user to interactively edit files from an Inferno console. It is particularly useful in installations of Inferno without graphics support. It is versatile and easy enough to use, so that it is even useful for the quick editing of files from within a graphical environment. The module definition and constants used by Pled:

```
TABCHAR          : con 16r88;
TABLEN           : con 8;

KEY_A            : con ('a'  | 'P' << 8);
KEY_BACKSPACE    : con ('\b' | 'E' << 8);
KEY_CTRLD        : con (4    | 'P' << 8);
KEY_DOT          : con ('.'  | 'P' << 8);
KEY_EESC         : con (27   | 'E' << 8);
KEY_ENEWLINE     : con ('\n' | 'E' << 8);
KEY_L            : con ('l'  | 'P' << 8);
KEY_N            : con ('n'  | 'P' << 8);
KEY_PESC         : con (27   | 'P' << 8);
KEY_PNEWLINE     : con ('\n' | 'P' << 8);
KEY_S            : con ('s'  | 'P' << 8);
KEY_TAB          : con ('\t' | 'E' << 8);

Line : adt
{
    str : string;
    ntabs   : int;
};

Pled : module
{
    init : fn (nil : ref Draw->Context, argv : list of string);
};
```

The implementation of Pled:

```
# File: pled.b

implement Pled;

include "sys.m";
include "draw.m";
include "bufio.m";
include "pled.m";

sys          : Sys;
bufio        : Bufio;
FD           : import sys;
Iobuf        : import bufio;

cctlfd                        : ref Sys->FD;
```

```
curlineidx, cursoridx     : int = 0;
numlines, mode            : int = 0;
stdin, stdout             : ref Sys->FD;


init (nil : ref Draw->Context, argv : list of string)
{
        sys = load Sys Sys->PATH;
    bufio = load Bufio Bufio->PATH;

        stdin = sys->fildes(0);
        stdout = sys->fildes(1);

        param := tl argv;
        while (param != nil)
        {
                (n, err) := pedit(hd param);
                if (n != 0)
                {
            sys->print("\nPled :: %s\n\n", err);
                }
                param = tl param;
        }

    cctlfd = sys->open("/dev/consctl", sys->OWRITE);
    sys->seek(cctlfd, 0, sys->SEEKSTART);
    sys->write(cctlfd, array of byte "rawoff", len "rawoff");
}

pedit (filename : string) : (int, string)
{
    buf           := array[1] of byte;
    consfd        : ref FD;
    key           : int = 0;
    lines         : array of Line;
    tmpstr        : string;

    cctlfd = sys->open("/dev/consctl", sys->OWRITE);
    if (cctlfd == nil)
    {
        return (-1, sys->sprint("Could not open /dev/consctl : %r"));
    }
    sys->write(cctlfd, array of byte "rawon", len "rawon");

    consfd = sys->open("/dev/cons", sys->OREAD);
    if (consfd == nil)
    {
        return (-1, sys->sprint("Could not open /dev/cons : %r"));
    }

    filebuf := bufio->open(filename, sys->OREAD);
    if (filebuf == nil)
    {
        return (-1, sys->sprint("Could not open [%s] : %r", filename));
    }
```

```
#   Determine number of lines in input file
numlines = 0;
while (filebuf.gets('\n') != nil)
{
    numlines++;
}

filebuf = bufio->open(filename, sys->ORDWR);
lines = array [numlines+1] of Line;
numlines = 0;

while ((tmpstr = filebuf.gets('\n')) != nil)
{
    lines[numlines].str = cleanends(tmpstr);
    lines[numlines].ntabs = counttabs(tmpstr);
    numlines++;
}

#   Peruse mode by default
mode = 'P';

sys->fprint(stdout, "\n\nFile [%s], [%d] lines total\n\n",
            filename, numlines);
sys->fprint(stdout, "[0][P]%s", lines[curlineidx].str);
cursoridx = len lines[curlineidx].str;

while (sys->read(consfd, buf, 1) == 1)
{
    key = int buf[0];
    case (key | (mode << 8))
    {
        #   Ctrl-d : Exit
        KEY_CTRLD =>
        {
            sys->fprint(stdout, "\n\n");
            return (0, "");
        }

        #   "s" or ENTER in peruse mode : Next line
        KEY_S or KEY_PNEWLINE =>
        {
            if (curlineidx < numlines-1)
            {
                tmp := "[" + string curlineidx + "][ ]";
                clear(len lines[curlineidx].str + len tmp +
                    lines[curlineidx].ntabs*(TABLEN-1));

                curlineidx++;

                sys->fprint(stdout, "[%d][%c]%s",
                    curlineidx, mode, lines[curlineidx].str);
            }
        }

        #   ENTER in edit mode
        KEY_ENEWLINE =>
```

```
{
    if (curlineidx < numlines-1)
    {
        tmp := "[" + string curlineidx + "][ ]";
        clear(len lines[curlineidx].str + len tmp +
            lines[curlineidx].ntabs*(TABLEN-1));

        curlineidx++;

        sys->fprint(stdout, "[%d][%c]%s",
            curlineidx, mode, lines[curlineidx].str);
    }
    else
    {
        #insert_line(lines, cur_line_index);
    }
}

#   'a' : Previous line
KEY_A =>
{
    if ((curlineidx > 0) && mode != 'E' )
    {
        tmp := "[" + string curlineidx + "][ ]";
        clear(len lines[curlineidx].str + len tmp +
            lines[curlineidx].ntabs*(TABLEN-1));

        curlineidx--;

        sys->fprint(stdout,"[%d][%c]%s",
            curlineidx, mode, lines[curlineidx].str);
    }
}

#   ESC : Toggle edit mode
KEY_PESC or KEY_EESC =>
{
    if (mode == 'P')
    {
        mode = 'E';
    }
    else
    {
        mode = 'P';
    }

    tmp := "[" + string curlineidx + "][ ]";
                clear(len lines[curlineidx].str + len tmp +
            lines[curlineidx].ntabs*(TABLEN-1));

    sys->fprint(stdout, "[%d][%c]%s",
        curlineidx, mode, lines[curlineidx].str);
    cursoridx = len lines[curlineidx].str;
}

#   Save
```

```
KEY_DOT =>
{
    save(filebuf, lines);
}

#   Backspace
KEY_BACKSPACE =>
{
    if (cursoridx >= 1)
    {
        sys->fprint(stdout,"\b");
        cursoridx--;
    }
}

#   Tabs
KEY_TAB =>
{
    sys->fprint(stdout, "%c", TABCHAR);
    lines[curlineidx].str[cursoridx] = key;
    cursoridx++;
}

#   List lines
KEY_L =>
{
    cctlfd = nil;
    cctlfd = sys->open("/dev/consctl", sys->OWRITE);

    sys->seek(cctlfd,0, sys->SEEKSTART);
    sys->write(cctlfd, array of byte "rawoff", len "rawoff");

    lbuf := array [Sys->ATOMICIO] of byte;

    sys->fprint(stdout,"\nLines to List: ");
    sys->read(stdin, lbuf, len lbuf);

    (n, llist) := sys->tokenize(string lbuf, " \n\r");

    if ( (int hd llist > numlines) ||
         (int hd llist < 0) ||
         (int hd tl tl llist > numlines) ||
         (int hd tl tl llist < int hd llist) ||
         (hd tl llist != "-")
       )
    {
        if (hd tl llist != "-")
        {
            sys->fprint(stdout, "Wrong Format : \"%s\"\n",
                string lbuf);
        }
        else
        {
            sys->fprint(stdout,
                "Out of range. File Contains %d lines.\n",
                numlines);
```

```
                    sys->fprint(stdout, "[%d][%c]%s",
                        curlineidx, mode, lines[curlineidx].str);
                }
            }
            else
            {
                start := int hd llist;
                finish := int hd tl tl llist;

                sys->fprint(stdout,"\n\n");
                for (i := start; i <= finish; i++)
                {
                    sys->fprint(stdout, "%s\n","|"+ string i +"> "+
                        lines[i].str);
                }
                sys->fprint(stdout,"\n\n");
                sys->fprint(stdout,"[%d][%c]%s",
                        curlineidx, mode, lines[curlineidx].str);
            }
            sys->seek(cctlfd,0, sys->SEEKSTART);
            sys->write(cctlfd, array of byte "rawon", len "rawon");
        }

        KEY_N =>
        {
            sys->fprint(stdout,
                "\n\nFile Contains %d lines total.\n\n",
                numlines);
            sys->fprint(stdout, "[%d][%c]%s",
                curlineidx, mode, lines[curlineidx].str);
        }

        * =>
        {
            if (mode == 'E')
            {
                if (cursoridx < len lines[curlineidx].str)
                {
                    lines[curlineidx].str[cursoridx] = key;
                }
                else
                {
                    lines[curlineidx].str[len lines[curlineidx].str]
                        = key;
                }

                cursoridx++;
                sys->fprint(stdout,"%c", key);
            }
        }
    }
}
sys->fprint(stdout,"\n");

return (0, "");
}
```

```
cleanends(tmpstr : string) : string
{
    CR := max(len tmpstr - 2, 0);
    LF := max(len tmpstr - 1, 0);

    if (tmpstr[CR] == '\r')
    {
        return tmpstr[: CR];
    }
    else if (tmpstr[LF] == '\n')
    {
        return tmpstr[: LF];
    }

    return tmpstr;
}

counttabs(line : string) : int
{
    ntabs := 0;

    for (i := 0; i < len line; i++)
    {
        if (line[i] == '\t') ntabs++;
    }

    return ntabs;
}

clear(delwidth : int)
{
    delete := string (array [delwidth] of {* => byte '\b'});
    blank := string (array [delwidth] of {* => byte ' '});
    sys->print("%s", delete);
    sys->print("%s", blank);
    sys->print("%s", delete);
}

save(filebuf : ref Iobuf, lines : array of Line)
{
    filebuf.seek(0, 0);
        for (i := 0; i < numlines; i++)
    {
        #   We had stripped the newlines of the ends
        if (lines[i].str == "\n")
        {
                    filebuf.puts(lines[i].str);
        }
        else
        {
            filebuf.puts(lines[i].str+"\n");
        }
    }
    filebuf.flush();
```

```
    tmp := "[" + string curlineidx + "][ ]";
    clear(len lines[curlineidx].str + len tmp +
        lines[curlineidx].ntabs*(TABLEN-1));

    sys->fprint(stdout, "[%d][%c]%s",
        curlineidx, 'S', lines[curlineidx].str);
}

max(a, b : int) : int
{
    if (a > b)
    {
        return a;
    }

    return b;
}
```

Discussion   In order to enable the user to browse through text using the cursor keys, the console is placed in 'raw' mode by writing the string 'rawon' into /dev/consctl as described in Section 5.15, and is returned to 'cooked' mode when the application exits.

The implementation of Pled employs a Limbo module that we have hitherto not discussed, the *bufio(2)* module. Bufio provides facilities to Limbo programs to perform buffered input and output. It builds upon the facilities provided in the Sys module to provide this functionality, and unlike Sys, Bufio is not a built-in module but rather is written in Limbo.

The functionality of the Bufio module revolves around the Iobuf ADT. This ADT contains methods for a variety of tasks such as retrieving (and returning) data from a buffer, seeking to a position in a buffer, etc.

Since we shall be using these member functions of the Iobuf ADT contained in Bufio (which is external to the Pled module), we must import the Iobuf ADT from an instance of Bufio as described in Chapter 4:

```
include "bufio.m";

#   ...

bufio : Bufio;
Iobuf : import bufio;
```

The following code segment from Pled illustrates using the Bufio module to open a file and read in its contents, line by line. After loading the implementation for Bufio, we obtain a new Iobuf instance by using the **open** routine of the Bufio module, which returns a reference to a initialized Iobuf and is placed in the variable filebuf:

```
bufio = load Bufio Bufio->PATH;
if (bufio == nil)
{
    return (-1, sys->sprint("Could not load Bufio : %r"));
}

filebuf := bufio->open(filename, sys->OREAD);
if (filebuf == nil)
{
    return (-1, sys->sprint("Could not open [%s] : %r", filename));
}

#   Determine number of lines in input file
numlines = 0;
while (filebuf.gets('\n')!= nil)
{
    numlines++;
}
```

Strings of text from the file whose name was supplied in the open call are read with the gets method of the Iobuf ADT, whose sole parameter specifies the delimiting character for lines. In the above, the delimiting character is a newline, thus each string read from the buffer is one line of the file.

Problems

5.1   Implement a utility to format text supplied to it such that the lines of text have a bounded width.

5.2   Implement a utility to determine the type of a file, e.g. text, Dis executable, image, etc.

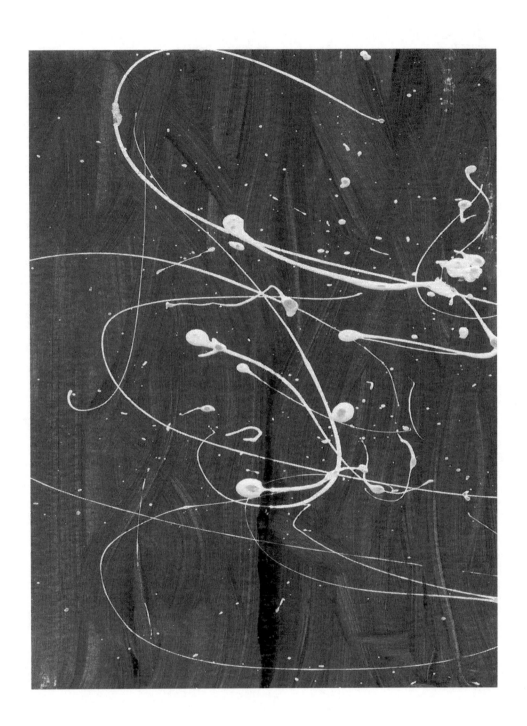

6

Programming with Threads

6.1 Introduction

During execution, Limbo applications run as one or more *threads*. This chapter details the properties of Limbo threads, how they are created and run, and the interfaces through which they may be controlled. Throughout this chapter, the term *thread* will be used to refer to a thread of execution of a Dis executable over the Dis VM, created via a Limbo spawn statement, i.e. a Limbo thread. The term *process* will be used to refer to an instance of the Dis VM running over a native kernel or host operating system. The next chapter describes *channels*, which are a facility by which threads often communicate or otherwise interact with each other.

Limbo applications on Inferno execute over the Dis VM. Such applications may be run in one of two ways: they may either be interpreted or on-the-fly compiled by the virtual machine. At any given time there may be several applications running, due, for example, to a user logged into the emulator and running the window manager, Web browser and a handful of Inferno network services. Each of these applications will comprise one or more threads; thus there will be several threads running over the virtual machine, some or all of which may be on-the-fly compiled or interpreted. As described in Chapter 1, individual applications may be marked during compilation so that they will always be on-the-fly compiled during execution, or, alternatively, the system may be started with an option to force on-the-fly compilation of all applications which are not explicitly marked otherwise—applications compiled with the Limbo compiler's '-C' flag are marked to prevent them from being on-the-fly-compiled at runtime.

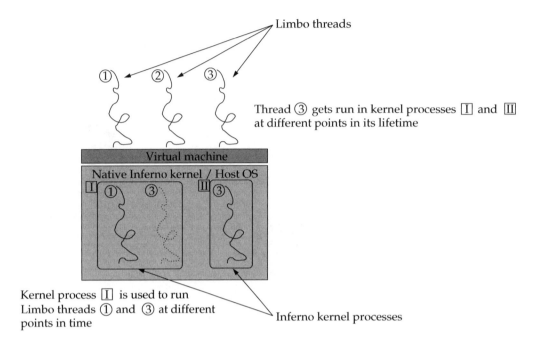

Figure 6.1   Limbo threads versus Dis VM processes.

Thread Scheduling   The Dis VM runs over either the Inferno native kernel or over a host operating system in the case of the Inferno emulator, as described in Chapter 1. To perform the task of running the multiple available Dis threads, the virtual machine employs one or more system processes. These system processes are processes on either the native kernel or processes over a host operating system. They are scheduled as per the scheduling policies of either the native kernel or the host operating system. These should not be confused with Dis threads, which are executing compiled Limbo applications[1].

Limbo threads are scheduled in a round-robin manner in the virtual machine by the virtual machine's own internal scheduler. This scheduler may use one or more system processes to run a Limbo thread. During its lifetime, a Limbo thread may be run in one or more different Dis VM processes. This is illustrated in Figure 6.1.

All Limbo threads share a common heap, from which memory is allocated for module instances and stack frames. Though there may be several Dis VM processes created over time, only one instance of Dis controls the heap[2]. New Dis VM processes

---

[1]The virtual machine processes may be implemented as threads on some host operating systems, but throughout this chapter the term *thread* will be used to refer to a thread of execution of a Dis executable over the Dis VM, created via a Limbo **spawn** statement, and *process* will be used to refer to an instance of the Dis VM running over a native kernel or host operating system.

[2]The size of the heap may be controlled by flags to the emulator at startup, described in *emu(1e)* or by configuration parameters in the native Inferno kernel.

are created when, for example, a Limbo thread executing in the main Dis process performs a call to one of the Sys module's functions that will cause a new Dis process to be created to service that request. For example, to jump a bit ahead of the content of this chapter, a Limbo thread that makes a call to the export system call with flags Sys->EXPASYNC will cause a new Dis process to be created.

6.2   Thread Creation

Threads are created using a spawn statement. For example, the following creates a new thread to run the function my_function which takes four parameters:

```
spawn my_function(1, d, 12, f->rg);
```

The function being spawned as a new thread must not have a return value. The function can also not be a method from a built-in module. Functions in built-in modules must be called synchronously, and the call will block until the called function completes. If necessary, a new thread can be spawned exclusively to perform such a function call, thus providing equivalent functionality to being able to spawn the built-in function. For example, the following snippet of code will compile, but will lead to a runtime error:

```
Display : import draw;

init(ctxt : ref Draw->Context, args : list of string)
{
    display     : ref Display;

    if (ctxt == nil)
    {
        display = Display.allocate(nil);

        #   This spawn will fail at runtime.
        spawn display.startrefresh();

        #   Instead, wrap the built-in function in the Limbo
        #   function 'refresh()', and spawn that instead:
        spawn refresh(display);
    }
}

refresh(display : ref Display)
{
    display.startrefresh();
}
```

Table 6.1 Limbo thread states.

Thread state	Description
`alt`	Thread is engaged in inter-thread communication, monitoring a set of communication channels for the ability to send or receive.
`broken`	Thread is broken.
`exiting`	Thread terminated or encountered an error.
`ready`	Thread is ready to execute.
`recv`	Thread is blocked waiting to receive on a communication channel.
`release`	Thread has been removed from virtual machine's ready queue to complete a call to a built-in module.
`send`	Thread is blocked on a send down a communication channel.

In the above, the variable `display` is a ref ADT, with a method, `startrefresh()`. Although syntactically correct, the spawn statement is illegal since `draw` is an instance of a built-in module, and `Display` is an ADT defined in the `draw` module. The `spawn` statement maps onto an instruction in the Dis VM, and since built-in modules do not run *over* the virtual machine (they are implemented in the C language and are at a layer logically below the VM), 'spawning' a function from a built-in module is not possible.

Once a thread has been spawned, all interaction with it will be through global variables, any channels it might listen on, file interfaces it might serve or read, and through the `/prog` filesystem. By default, a spawned thread and its parent share all global variables, open file descriptors and current working directory. Since the spawned thread and its parent execute concurrently, care should be taken to synchronize accesses to these shared resources. A spawned thread will also inherit the name space, file descriptor group and process group of its parent. This default behavior can be overridden with the `pctl` system call, discussed shortly.

6.3 Thread States

During its execution lifetime, a Limbo thread may traverse through one of many states, based on the operations it performs, such as system calls through the Sys module, inter-thread communication as described in the next chapter, etc. Table 6.1 shows the possible states in which a thread may exist.

When a thread is created through a `spawn` statement, it is initially in the *ready* state. It is placed on the virtual machine's ready queue and will be executed in turn in a round-robin manner. When a thread performs a system call through the Sys module to do file manipulation, network or name space operations, the thread is removed from the run queue, and a new Dis VM process may get scheduled to service the request. Once the operation performed by the system on behalf of the thread call to the Sys module has completed, the thread is placed at the head of the ready queue. As discussed in the previous section, it is not possible to spawn a function defined in a built-in module—it is only possible to synchronously invoke such functions, and block until the call completes. Threads that are blocked waiting for a call to a built-in module to complete are in the *release* state.

The *alt*, *recv* and *send* states are related to threads performing inter-thread communication. In abstract terms, a thread is placed in the *send* state if it is ready to send data to another thread. Similarly, a thread is placed in the *recv* state if it is ready to receive data. A thread may simultaneously monitor several communication channels for the ability to send or receive on them. A thread in such a situation is placed in the *alt* state. The details of inter-thread communication with channels are covered in the next chapter.

Sometimes, as you are well aware, programmers screw up and their programs 'crash'. When a thread bites the dust on Inferno, the thread is suspended in the *broken* state rather than just being kicked out of memory. This facilitates post-mortem analysis on misbehaving programs. A frustrated, sleep-deprived programmer can then attach a debugger to the broken thread and view its viscera. A thread that has been forcefully terminated (for example, by means of the /prog filesystem described later in this chapter) or which has encountered an error is placed in the *exiting* state. Lastly, a thread that is being manipulated by the thread debugging interface (the /prog filesystem) is placed in the *debugged* state. The transitions between states are depicted pictorially in Figure 6.2.

6.4 Thread Name Spaces

A thread's *name space* is the hierarchy of files visible to the thread. A central tenet of Inferno is that all resources have a file interface to them. Thus manipulating the file name space is often inevitable when programming applications for Inferno. More importantly, the name space is *per-thread*, so a thread may manipulate its name space without necessarily affecting other threads. Likewise, untrusted applications may be run in restricted name spaces to prevent them from wreaking havoc on the rest of the system. The implications of this permeate every pore of the design of Inferno.

If name spaces are that important, are they also arcane, with understanding reserved for those who toil many stormy nights, drinking mud-thick coffee and enduring insults from bearded wise men and dirty, smelly, scary, scantily clad beasts of burden? No. Not at all. Actually, very much to the contrary. The file interface to resources in Inferno was chosen because file semantics are well understood, and file manipulation is very much invariant across many different computing platforms. Name space manipulation (besides file creation) can be accomplished *completely* with

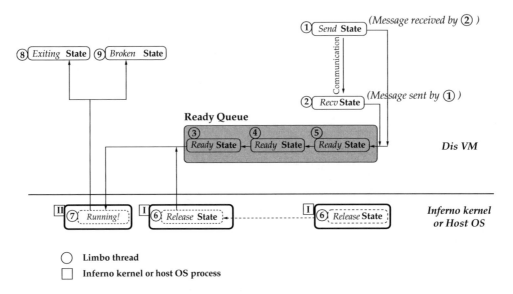

Figure 6.2 Limbo thread states.

two system calls: `bind` and `pctl`. There are several ways to create new entries in the name space, some of which include creating a real disk file, creating a synthesized file with `file2chan` and attaching a name space served by a Styx server using `mount`.

6.4.1 Thread Control: The pctl System Call

Syntax : pctl(*flags* : int, *movefd* : list of ref FD) : int

A thread is usually part of an application that cooperates with other threads to achieve a common goal. Threads which are part of an application typically need to share the same name space or might specifically need to execute in an isolated name space and are organized into *name space groups*. Likewise, threads may be organized into *thread groups* (sometimes referred to as process groups, but that is a misnomer), *environment groups* and *file descriptor groups*.

The `pctl` system call enables the modification of a thread's set of file descriptors, its name space attributes, environment variables and thread group ID, shared with other threads. The return value is the thread ID of the calling thread:

```
#   Determine our thread ID
my_id := sys->pctl(0, nil);

sys->print("My thread ID is [%d]\n", my_id);
```

The *flags* parameter to `pctl` determines how the thread's name space will be modified, and can be one of NEWFD, FORKFD, NEWNS, FORKNS, NODEVS, NEWENV, FORKENV or NEWPGRP, which are all constants defined in /module/sys.m.

The NEWFD flag causes a new file descriptor group to be created and the current thread placed in that file descriptor group. All currently open file descriptors are closed, except those specified in the *movefd* parameter to `pctl`, which are kept open in the new file descriptor group:

```
#  Keep file descriptors 0, 1 and 2 open, copy to new group
move_fd := list of {0, 1, 2};

sys->pctl(Sys->NEWFD, move_fd);
```

The FORKFD flag causes the creation of a new file descriptor group, for the current thread. All file descriptors are copied to the new group. The file descriptors listed in *movefd* are closed in the old file descriptor group:

```
#  Close file descriptors 0, 1 and 2
#  Copy everything else to new group
move_fd := list of {0, 1, 2};

sys->pctl(Sys->FORKFD, move_fd);
```

The NEWNS flag causes the creation of a new name space group, with the root of the name space for this name space group set to the current directory. This is typically useful in creating a new restricted name space from scratch:

```
#  The second parameter, movefd, has no meaning here
#  so set it to nil
sys->pctl(Sys->NEWNS, nil);
```

The NEWENV flag causes the placement of the thread in a new *empty* environment group. The FORKENV flag causes the creation of a new environment group that is a copy of the current environment group (i.e. all current environment variables are copied over to the new environment group). Changes made to the new environment are not seen by the old environment group:

```
#  The second parameter, movefd, has no meaning here
#  so set it to nil
sys->pctl(Sys->NEWENV, nil);
```

The NEWPGRP flag causes the creation of a new thread group, with the thread group ID set to the thread ID of the calling thread:

```
#   The second parameter, movefd, has no meaning here
#   so set it to nil
my_thread_group := sys->pctl(Sys->NEWPGRP, nil);

sys->print("My thread group ID is [%d]\n", my_thread_group);
```

6.5 Caveats

Threading and just-in-time compiled modules   When modules are just-in-time compiled, the Dis VM instructions for the module are converted into native machine code in fixed-size quanta. Limbo programs running in just-in-time compiled mode will therefore take over the virtual machine for the duration of these quanta, during which no other threads will execute. This can sometimes be problematic in situations where threads depend on fine-grained interleaving of execution.

Cleanly exiting from multi-threaded applications   When applications consist of a collection of threads, it is often desirable to be able to exit from the application cleanly, terminating all the running threads that make up the application. There are two main approaches to this. In the first, the application could be constructed so that all its constituent threads listen on a communication channel which is used to send termination messages and possibly perform other synchronization as the application exits. The use of communication channels in Limbo is the subject of the next chapter. The other alternative is to forcefully terminate threads using the facilities of the /prog filesystem interface to threads. This is necessary, for example, if one or more of the threads that comprise an application is blocked on a system call.

6.6 The /prog Filesystem Interface to Threads

Associated with each running thread is a subdirectory of the /prog filesystem, the name of the directory being the ID of the thread. Each such directory is populated with 12 files: ctl, dbgctl, heap, ns, nsgrp, pgrp, stack, status, text, wait, fd and env. So, for example, the /prog filesystem portion for the thread with ID 3516 will look like:

```
; ls -ls /prog/3516
--w-------  p 0 pip pip 0 Apr 19 06:24 /prog/3516/ctl
-rw-r--r--  p 0 pip pip 0 Apr 19 06:24 /prog/3516/dbgctl
-rw-r--r--  p 0 pip pip 0 Apr 19 06:24 /prog/3516/heap
-r--r--r--  p 0 pip pip 0 Apr 19 06:24 /prog/3516/ns
-r--r--r--  p 0 pip pip 0 Apr 19 06:24 /prog/3516/nsgrp
-r--r--r--  p 0 pip pip 0 Apr 19 06:24 /prog/3516/pgrp
```

```
-r--r--r-- p 0 pip pip 0 Apr 19 06:24 /prog/3516/stack
-r--r--r-- p 0 pip pip 0 Apr 19 06:24 /prog/3516/status
---------- p 0 pip pip 0 Apr 19 06:24 /prog/3516/text
-r--r--r-- p 0 pip pip 0 Apr 19 06:24 /prog/3516/wait
-r--r--r-- p 0 pip pip 0 Apr 19 06:24 /prog/3516/fd
-r--r--r-- p 0 pip pip 0 Apr 19 06:24 /prog/3516/env
;
```

The Inferno *ps(1)* utility uses the /prog/ filesystem to provide information at the command interface about the threads running on a system. The output of the *ps* command consists of one line per running thread in the system. Each line consists of six columns: *thread ID*, *thread group ID*, *thread owner* (user ID of the user that created the thread), *thread state*, *memory usage* and lastly the module containing the function running as the thread. An example of the output of the *ps* command is shown below:

```
; ps
       1       1       pip    release    114K Sh
       4       1       pip        alt     14K Cs
       5       5       pip    release     22K Virgild
      91      90       pip    release    142K Sh
      99       1       pip      ready    113K Ps
;
```

6.6.1   /prog/n/ctl: Write Only

The ctl file is used to control the execution of a thread. By writing control messages into this file, you can stop the execution of a thread. Writing the string 'kill' into the ctl file of a thread will cause the thread to exit. Writing 'killgrp' into the ctl file will cause all threads in the same thread group to exit; however, if a thread writes 'killgrp' to its own ctl file, it does not kill itself.

In the example of Figure 6.3, there are initially 11 threads running in the system (with thread IDs 1, 3, 4, 5, 6, 7, 9, 11, 12, 14 and 19), as can be determined from the first column of the output of the *ps* command. These threads are grouped into three process groups, corresponding to the thread ID of the parent thread of each group—1, 3 and 5—and is likewise shown in the second column of the output of *ps*. Thread group 1 corresponds to all threads spawned directly from the module Sh, the command shell. Writing the string "kill" into the control file of thread 14, which belongs to thread group 3, kills it, as is shown by the subsequent *ps*. Writing "killgrp" into the control file of thread 12, which belongs to thread group 3, kills all threads in that thread group.

```
; ps
        1           1       narteh      release     67K Sh[$Sys]
        3           3       narteh      release      8K Server[$Sys]
        4           1       narteh          alt      8K Cs
        5           5       narteh      release     11K Virgild[$Sys]
        6           3       narteh      release      8K Server[$Sys]
        7           3       narteh      release      8K Server[$Sys]
        9           3       narteh      release      8K Server[$Sys]
       11           3       narteh      release      8K Server[$Sys]
       12           3       narteh      release      8K Server[$Sys]
       14           3       narteh      release      8K Server[$Sys]
       19           1       narteh        ready     66K Ps[$Sys]

; lc /prog
1/ 11/ 12/ 14/ 20/ 3/ 4/ 5/ 6/ 7/ 9/

; echo -n kill > /prog/14/ctl
; ps
        1           1       narteh      release     67K Sh[$Sys]
        3           3       narteh      release      8K Server[$Sys]
        4           1       narteh          alt      8K Cs
        5           5       narteh      release     11K Virgild[$Sys]
        6           3       narteh      release      8K Server[$Sys]
        7           3       narteh      release      8K Server[$Sys]
        9           3       narteh      release      8K Server[$Sys]
       11           3       narteh      release      8K Server[$Sys]
       12           3       narteh      release      8K Server[$Sys]
       23           1       narteh        ready     66K Ps[$Sys]

; echo -n killgrp > /prog/12/ctl
; ps
        1           1       narteh      release     67K Sh[$Sys]
        4           1       narteh          alt      8K Cs
        5           5       narteh      release     11K Virgild[$Sys]
       28           1       narteh        ready     66K Ps[$Sys]

;
```

Figure 6.3   Thread control via /prog/n/ctl.

6.6.2 /prog/n/dbgctl: Read/Write

The dbgctl file provides a debugging interface to already executing threads. Reading dbgctl returns information on the state of the thread being debugged. The returned string, on a line terminated by a newline, may be one of the following.

- exited—the thread exited cleanly.

- broken *error*—the thread exited due to the cause described by *error*, which is a string of up to 64 UTF-8 bytes.

- send—the thread is blocked on sending data down a channel.

- `recv`—the thread is blocked on receiving data from a channel.

- `alt`—the thread is blocked in an alt statement.

- `run`—the thread is ready to run.

- new *pid*—the thread has spawned a new sub-thread, with process ID *pid*.

The execution of a thread can be controlled by writing command strings into the `dbgctl` file. The commands are detailed below.

- `step` *n*—writing the string `"step n"` into dbgctl causes the interpreter to step through the application for at most *n* instructions or until a breakpoint is reached, whichever is sooner.

- `toret`—this causes the interpreter to continue execution until the current function returns or until a breakpoint is reached, whichever is sooner.

- `cont`—this instructs the interpreter to continue execution until the next breakpoint is reached.

- `bpt set` *path pc*—this sets a breakpoint at program counter value *pc* for the module specified by *path*. The module path is the location of the Dis executable corresponding to this module.

- `bpt del` *path pc*—this removes a breakpoint at program counter value *pc* for the module specified by *path*, if one exists. It is ignored otherwise. The module path is the location of the Dis executable corresponding to this module.

- `detach`—stop debugging thread.

- `stop`—stop the execution of the thread.

- `unstop`—permit a thread which has been halted with a prior `stop` to resume execution.

6.6.3 /prog/n/fd: Read Only

The file `fd` returns information on open file descriptors of the thread's file descriptor group. The data returned on a read of `fd` is laid out with entries for each file descriptor separated by a newline. Each entry consists of five columns: (1) the file descriptor index; (2) the open mode (read only (`r`), write only (`w`), read/write (`rw`)) associated with that descriptor; (3) the two fields of the unique ID assigned to the corresponding file by the filesystem driver, *qid.path* and *qid.vers*, separated by a dot (Each qid field is 8 hexadecimal digits long); (4) the file offset in bytes; and (5) the path of the file:

```
; cat /prog/50/fd
  0 r  00000010.00000000        51 #s/cons.45
  1 w  00000010.00000000      1379 #s/cons.45
  2 w  00000010.00000000        20 #s/cons.45
;
```

6.6.4 /prog/n/heap: Neither Read/Write

This interface is implemented, but disabled in production versions of Inferno. Reading it and writing to it will result in an error.

6.6.5 /prog/n/ns: Read Only

This file contains a description of the operations performed to construct the name space of the current thread. This includes all the operations performed by any of the ancestors which were passed on. Each line of the returned contents corresponds to one operation on the name space, and has the format:

flag   destination   source

The *source* field is the name of a directory or device, and the *destination* field is the name of the directory to which that source directory or device is bound. The *flag* is an integer constant that represents one of the constants MREPL, MBEFORE, MAFTER, representing the integer values 0, 1, 2, defined in sys.m, possibly OR'ed with the MCREATE flag, also defined in /module/sys.m. These represent the flags the *bind* operation used to perform the name space operation. Thus, for example, a *bind* operation with flags MAFTER | MCREATE will show up as the value 6, as occurs in the case of the bind of the root filesystem, #U to '/' in the second line of the output below.

```
; cat /prog/1/ns
0 #/ #/
6 #/ #U
0 #//dev #//dev
1 #//dev #c
2 #//dev #U/dev
4 #U/env #e
2 #/ #C
0 #U/n/remote #M1
0 #//net #M1/net
1 #//dev #d
2 #/ #C
0 #//prog #p
0 #//chan #//chan
1 #//chan #s
;
```

6.6.6 /prog/n/nsgrp: Read Only

Reading the nsgrp file returns the thread's name space group. A thread may have a name space group identifier different from its parent if it forks its name space using the pctl system call, with the FORKNS or NEWNS flags. In the example below, the thread Cs with thread ID 4 is in name space group 2:

```
; ps
      1         1         pip     release   129K Sh
      3         3         pip     release   17K Server
      4         1         pip     alt       16K Cs
;
; echo; cat /prog/4/nsgrp; echo

      2
```

6.6.7 /prog/n/pgrp: Read Only

The pgrp file contains an integer value that is the thread group identifier of the thread. The thread group of a thread is the thread ID of its parent thread, unless the child thread modified its thread group ID via the pctl system call with the NEWPGRP flag to set its thread group ID to its own thread ID, diverging the thread group from its parent:

```
; ps
      1         1         pip     release   129K Sh
      3         3         pip     release   17K Server
      4         1         pip     alt       16K Cs
;
; echo; cat /prog/4/pgrp; echo

      1
```

6.6.8 /prog/n/stack: Read Only

Reading stack gives you the dynamic call stack trace for a thread. Each newline delimited field read from stack corresponds to one activation frame, and has six fields separated by a single whitespace. The fields are (1) frame pointer, (2) program counter, (3) module data pointer, (4) module code pointer, (5) execution method for the module, and (6) the path name of the module. All these fields, except the execution method and path, are eight hexadecimal digits long. The execution method is an integer, 0 or 1, for interpreted modules and on-the-fly compiled modules, respectively. The path field is the absolute path string of the location of the Dis executable for the module containing the function which the thread is executing:

```
; cat /prog/1/stack
08176638 15556094 082203d4 081434c8 1 /dis/sh.dis
081765c0 15556414 082203d4 081434c8 1 /dis/sh.dis
081764f8 00000b4c 082203d4 081434c8 1 /dis/sh.dis
08121780 eaaabcbd 082203d4 081434c8 1 /dis/sh.dis
08121728 eaaab534 082203d4 081434c8 1 /dis/sh.dis
081216c8 155559ff 082203d4 081434c8 1 /dis/sh.dis
08121658 eaaaae24 082203d4 081434c8 1 /dis/sh.dis
081215f8 0000016e 082203d4 081434c8 1 /dis/sh.dis
081215b8 eaaaab2a 0821bdf4 08122e68 1 /dis/emuinit.dis
;
```

6.6.9 /prog/n/status: Read Only

The status file contains information on the status of the thread. It has six fields that represent (1) the thread identifier, (2) the thread group identifier, (3) the username of the user that launched the thread, (4) the state of the thread, (5) the amount of memory used by the thread, rounded up to the nearest kilobyte, with the letter 'K' appended, and, lastly, (6) the name of the module containing the function which was spawned as a thread. For compiled modules, the module name is just the module name as it was defined in the implement statement of the Limbo implementation. For interpreted modules, if the module is in the *release* state, i.e. not executing in the virtual machine but blocked waiting for a system call to complete, the name of the module in which this blocking occurred is printed appended to the thread's module name in brackets (e.g. Sh[$Sys]). So, for example, a thread that performs a file manipulation, name space operations or network accesses will block in the virtual machine and be put in the *release* state, as described previously in Section 6.1. The thread's status will thus be similar to that shown below:

```
    1        1        pip    release    1K Sh[$Sys]
```

The format of the status file is identical to that of a line of output of the *ps(1)* utility, corresponding to the thread in question.

6.6.10 /prog/n/text: Neither Read/Write

This interface is not implemented. Reading it and writing to it will result in an error.

6.6.11   /prog/n/wait: Read Only

A read of the wait file of a thread will block until a child thread, created after the wait file was opened, exits. When a read succeeds, the format of the data read is three fields containing (1) the thread ID of the exiting thread, (2) the module name of the thread's module, followed by a single whitespace and a colon, and (3) a possibly empty error string which may be 0–64 characters long:

```
100 "Wm" :
```

In the above example, the exiting thread was running the module Wm, had thread ID 100, and exited without any errors.

6.6.12   /prog/n/env: Read Only

Reading the env file of a thread returns the set of environment variables in the thread's environment group, one per line, with the variable name separated from its value by an '=':

```
; cat /prog/766/env
prompt='% ' ''
autoload=std
fn-%='{$*}'
fn-cd='{builtin cd $*;echo cwd '{pwd} >/chan/shctl}'
fn-wmrun=
home=/usr/pip
apid=439
args=charon
```

6.7   Summary

This chapter described the interface to threads running on an Inferno system. Like other resources in Inferno, the interface to threads is represented as a filesystem, the /prog filesystem. Programs that provide information to the user about threads (such as *ps*) and those that provide debugging interfaces to threads (such as a debugger) do so by manipulating files in the /prog filesystem. Since it is possible to access the name space of a remote machine, it is possible to debug threads and obtain thread execution statistics for threads running on a remote machine.

Bibliographic Notes

A coverage of the traditional concepts of threads versus processes can be found in operating systems and computer systems textbooks such as [7, 76, 77]. Most other systems that employ multithreading typically employ an implementation of POSIX threads (*pthreads*). Comprehensive coverage of pthreads can be found in [9, 47]. The /prog filesystem interface to threads is a descendant of the Unix /proc filesystem, described in [29]. The scheduling of threads is described in the Inferno system manuals [79]. The design, implementation and use, of Limbo's direct ancestors, Alef and Newsqueak, are described in [81] and [50] respectively.

6.8 Chapter Example: Broke—Culling Broken Threads

For the chapter example, we will examine the *broke* program, which searches for broken threads and kills them[3].

```
# File : broke.b

implement Broke;

include "sys.m";
include "draw.m";

sys: Sys;
stderr : ref Sys->FD;

Broke: module
{
    init:   fn(nil: ref Draw->Context, args: list of string);
};

init(nil: ref Draw->Context, nil: list of string)
{
    sys = load Sys Sys->PATH;
    fd := sys->open("/prog", Sys->OREAD);
    if (fd == nil)
    {
        err(sys->sprint("can't open /prog: %r"));
    }

    stderr = sys->fildes(2);

    killed := "";
    dir := array[100] of Sys->Dir;
    while((n := sys->dirread(fd, dir)) > 0)
    {
        for(i := 0; i < n; i++)
        {
            if(isbroken(dir[i].name) && kill(dir[i].name))
            {
                killed += sys->sprint(" %s", dir[i].name);
            }
        }
    }

    if (n < 0)
    {
        err(sys->sprint("error reading /prog: %r"));
    }

    if(killed != nil)
    {
        sys->print("%s\n", killed);
    }
```

[3]An earlier version of *broke* was called 'Slayer'!

```
}

isbroken(pid: string): int
{
    statf := "/prog/" + pid + "/status";
    fd := sys->open(statf, Sys->OREAD);
    if (fd == nil)
    {
        return 0;
    }

    buf := array[256] of byte;
    n := sys->read(fd, buf, len buf);
    if (n < 0)
    {
        sys->fprint(stderr, "broke: can't read %s: %r\n", statf);
        return 0;
    }

    (nf, l) := sys->tokenize(string buf[0:n], " ");

    return (nf >= 4 && hd tl tl tl l == "broken");
}

kill(pid: string): int
{
    ctl := "/prog/" + pid + "/ctl";
    fd := sys->open(ctl, sys->OWRITE);
    if(fd == nil || sys->fprint(fd, "kill") < 0)
    {
        sys->fprint(stderr, "broke: can't kill %s: %r\n", pid);
        return 0;
    }

    return 1;
}

err(s: string)
{
    sys->fprint(sys->fildes(2), "broke: %s\n", s);
    sys->raise("fail:error");
}

user(): string
{
    fd := sys->open("/dev/user", sys->OREAD);
    if(fd == nil)
    {
        return "inferno";
    }

    buf := array[Sys->NAMELEN] of byte;
    n := sys->read(fd, buf, len buf);
    if(n <= 0)
    {
        return "inferno";
```

```
    }

    return string buf[0:n];
}
```

Discussion   The *broke(1)* utility searches through the /prog filesystem for threads in the *broken* state and terminates them.

Problems

6.1   Write a simple command-line debugger that enables users to access all the facilities of the /prog filesystem.

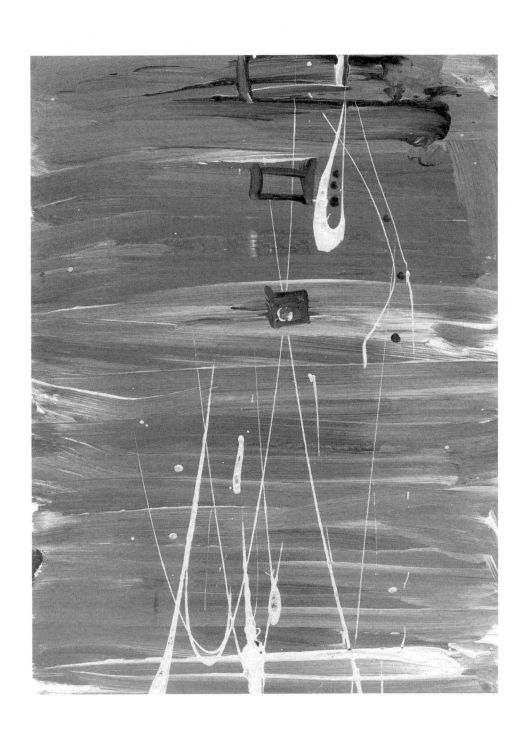

7

Channels

7.1 Introduction

Channels in Limbo are communication paths; they can be used to transfer information between threads or to synchronize threads.

Limbo channels are typed, and are thus much more versatile than pipes (which Inferno also implements with the pipe device, #|). Typed channels enable threads to communicate arbitrary information, using whichever data structure is most suitable. Anything from simple integers to complex abstract data types may be sent over a channel, and arbitrarily complex communication paths may be set up.

Limbo enforces strong type checking both at compile time and at runtime—you can only send data of one type down a channel with the same type, thus applications are responsible for marshaling data into channels. Serialization of data objects down a channel is, however, automatically performed by the Limbo runtime environment. For example, if you have a picture that you wish to send from one thread to another using a channel, you would first decide on an abstract data type to hold the data of the picture, say, a Pict ADT. You would then declare a channel of type Pict and send the ADT instance down the channel. The thread on the other end would perform a receive operation from the channel, into a variable of type Pict. You, however, would not need to bother about how the bits of the ADT instance are actually communicated, i.e. you would not have to worry about the manner in which the Pict ADT instance is converted into a bit-stream to be sent down the channel. Figure 7.1 illustrates how an allocated channel can be used to communicate between two threads. In the figure, the thread executing the function writer writes the value 42 down a channel,

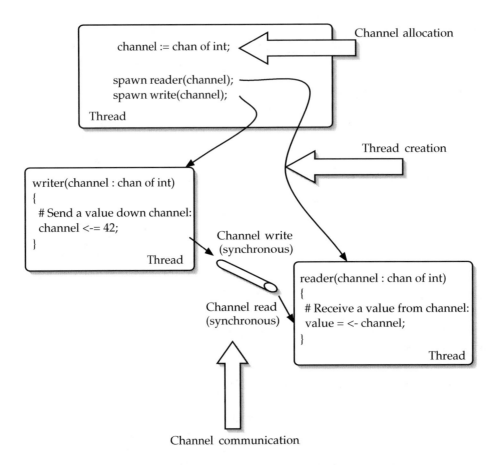

Figure 7.1 Illustration of Limbo channels.

imaginatively named `channel`, of type `chan of int`, while the thread executing the function `reader` reads from the selfsame channel, into a variable of type `int`.

A write to a channel will block until a matching read from the channel is performed by a thread at the other end of the channel; thus the reads from and writes to a channel must be performed by different threads.

A thread that is blocked on a write to a channel is placed in the *send* state and is taken off the virtual machine's ready queue until a matching receive is posted on the other end of the channel. Conversely, a read from a channel will block until a matching write to the channel is performed by another thread. A thread blocked on a read from a channel is placed in the *recv* state and taken off the virtual machine's ready queue until a matching write is posted on the other end of the channel.

The opposite ends of a channel will usually be serviced by separate threads, due to the requirement of matching operations on the other end of the channel. For this reason, channels provide an excellent means of synchronizing threads. The simplest application of channels is to pause an application until some event occurs.

In the example below, a simple application sleeps until the spawned process has completed, and then prints out a message and exits. This example illustrates the use of channel communication for synchronization between threads.

```
# File : chanexample.b

implement Fibonacci;

include "sys.m";
include "draw.m";

sys : Sys;
MAX : con 50;
x : chan of int;

Fibonacci : module
{
    init : fn(nil : ref Draw->Context, nil : list of string);
};

init(nil : ref Draw->Context, nil : list of string)
{
    sys = load Sys Sys->PATH;

    x = chan of int;
    sys->print("0  .\n1  ..\n");
    spawn f(0, 1);

    <-x;
    sys->print("Spawned thread completed.\n");
}

f(a, b : int)
{
    sys->print("%-3d", a + b);
    for (i := 0; i <= a+b; i++)
    {
        sys->print(".");
    }
    sys->print("\n");

    if (a+b < MAX)
    {
        f(b, a+b);
    }

    x <-= 0;
}
```

The example demonstrates the basic features of programming with channels. The main thread (function `init`) creates another thread, worker, which prints out the first *n* Fibonacci number smaller in value than 2^{16}. The main thread then performs a read from a global channel, which will block until the worker thread has completed and sent data on the channel. The actual data received on the channel by the `init` thread is thrown away, but it could have been stored in a variable with the same type as the channel (i.e. with type int).

The channel used for communication between the main thread and the worker thread is defined to be in global scope of both threads:

```
x : chan of int;
```

Subsequent to the definition of the channel *type*, storage for the channel must actually be allocated, and this is performed in the `init` thread:

```
x = chan of int;
```

Channels, like arrays, are reference types and do not have storage allocated automatically.

The operator for performing channel communication is '<-'. The '<-' operator always goes next to the channel, with the source of the operation on the right and the destination on the left. Thus if the channel is on its left, we are writing to the channel, and if the channel is on its right, we are reading from the channel:

```
#   Write the tuple (2,"test") to the channel
x <- = (2, "test");

#   Read from the channel into the tuple (a, b)
(a, b) = <- x;
```

7.2 Multi-Way Selection on Channels with alt and Arrays of Channels

You can have multiple threads read from a channel or have a thread read from multiple channels. The latter is enabled by the alt[1] construct, illustrated below:

```
alt
{
    a := <- chan1 =>
    {
```

---

[1]The Inmos Transputers have hardware facilities for alternating on communication channels, and the ALT statement in Occam is also equivalent to this.

```
        sys->print("Read on chan1\n");
    }
    b := <- chan2 =>
    {
        sys->print("Read on chan2\n");
    }
    chan3 <- = "Square Circle Zine" =>
    {
        sys->print("Send on chan3\n");
    }
}
```

The *alt* statement above will block until either chan1 or chan2 is ready to send data or chan3 is ready to receive data. Like a case statement, the alt statement is processed once-through; thus to continue to monitor a set of channels for the ability to communicate, you would have to enclose your alt statement in a loop. If the above block of code was in a loop and we wanted to have some default action taken when none of the channels were ready to send or receive data, we could write:

```
for (;;)
alt
{
    a := <- chan1 =>
    {
        sys->print("Read from chan1\n");
    }

    b := <- chan2 =>
    {
        sys->print("Read from chan2\n");
    }

    chan3 <- = "Orange" =>
    {
        sys->print("Send on chan3\n");
    }

    * =>
    {
        sys->print("Default action.\n");
    }
}
```

Another way to perform multi-way selection of channels that are ready to communicate (for reads only) is to perform an assignment from an array of channels—the read results in a tuple consisting of the index of the channel that was ready to send and the data that were received in the communication:

```
channels := array [10] of chan of int;

#  ...

(index, value) := <- channels;
```

7.2.1 Peculiarities of alt

In the current implementation of Limbo, only one process may `alt` on a send or receive for a given channel at a time. This restriction also existed in one of the predecessors of Limbo, Winterbottom's *Alef* [81] language, where the restriction was placed, supposedly due to the difficulty of handling such a situation in a multiprocessor environment. Having multiple threads `alt` on a channel send or receive operation will therefore currently elicit a "`channel busy`" error. The following example illustrates this. This seemingly well-formed application does not behave as expected and dies with a "`channel busy`" error.

```
# File : altchanbusy.b

implement Test;

include "sys.m";
include "draw.m";

Test : module
{
    init : fn(nil : ref Draw->Context, nil : list of string);
};

init(nil : ref Draw->Context, nil : list of string)
{
    channel := chan of int;

    spawn write(channel);
    spawn write(channel);

    spawn read(channel);
    spawn read(channel);
}

write(channel : chan of int)
{
    while ()
    alt
    {
        channel <-= 1 =>
            ;
    }
}
```

```
read(channel : chan of int)
{
    while ()
    alt
    {
        <-channel =>
            ;
    }
}
```

7.3 Pipelining Computation with Channels

Channels can be used to solve problems that would be difficult to implement otherwise. To be fair, it is not channels alone that enable what we shall discuss next but the combination of channels and threads (a single thread cannot communicate with itself by a channel!).

Consider the following example. Can you tell what the nature of the values printed out are?

```
# File : sieve-naive.b

implement Eratosthenes;

include "sys.m";
include "draw.m";

sys : Sys;

Eratosthenes : module
{
    init : fn(nil : ref Draw->Context, nil : list of string);
};

init(nil : ref Draw->Context, nil : list of string)
{
    sys = load Sys Sys->PATH;

    i := 2;
    sourcechan := chan of int;
    spawn sieve(i, sourcechan);

    while ()
    {
        sourcechan <-= i++;
    }
}

sieve(ourprime : int, inchan : chan of int)
{
    n : int;
```

```
    sys->print("%d ", ourprime);
    newchan := chan of int;

    while (!((n = <-inchan) % ourprime))
    {
    }

    spawn sieve(n, newchan);

    while ()
    {
        if ((n = <-inchan) % ourprime)
        {
            newchan <-= n;
        }
    }
}
```

As you might have figured out by perusing the code, the application prints out prime numbers, starting from the number 2, by the method of the *Sieve of Eratosthenes*[2].

The method works as follows. To find all the prime numbers between the smallest prime, 2, and some number n, we look at all the numbers in the range in several passes. On each pass, we strike out any number divisible by the first number not stricken out. So for example, we would first strike out any number divisible by 2, then all those divisible by 3, then 5, etc., stopping at $\sqrt{n}$. Thus for example, to find all primes between 1 and 20, the sequence of numbers we will have on each pass over our list will be as follows:

```
Our initial list. We omit 1 since it is neither a composite nor a prime:
2 3 4 5 6 7 8 9 10 11 12 13 14 15 16 17 18 19 20

After deleting all multiples of 2:
2 3 5 7 9 11 13 15 17 19

After deleting all multiples of 3:
2 3 5 7 11 13 17 19

We stop here because 5 is greater than square root of 20
```

In the example, rather than representing the range of numbers from 2 to n statically, we think of them as a stream of numbers, and each pass of the method described above as a stationary sieve that strikes out multiples of a specific prime number and lets the rest through. Each such 'sieve' is a thread which first prints out the prime number whose multiples it will be filtering out of the stream (the next prime number in sequence), then likewise spawns a thread to filter out multiples of the next prime in the sequence.

---

[2]This method for identifying prime numbers was conceived by Eratosthenes of Cyrene, who lived *circa* 275–195 BC.

Such a modeling of an iterative algorithm (going over the list of numbers in several passes) as a pipelined computation (each stage in the pipeline is a thread, and the length of the pipeline grows dynamically) is interesting: however, our initial implementation suffers from a major problem: the creation of new threads is unbounded.

To stop the growth of the pipeline and cause termination once a certain upper bound on the value of the primes has been reached, we could employ several approaches. The idea would be to have each thread check to see if the upper bound has been reached before printing its prime, and, if so, terminate itself and all the other threads in the pipeline. We could use the facilities described in Chapter 6 to forcibly kill all the threads in the thread group, or use another channel to deliver a termination message to all the threads.

7.4 User-Level Filesystems: Files Connected to Channels

Servers presenting filesystem interfaces to resources are communicated with, at the lowest level, via the Styx protocol. Applications that wish to export filesystem interfaces, however, do not generally have to deal with the details of the Styx protocol explicitly. The creation and management of simple to complex filesystem interfaces is facilitated by methods provided by the Inferno system modules. One facility for applications to create such application level filesystems is the `file2chan` method in the Sys module. Using this facility, an application can create *synthetic file* entries in the name space, such that reads from and writes to these synthetic file entries are seen by applications as interactions on channels.

Synthetic entries in the filesystem do not exist on the disk, but appear to users in the name space and can be manipulated just as disk files would. Reads of these synthetic files will return data as determined by the application that created them, and writes to these synthetic files will be received by the corresponding applications. This behavior of synthetic versus disk files is illustrated in Figure 7.2.

To permit applications to create such synthetic entries in the name space requires, as might be apparent, a means of intercepting all accesses to the name space and diverting those that refer to synthetic files to an appropriate entity. Once these accesses have been intercepted, they must somehow be delivered to applications. Such accesses to the name space actually cause the generation of Styx messages, and these could be sent directly to applications for interpretation. Such an approach of handling Styx messages at the application level is the subject of Chapter 8. This section presents a much simpler (though limited) facility.

Rather than handling Styx messages directly, applications may employ a combination of the *Srv device* and the `file2chan` methods of the Sys module.

The creation of synthetic files using this combination works as follows. The Srv device (#s), also referred to as the *server registry*, is first bound into the directory in which the application wishes to create synthetic files. All accesses to a directory in Inferno will be seen by all devices bound into that location of the name space. This is the default behavior of union directories (see the manual pages for *bind(1)* for details

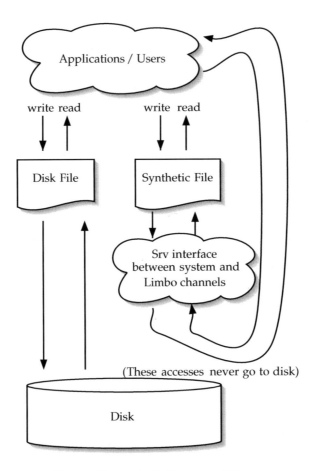

Figure 7.2 Synthetic files versus disk files.

of this behavior). The point of relevance here is that if the device is bound in the name space to appear *before* other entries in the union directory, then it will see all accesses to the union directory.

Once the Srv device has been bound into a directory, synthetic entries in the name space can be created with the `sys->file2chan` method of the `Sys` module. The syntax is:

```
file2chan(dir, file: string):   ref FileIO
```

A synthetic file with name specified by the string `file` is created in the directory `dir`. The information in this call is passed on to the Srv device, which will then synthesize the named entry in the name space. Accesses to this synthesized file will be converted to messages on channels contained in the `ref FileIO` ADT that is returned by the `file2chan` call. A more detailed version of Figure 7.2 showing this behavior is shown in Figure 7.3.

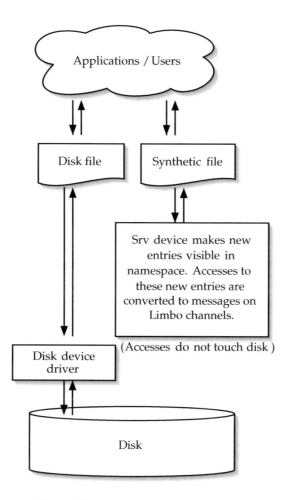

Figure 7.3 The Srv device and synthetic files.

The Srv device thus acts as a proxy for applications wishing to serve entries in a name space. The applications bind the Srv device into a directory, in a similar manner to what would be done for a more complicated file server that actually handled Styx messages. Subsequent to this, the application calls file2chan to notify the Srv device to create entries in the name space and respond to accesses on them. The Srv device passes read and write requests on to the application when such accesses occur. The details of the channel interaction between the Srv device and the application lie in the FileIO structure, a reference to an instance of which the application receives as the return value of a file2chan call.

The FileIO ADT contains a pair of channels: one corresponding to read operations on the file, and the other corresponding to write operations. Each of the read and write channels is a channel of a four-member tuple:

```
Rread: type chan of (array of byte, string);
Rwrite: type chan of (int, string);

FileIO: adt
{
    read:    chan of (int, int, int, Rread);
    write:   chan of (int, array of byte, int, Rwrite);
};
```

On a read from the synthetic file, the tuple sent down the read channel consists of the following.

- A read offset.

- Count of bytes read.

- A unique identifier, *fid*, maintained by the client, of the file being read. This is especially useful if the application wishes to discern between multiple readers of the synthetic file and handle them accordingly.

- A channel on which the server should send a reply for this request. The reply channel has type Rread, being a channel of an array of bytes (representing the data to be send back to the reader of the synthetic file) and a string (representing a possible error message). The convention employed is that on a successful read, the error string is set to nil, and otherwise it is set to an appropriate error message, and the byte array should contain zero bytes. If the file is closed for reading, the rc reply channel for the read request will be nil.

On a write to the synthetic file, the application serving the file receives a tuple consisting of the following.

- The offset of the write.

- An array of bytes representing the data of the write.

- A unique identifier, *fid*, maintained by the client, of the file being written. This is useful if the application wishes to discern between multiple readers of the synthetic file.

- A channel, wc, on which to return the status of the write. This can be used by the application, for example, to enforce a size limit on data written into the synthetic file and to inform clients of the interface when a write error (as determined by the application) has occurred. On a write error, the count field of the response sent on wc is set to zero, and the error field set to an appropriate error message. If the file is closed for writing, the wc reply channel for the write request will be nil, and appropriate action can be taken by the application (e.g. terminate).

7.5   Example: A Simple File Server

The discussion of the facilities to serve synthetic files is best made concrete with an example. In this section, we will look at a simple application that serves a single synthetic file. Writes to the file are discarded and reads from the file return a string stating the number of times the file has been read. This simple example does not use all the functionality possible for such synthetic files, for example, for handling multiple readers and writers. In another example at the end of the chapter, we extend the simple server described in this section to cater for multiple readers and writers. The complete simple file server application is shown below:

```
# File : simplefileserver.b

implement FileServer;

include "sys.m";
include "draw.m";

FileServer : module
{
    init : fn(nil : ref Draw->Context, nil : list of string);
};

sys : Sys;

init(nil : ref Draw->Context, nil : list of string)
{
    sys = load Sys Sys->PATH;

    sys->bind("#s", "/usr/pip", sys->MBEFORE);
    chanref := sys->file2chan("/usr/pip", "synthetic.file");

    if (chanref == nil)
    {
        sys->print("Error - Could not create chan file : %r\n");
        exit;
    }

    spawn worker(chanref);
}

worker(chanref : ref sys->FileIO)
{
    data    : array of byte;
    index   : int = 0;
    count   : int = 1;

    while (1)
    alt
    {
        (off, nbytes, fid, rc) := <-chanref.read =>
        {
            if (rc == nil) break;
```

```
          #   If this is a new read, generate new data
          if (index == 0)
          {
              data = array of byte ("File read "+
                  string count+" times.\n");
          }

          if (index < len data)
          {
              end := min(index+nbytes, len data);

              #   Serve the reader with data that are left
              rc <-= (data[index:end], "");
              index = end;
          }
          else
          {
              #   Finished serving contents of data[]
              rc <-= (nil, "");

              #   So next read of data will start afresh
              index = 0;
              count++;
          }
      }

      (offset, writedata, fid, wc) := <-chanref.write =>
      {
          if (wc == nil)
          {
              break;
          }

          wc <-= (len writedata, "");
      }
    }
}

min (a, b : int) : int
{
    if (a < b)
        return a;
    return b;
}
```

Our file server serves a file out of the directory /usr/pip. We must therefore bind the Srv device, #s, into that directory before subsequently calling file2chan with the name of the directory (in which we bound the Srv device) and the name of the file (imaginatively named 'synthetic.file') that we wish the Srv device to synthesize on our behalf. The second argument to the bind call specifies that we want the Srv device to appear first in the union directory, ensuring that all requests for entries in the name space will be seen by Srv. In return, the call to file2chan provides a reference to a

FileIO ADT which the application will use for its interaction with its proxy, the Srv device:

```
sys->bind("#s", "/usr/pip", sys->MBEFORE);
chanref = sys->file2chan("/usr/pip", "synthetic.file");
```

Once this name space entry creation is successful, we can just wait for read and write requests and service them accordingly. This task is performed by a separate thread, worker, which receives a reference to the FileIO ADT, chanref, as its argument.

The FileIO ADT, as previously shown, contains two channels, read and write. On a read from the synthesized file, a tuple describing the read request can be read off this channel. Similarly, on a write to the synthesized file, a tuple describing the write can be read off the write channel of the chanref ADT instance. The worker thread thus forever iterates waiting on an event on either the read or write channel:

```
while (1)
alt
{
    (offset, nbytes, fid, rc) := <-chanref.read =>
    {
        if (rc == nil) break;

        #   If this is a new read, generate new data
        if (index == 0)
        {
            data = array of byte ("File read "+
                string count+" times.\n");
        }

        if (index < len data)
        {
            end := min(index+nbytes, len data);

            #   Serve the reader with data that are left
            rc <-= (data[index:end], "");
            index = end;
        }
        else
        {
            #   Finished serving contents of data
            rc <-= (nil, "");

            #   So next read of data will start afresh
            index = 0;
            count++;
        }
    }

    (offset, writedata, fid, wc) := <-chanref.write =>
    {
```

```
        if (wc == nil)
        {
            break;
        }

        wc <-= (len writedata, "");
    }
}
```

In both the case of a read and a write, `offset` and `fid` represent the offset in the synthetic file of the request and the unique identifier provided by the client in the request, respectively. Our application ignores both of these pieces of information—writes are discarded, reads always return the same string no matter the offset, and we do not cater for multiple readers or writers (which the `fid` would be useful for).

The tuple members `nbytes` and `writedata` in the read and write requests denote the number of bytes requested in the read and the written data, respectively.

The channels `rc` and `wc` are used to communicate the status of the operation back to the client. Although we ignore the offset in the read, we track how much data has been read using the variable `index`.

If, for example, the synthetic file is being read by the Inferno utility *cat(1)*, each read request will be 8192 bytes in size. The first read will return to `cat` the number of bytes in the string we synthesize. This will be followed by one more read by `cat` (at an offset depending on the number of bytes returned in the previous read), and we want this read to return an end-of-file status to the reader, so that it completes. It would be insufficient to rely on the `offset` to determine when to return this EOF status. For one, there is no guarantee that the offset will ever be non-zero. Second, our string will not always be of the same length in bytes, due to the string representation of the total number of bytes read.

We use `index` as a local counter of the read offset. If it is less than the size of our synthesized string, we return as many bytes as remain in the string or the requested number of bytes, whichever is smaller. If we detect by the value `index` that the entire synthesized string has already been delivered, we return a `nil` byte stream and an empty error string to the reader. Note that this use of `index` falls on its face in the presence of multiple concurrent readers of the file. The end-of-chapter example provides a solution to this.

Note that all the events on the `read` and `write` channels were generated as a result of our proxy, the Srv device, in response to Styx messages it intercepted on our behalf. Likewise, the responses delivered on the `rc` and `wc` channels by our simple file server are converted into Styx messages by the Srv device. The nature of the Styx protocol, and the construction of Limbo applications to handle these Styx messages directly (without the help of Srv and the `file2chan` mechanism), is the subject of the next chapter.

7.6 Summary

This chapter introduced the Limbo channel, which provides synchronous communication paths between threads. Channels in Limbo are *typed*, and thus channels can be declared to be of any of the data types discussed so far. It is possible to have channels of ADTs, channels within ADTs, and even channels which are of the type of ADTs which contain channels, as was seen in the case of the `read` and `write` components of the `FileIO` ADT. Channels are data types—just as integers, ADTs, etc., are—and they may be passed as arguments to functions, or one may even pass channels down channels (demonstrated above for the `rc` and `wc` channels). We illustrated the construction of simple file servers using the `file2chan` facility in conjunction with the Srv device, laying the foundation for the next chapter on the Styx protocol.

Bibliographic Notes

The concept of channels in Limbo are descended from Hoare's *Communicating Sequential Processes* (CSP) [25]. Calculi for reasoning about concurrent systems include Milner's CCS [39] and π-calculus [41, 70], a good introduction to these ideas being [40]. An early language that incorporated ideas from CSP is Occam [37, 38], which run on the Inmos Transputers [36]. The concept of constructing applications as filters acting on *streams* of data is familiar in other languages [2]. A lucid description that is closely related to Limbo through Pike's Newsqueak [50] is [33].

7.7   Chapter Example: Multiplexing Readers in Simple File Server

The chapter example extends the simple file server described previously to cater for multiple readers:

```
# File : multiplexfs.b

implement FileServer;

include "sys.m";
include "draw.m";

sys : Sys;

FileServer : module
{
    init : fn(nil : ref Draw->Context, nil : list of string);
};

Reader : adt
{
    index, fid : int;
    data : array of byte;
};

MAXREADERS : con 1024;

init(nil : ref Draw->Context, nil : list of string)
{
    sys = load Sys Sys->PATH;

    sys->bind("#s", "/usr/pip", sys->MBEFORE);
    chanref := sys->file2chan("/usr/pip", "synthetic.file");

    if (chanref == nil)
    {
        sys->print("Error - Could not create chan file : %r\n");
        exit;
    }

    spawn worker(chanref);
}

worker(chanref : ref sys->FileIO)
{
    readers := array [MAXREADERS] of Reader;
    i, nfids, count    : int = 0;

wlabel:
    while (1)
    alt
    {
        (off, nbytes, fid, rc) := <-chanref.read =>
        {
```

```
if (rc == nil)
{
    break;
}
for (i = 0; i < nfids; i++)
{
    if (readers[i].fid == fid)
    {
        if (readers[i].index < len readers[i].data)
        {
            end := min(readers[i].index+nbytes,
                len readers[i].data);

            #    Serve the reader with data that's left
            rc <-=(readers[i].data[readers[i].index:end],
                "");
            readers[i].index = end;
        }
        else
        {
            #    Finished serving contents of data[]
            rc <-= (nil, "");

            #    So next read of data will start afresh:
            readers[i].index = 0;
            readers[i].fid = -1;
            readers[i].data = nil;

            #    Recycle entry
            if (i == (nfids-1))
            {
                nfids--;
            }
            count++;
        }
        continue wlabel;
    }
}

if (i == nfids)
{
    readers[nfids].fid = fid;
    readers[nfids].index = 0;
    nfids++;

    #    This is a new read, generate new data
    readers[i].data = array of byte
        ("File read "+string count+" times.\n");

    end := min(readers[i].index+nbytes, len readers[i].data);

    #    Serve the reader with data
    rc <-= (readers[i].data[readers[i].index:end], "");

    readers[i].index = end;
}
```

```
            }

            (offset, writedata, fid, wc) := <-chanref.write =>
            {
                if (wc == nil)
                {
                    break;
                }

                wc <-= (len writedata, "");
            }
        }
}

min (a, b : int) : int
{
    if (a < b)
        return a;
    return b;
}
```

Discussion   The above example is a reworked version of the example presented in the body of the chapter. The primary addition is the data structure, readers, to keep track of the *fids* which have been supplied in the read channel. After a read is completed, that entry in the readers data structure is recycled.

Problems

7.1   Write a Limbo program to intercept the Styx messages that are generated when a name space is traversed. To begin, you will need to create a file with sys->file2chan, then open that file and do a sys->export on the open file descriptor. There is a much easier way to do this using a pipe device, but the implementation with file2chan is instructive!

Appendix: Modeling and Verification of Concurrent Applications with SPIN

In the last two chapters, we have learnt how to build applications consisting of multiple *threads*, and how to connect these threads with communication *channels*. These multiple threads execute concurrently and share resources such as global variables, name spaces and the like. Inferno makes it safe for applications to share these resources, and provides facilities for explicitly controlling how some of this sharing occurs (such as `sys->pctl` discussed in Chapter 6).

These facilities are, however, not a panacea for constructing correct programs. The questions of *what is a correct program* and how we can verify that an implementation conforms to a conceptual design lead us to the subject of this appendix. There are many approaches to automated validation of models against specifications, but we will focus on only one particular tool, SPIN.

SPIN, which stands for Simple Promela INterpreter, is a tool developed by Gerard Holzmann for the verification of protocols. It is publicly available from `http://cm.bell-labs.com/cm/cs/what/spin/`. Although it currently does not run over Inferno, it is still quite useful for analyzing concurrent Limbo applications, albeit from a separate host platform. This appendix does not delve into the theory and the inner workings of SPIN, but rather looks at its use, by example, to seed your thoughts.

A.1   Using SPIN

To use SPIN, a model of the application is constructed in the modeling language of SPIN, called *Promela*, for Protocol meta language.

Many of the constructs in Limbo map directly to counterparts in Promela. Promela provides means of representing and creating processes, communicating via buffered or rendezvous channels and specifying control flow.

To illustrate how one could model Limbo applications using Promela and SPIN, we will look at a very simple example. The aim here is not to provide a tutorial on using SPIN, but rather to give you a sense of some of the facilities available, should you be interested in pursuing this further.

As an example, the following is a Promela model for an application consisting of six threads. One of the threads acts as a master, periodically sending typed messages to all the remaining five threads (which act as slaves), then waits until it has received responses from all the slaves. Upon receipt of the queries from the master, each slave tries to send a response to the master.

The communication going from the master to the slaves is performed on five distinct communication channels, while the responses from the slaves to the master occur on a single channel. Channels in Promela can be defined to be synchronous or buffered, and in the following we can define them to be synchronous to mirror the behavior of Limbo channels:

```
# File : limbochannels.pr

#define   NUMCHANS   6
#define   NUMSLAVES  5
#define SAMPLEDCHAN 5


/*        Message Types:              */
mtype = {SAMPLE, SAMPLED};

/*   Synchronous Communication Medium:  */
chan netseg[NUMCHANS] = [0] of {mtype};

proctype slave(byte my_id)
{
    byte got_sample;

    got_sample = 0;
    printf("Node %d startup\n", my_id);

    do
        /*   Wait for message type 'SAMPLE'          */
    ::  netseg[my_id]?SAMPLE ->
            got_sample = 1;

    ::  got_sample ->
            /*   Send a 'SAMPLED' message */
            netseg[SAMPLEDCHAN]!SAMPLED;
            got_sample = 0;
    od
}

proctype master()
{
    byte nreceipts, nsent, nperiods;

    nperiods = 0;
    printf("Master started up\n");

    do
    ::  ((nreceipts % NUMSLAVES) == 0) ->
            nreceipts = 0;
            nsent = 0;

            do
            ::  nsent < NUMSLAVES ->
                    netseg[nsent]!SAMPLE;
                    nsent++;
            ::  nsent == NUMSLAVES ->
                    nperiods++;
                    break;
            od

    ::  netseg[SAMPLEDCHAN]?SAMPLED ->
            nreceipts++;
    od
```

```
}
/*          Initial process creates processes   */
init
{
    run slave(0);
    run slave(1);
    run slave(2);
    run slave(3);
    run slave(4);

    run master();
}
```

The `init` thread is run by default, and it instantiates the master and slave threads using the `run` statements. Each created slave thread is supplied with a parameter to identify which of the slaves it will act as, and this is used by the slaves to choose which communication channel to listen on for requests from the master.

The specification can be supplied to SPIN to perform *random simulation*, in which the instantiated threads are run in random interleavings. Figure A.1 shows a *message sequence chart* of the messages that transpire during this random simulation. The amount of time steps for which each thread makes progress can also be obtained from random simulation, and is shown as a bar graph in Figure A.2. Both figures were generated automatically by SPIN during simulation of the Promela description by SPIN.

Each of the threads in the example can be modeled by a finite-state automaton; we can also use SPIN to study the automaton for each `proctype`. The automata for the `init`, `master` and `slave` proctypes are shown in Figure A.3. The three figures were automatically generated by SPIN from the Promela description above.

The above description of the use of SPIN was purposefully shallow, and meant only to give you a flavor of the kinds of things that can be done with SPIN. The actual details of verifying models, specifying correctness properties of models and verifying these properties, have been purposefully left out.

It is fairly straightforward to convert the Promela specification into a Limbo module once a design is deemed satisfactory. The Limbo module implementing the Promela model above is shown below:

```
# File : limbopromela.b

implement PromelaLimbo;

include "sys.m";
include "draw.m";

PromelaLimbo : module
{
    init : fn(nil : ref Draw->Context, nil : list of string);
};
```

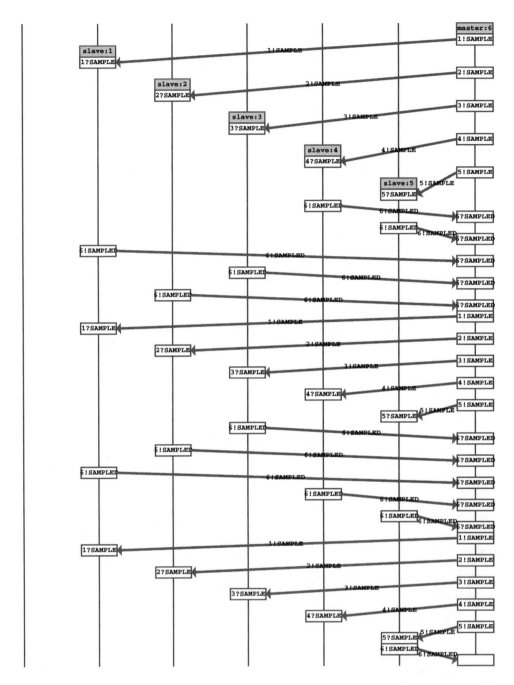

Figure A.1 Message sequence chart from SPIN simulation of the Promela model, generated by SPIN during simulation.

Percentage of 266 system steps
executed per process (7 total)

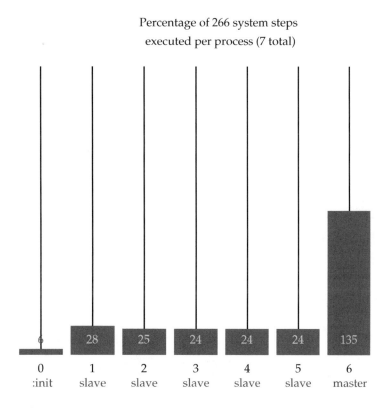

0	1	2	3	4	5	6
:init	slave	slave	slave	slave	slave	master

Figure A.2 Bar graph of time steps executed by each thread during random simulation, generated automatically by SPIN.

```
sys        : Sys;

NUMCHANS   : con 6;
NUMSLAVES  : con 5;
SAMPLEDCHAN     : con 5;
SAMPLE, SAMPLED : con 1 << iota;

#    Synchronous Communication Medium:
netseg := array [NUMCHANS] of chan of int;

slave(my_id : int)
{
    got_sample := 0;
    sys->print("Node %d startup\n", my_id);

    while ()
    alt
    {
        #    Wait for message type 'SAMPLE'
        msg := <-netseg[my_id] =>
```

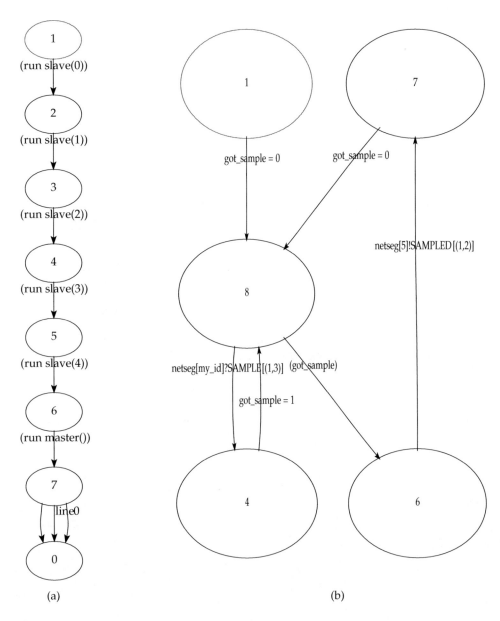

Figure A.3   Automata for the (a) init and (b) master. The figures were generated automatically by SPIN from the Promela specification.

```
    {
        if (msg == SAMPLE)
            got_sample = 1;
    }
```

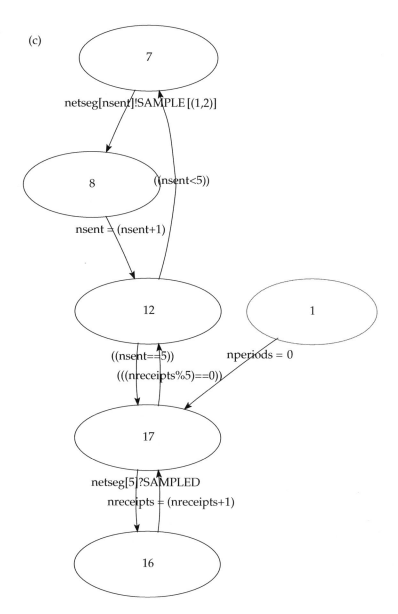

Figure A.3 (*Cont.*) Automata for (c) the slave proctypes. The figures were generated automatically by SPIN from the Promela specification.

```
* =>
{
     if (got_sample)
     {
```

```
                        #     Send a 'SAMPLED' message
                        netseg[SAMPLEDCHAN] <-= SAMPLED;
                        got_sample = 0;
                    }
                }
            }
        }

master()
{
    nreceipts, nsent, nperiods : int = 0;

    sys->print("Master started up\n");

    while ()
    alt
    {
        * =>
        if ((nreceipts % NUMSLAVES) == 0)
        {
            nreceipts = 0;
            nsent = 0;

            while ()
            {
                if (nsent < NUMSLAVES)
                {
                    netseg[nsent] <-= SAMPLE;
                    nsent++;
                }
                if (nsent == NUMSLAVES)
                {
                    nperiods++;
                    break;
                }
            }
        }

        msg := <-netseg[SAMPLEDCHAN] =>
        {
            if (msg == SAMPLED)
                nreceipts++;
        }
    }
}

#       Initial process creates processes
init (nil : ref Draw->Context, nil : list of string)
{
    sys = load Sys Sys->PATH;

    for (i := 0; i <= SAMPLEDCHAN; i++)
    {
        netseg[i] = chan of int;
    }
```

```
        spawn slave(0);
        spawn slave(1);
        spawn slave(2);
        spawn slave(3);
        spawn slave(4);

        spawn master();
}
```

The Limbo module above was obtained by attempting to faithfully capture the structure of the original Promela specification, so that you may see the correspondence between the two.

There is a wealth of information on using SPIN available on the Web, and there are annual workshops devoted to SPIN held all over the world. The URL supplied above or a search of the Web should provide ample information should you seek to probe further.

8

Styx Servers

Inferno uses two simple yet powerful ideas to achieve the distribution of resources in a network. The first idea is the representation of system resources as files in a hierarchical name space. This means not just having entries in the name space that represent various resources, but also being able to access and control those resources entirely through entries in the name space. An Inferno Styx server may serve a name space consisting of files that reside on a permanent store, as is the case with what are traditionally thought of as file servers, or it may serve a name space in which entries are dynamically created or whose content is dynamically generated by the file server. Accesses to such dynamically generated entries in the name space do not go through disk files and are purely interfaces to the programs that synthesize them.

Representing resources by files is an idea that exists to a limited extent in Unix, for example, in the /dev and /proc [29] filesystems. In contrast, however, to the /dev filesystem in Unix, Inferno's /dev filesystem permits complete interaction with devices. While its Unix counterpart requires `ioctl` system calls for configuring devices, both the device control and I/O can be performed entirely through an entry in the name space in the case of Inferno.

The second idea, which makes this representation of resources even more powerful, is the use of a single, simple protocol for accessing entries in the name space, whether they are local or are accessed on a remote device over the network. That protocol is *Styx*, the subject of this chapter. Styx is a lightweight remote procedure call (RPC) protocol by which Inferno name space servers are accessed. Compared to other remote procedure protocols such as NFS [69], it is significantly simpler, and is meant to be used across a wide variety of platforms, from embedded systems to high-performance servers, for exporting resources. Table 8.1 provides a brief comparison between Styx and the NFS version 2 RPC protocol.

When a user performs an operation such as reading a file, changing directories or deleting a file on an Inferno system, these operations are translated by a component of the system into local procedure calls, or Styx messages, which are sent to a Styx server on the other side of a connection, depending on whether the entry in the name space is served by the kernel or a Styx server on the other end of a connection, respectively. The entity which performs this conversion from system calls to Styx messages is called the *mount driver*, the #M device. A similar device, the *server registry*, #s, converts between filesystem operations and a channel in a user-level application, as shown in the description of *file2chan* in Chapter 7. Unlike the #s device, and most other devices, the #M device cannot be accessed from user space, and is accessed indirectly by applications, by performing system calls. The following illustrates what happens when an attempt is made to mount the #M device:

```
; bind '#M' /tmp
bind: cannot bind #M onto /tmp: mount/attach disallowed
;
```

8.1   #M, The Mount Driver

The *mount device*, #M, converts operations on the name space of a process as a result of system calls such as read, write, stat, etc., into messages to be sent on a channel internal to the emulator or the native kernel. In the case of accesses to entries in the name space served by the kernel, these messages end up as arguments to functions in the appropriate device driver. Each of these local procedure calls corresponds to a Styx transaction. When the local name space is being accessed from a remote location, the Styx messages delivered to the local host are converted into the corresponding local procedure calls, and the return values from these procedure calls are likewise converted into reply Styx messages to be sent back across the connection.

In the alternative case of accesses to remote resources, the messages are received as Styx messages on the remote end of the connection and the remote mount device behaves as described above. The mount driver thus performs the demultiplexing of name space accesses into the corresponding procedure calls to device drivers or bytes to be sent on a connection, and the multiplexing of the return values from procedure calls and received messages on connections into the return values for the open, read, write calls, etc., that are used to access the filesystem. It is important to note that even though Styx is the underlying protocol for accessing resources, be they local or remote, most applications will never explicitly generate or consume Styx messages, but will do so indirectly by mounting new servers into their name space, and reading and writing entries in the name space through system calls and so on.

Table 8.1 Comparison between NFS v2 RPC and Styx message types.

Action	Idempotent	Styx RPC	NFS RPC
Client authenticates with server and provides a **fid** to point to root of server's tree	Yes	**Attach**	—
Duplicate a **fid** to point to a given file	Yes	**Clone**	—
Traverse file tree a single step with **fid**	No	**Walk**	—
Discard (invalidate) a **fid**	No	**Clunk**	—
Return File Attributes	Yes	**Stat**	**GETATTR**
Set File Attributes	Yes	**Wstat**	**SETATTR**
Check permissions and open file	Yes	**Open**	—
Create and open a file step with **fid**	Yes	**Create**	**CREATE**
Read from file	Yes	**Read**	**READ**
Write to file	Yes	**Write**	**WRITE**
Remove file	No	**Remove**	**REMOVE**
No-op	Yes	**Nop**	—
Interrupt a pending operation	Yes	**Flush**	—
Error	—	**Error**	—
Look up a filename	Yes	—	**LOOKUP**
Read from symbolic link	Yes	—	**READLINK**
Rename file	No	—	**RENAME**
Create link to file	No	—	**LINK**
Create symbolic link	Yes	—	**SYMLINK**
Create directory	No	—	**MKDIR**
Remove directory	No	—	**RMDIR**
Read from directory	Yes	—	**READDIR**

8.2   #s, The Server Registry

The *srv device*, #s, provides a means for Limbo programs to serve entries in an Inferno name space through the `file2chan` Sys module call. The srv device provides a coupling between filesystem access and messages on Limbo channels in much the same manner as the mount device provides a coupling between such accesses and calls to functions in device drivers. The srv device is used by binding it into the name space *before* any other device, such that all accesses in the mount point (i.e. the directory in which #s is bound) are received by the srv device. It then performs multiplexing between multiple readers/writers of a possible multiplicity of entries in the name space connected to Limbo channels.

8.3 The Styx Protocol

The Styx RPC protocol consists of 14 message types that describe operations on files and directories containing them and the way a system should behave upon receipt of these messages. Styx messages may be exchanged between Inferno applications on a machine and also between Inferno machines across a network, as previously described. Styx is not defined to be exclusive to Inferno and an implementation of the Styx protocol could be provided for Unix, Windows or any other operating system. Styx must be implemented over a reliable communication protocol that preserves delimiters between messages and delivers messages reliably and in sequence. Reliability in the underlying protocol is necessary because Styx does not in itself define any mechanisms for retransmission or timeouts. Preservation of delimiters is important as Styx does not provide any means of segmentation and reassembly of messages. Lastly, due to the fact that connections to a Styx server are stateful, it is necessary that messages as seen by the Styx server must be in sequence.

The 14 types of Styx messages are Attach, Clone, Walk, Clunk, Stat, Wstat, Open, Create, Read, Write, Remove, Nop, Flush and Error. All of these except the Error type may either be sent to a Styx server from a Styx client or to a Styx client from a Styx server. Messages sent to a Styx server from a client are referred to as *T-messages* and replies from a server in response to a message from a client are referred to as *R-messages*, and such pairs are referred to as Styx *transactions*. A client cannot transmit an error message to a server; thus there is no Terror in Styx. Thus, all in all, there are 27 unique Styx message types.

Styx messages consist of streams of bytes, starting with a 1 byte field, the Type, identifying which of the 27 message types the message is, and one or more fields being parameters of the particular message type. The ordering of bytes within a multi-byte field in a Styx message is defined to be independent of the underlying host machine architecture. All multi-byte fields except the 28 and 64 byte fields are represented in little-endian byte order. The 28 byte fields are used for names (user IDs, file names) and are represented as strings and include a terminating null byte. The Rerror message type has a 64 byte ENAME field which is used to hold an error string, including a terminating null byte.

8.4 Types, Tags, Fids and Qids

Styx connections are initiated when a client sends a `Tattach` message to a Styx server. In this initial message, the client provides the user ID it wishes to access the file server as. Connections in Inferno are authenticated outside of the Styx protocol proper, and, subsequent to that external procedure, the Styx transactions only have the privileges of the user the connection was authenticated as. Thus privileges associated with the Styx transactions after a `Tattach` are the intersection of the privileges of the user the connection carrying the Styx messages was authenticated as and that of the UID provided in the `Tattach`.

T-messages from a client to a Styx server include a *tag* field to identify the message, and the R-messages received from the server have the same tags as their corresponding T-messages. Most T-messages contain a *fid*, which has an association with a particular file on a server. In the initial `Tattach` message, the client supplies a fid which it wishes to associate with the root of the name space on the server.

The client navigates the server's name space by performing *walks* on fids pointing to directories, which causes the fid to be associated with a particular file in the directory. In order to keep the relation between a fid and a particular directory on the server, before attempting to walk to a file in a directory a client can *clone* a fid, by providing an alternate fid ID to be associated with the directory, and then doing walks on the cloned fid. The association at the server between a fid supplied by the client and an entry in the name space can be removed by a *clunk* operation.

It is possible that many entries in the name space of the Styx server may represent the same resources. For example, if the file `/usr/pip/dis/spell.dis` is bound to `/dis`, the two entries in the name space actually represent the same resource. Each Styx server associates a *qid* with every unique entry in the name space it serves. This qid is provided in the R-messages for `Attach`, `Create`, `Open` and `Walk` transactions, permitting clients to distinguish unique entries—no two entries in the name space served by a Styx server should have the same qid.

8.5 Styx Message Formats

Tattach, Rattach

Client authenticates with server as user *UID* and provides a fid point to the filesystem *ANAME* of server's tree, server provides its unique identifier, *QID*, for the root of the filesystem to which the client is attached. This is usually the first message pair that transpires in a connection of a client to a server.

TYPE [1]	TAG [2]	FID [2]	UID [28]	ANAME [28]
Tattach				

TYPE [1]	TAG [2]	FID [2]	QID [8]
Rattach			

Tclone, Rclone

Have a new fid, *NEWFID*, associate with the file associated with an existing fid. This usually occurs right before a fid is moved to point to another entry in the current directory with a `Walk` transaction.

TYPE [1]   TAG [2]   FID [2]   NEWFID [2]

Tclone			

TYPE [1]   TAG [2]   FID [2]

Rclone		

Twalk, Rwalk

Associate *FID* with file named *NAME* in the current directory, server provides its unique *QID* for the file the *FID* now points to.

TYPE [1]   TAG [2]   FID [2]   NAME [28]

Twalk			

TYPE [1]   TAG [2]   FID [2]   QID [8]

Rwalk			

Tclunk, Rclunk

Remove the association between an entry in the name space of the server and a fid.

TYPE [1]   TAG [2]   FID [2]

Tclunk		

TYPE [1]   TAG [2]   FID [2]

Rclunk		

Tstat, Rstat

Retrieve file attributes.

TYPE [1]   TAG [2]   FID [2]

Tstat		

TYPE [1]   TAG [2]   FID [2]   STAT [116]

Rstat			

Twstat, Rwstat

Set file attributes.

TYPE [1]	TAG [2]	FID [2]	STAT [116]
Twstat			

TYPE [1]	TAG [2]	FID [2]
Rwstat		

Topen, Ropen

Check permissions and open file associated with fid, server returns its unique identifier for the file, the *QID*.

TYPE [1]	TAG [2]	FID [2]	MODE [1]
Topen			

TYPE [1]	TAG [2]	FID [2]	QID [8]
Ropen			

Tcreate, Rcreate

Create and open a file named *NAME* in the current directory, with permissions *PERM*, and associate it with fid. If the most significant bit of mode is set, the created file is a directory.

TYPE [1]	TAG [2]	FID [2]	NAME [28]	PERM [4]	MODE [1]
Tcreate					

TYPE [1]	TAG [2]	FID [2]	QID [8]
Rcreate			

Tread, Rread

Read *COUNT* byte from offset *OFFSET* from file associated with fid, server returns number of bytes read and data.

TYPE [1]	TAG [2]	FID [2]	OFFSET [8]	COUNT [2]
Tread				

TYPE [1]	TAG [2]	FID [2]	COUNT [2]	PAD [1]	DATA [COUNT]
Rread					

Twrite, Rwrite

Write *COUNT* bytes to file associated with fid at offset *OFFSET*, server returns number of bytes successfully written.

TYPE [1]	TAG [2]	FID [2]	OFFSET [8]	COUNT [2]	PAD [1]	DATA [COUNT]
Twrite						

TYPE [1]	TAG [2]	FID [2]	COUNT [2]
Rwrite			

Tremove, Rremove

Remove file associated with fid.

TYPE [1]	TAG [2]	FID [2]
Tremove		

TYPE [1]	TAG [2]	FID [2]
Rremove		

Tnop, Rnop

No operation.

TYPE [1]	TAG [2]
Tnop	

TYPE [1]	TAG [2]
Rnop	

Tflush, Rflush

Interrupt pending operation with message tag *OLDTAG*.

TYPE [1]	TAG [2]	OLDTAG [2]
Tflush		

TYPE [1]	TAG [2]
Rflush	

Rerror

Error message only from server to client. There is no `Terror`.

TYPE [1]	TAG [2]	ENAME [64]
Rerror		

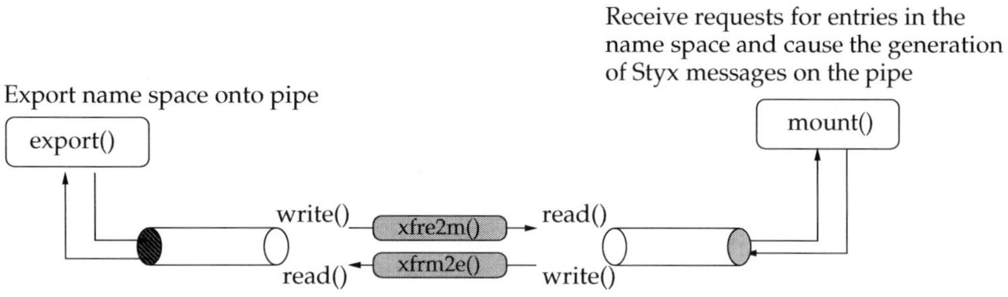

Receive requests for entries in the
name space and cause the generation
of Styx messages on the pipe

Export name space onto pipe

| export() |

| mount() |

write()   xfre2m()   read()

read()   xfrm2e()   write()

Figure 8.1   Snooping on Styx messages generated by filesystem operations.

8.6 Intercepting Styx Messages

To illustrate the Styx messages generated by filesystem accesses, it is instructive to build an application that reveals the generation of these messages. As has been mentioned previously, user applications do not have direct access to the mount driver, and even further for entries in the name space that are served locally, the mount driver translates the system calls into local procedure calls.

To force the generation of Styx messages, and to interlope on this generated stream, the local name space must be exported to an interloper, who must in turn export the interloped stream back to the name space. The general ideas used here will also be employed later in the chapter to construct a Limbo file server that serves an arbitrary file hierarchy. Exporting a portion of the name space to the interloper can be achieved with the `export` Sys module call. Export takes an open file descriptor and generates Styx messages on the reader of that descriptor for any operations on the exported name space, and these messages can be inspected or modified as needed by the reader on the file descriptor. The counterpart to `export` is `mount`, which mounts an exported filesystem from a file descriptor into a location in the name space. Building an interloper is therefore possible in the following manner.

- Create two pairs of file descriptors such that a read on either member in a pair must be serviced by a write on the other descriptor in the pair and vice versa. This can be achieved using the pipe device, '#|'. Consider one pair to be associated with the export that will eventually be done, and the other pair to be associated with the eventual mount of the exported name space.

- Create a thread that reads from one end of the export pipe and writes to the mount pipe, and another that reads from one end of the mount pipe and writes to the export pipe. These two threads are labeled as `xfrm2e` and `xfre2m` in Figure 8.1.

- Perform an `export` of a portion of a name space on the end of the export pipe that is not attached to the threads, shown hatched in Figure 8.1. Likewise do a mount of the end of the mount pipe not attached to the threads to a point in the name space, shaded dark gray in the figure.

- At this point, all filesystem requests on the exported name space will result in Styx messages being sent down the mount pipe and will be handled by xfrm2e and likewise replies from the export will be sent down xfre2m. The messages may be dumped or modified at will.

The following program implements the filesystem interloper discussed above:

```
# File : interloper.b

implement Interloper;

include "sys.m";
include "draw.m";

sys : Sys;

Interloper : module
{
    init : fn(nil : ref Draw->Context, nil : list of string);
};

msgtype := array [] of
    {
        "Tnop", "Rnop", "Terror", "Rerror",
        "Tflush", "Rflush", "Tclone", "Rclone",
        "Twalk", "Rwalk", "Topen", "Ropen",
        "Tcreate", "Rcreate", "Tread", "Rread",
        "Twrite", "Rwrite", "Tclunk", "Rclunk",
        "Tremove", "Rremove", "Tstat", "Rstat",
        "Twstat", "Rwstat", "Tsession", "Rsession",
        "Tattach", "Rattach"
    };

init(nil : ref Draw->Context, nil : list of string)
{
    sync := chan of int;


    sys = load Sys Sys->PATH;
    sys->bind("#|", "/chan", sys->MBEFORE);

    export_pipe := array [2] of ref Sys->FD;
    mount_pipe := array [2] of ref Sys->FD;

    sys->pipe(export_pipe);
    sys->pipe(mount_pipe);

    spawn xfre2m(export_pipe, mount_pipe, sync);
    spawn xfrm2e(export_pipe, mount_pipe, sync);

    <- sync;
    <- sync;

    if (sys->export(export_pipe[0], sys->EXPASYNC))
    {
        sys->print("Error - Could not export : %r\n");
```

```
            exit;
    }

    if (sys->mount(mount_pipe[1], "/n/remote", sys->MREPL, nil) == -1)
    {
            sys->print("Interloper : mount failed");
    }
}

xfre2m (export_pipe, mount_pipe : array of ref Sys->FD, sync : chan of int)
{
    sync <-= 1;

    buf := array [sys->ATOMICIO] of byte;

    while (1)
    {
            n := sys->read(export_pipe[1], buf, len buf);
            sys->write(mount_pipe[0], buf, n);
            sys->print("Message type [%s] length [%d] from EXPORT --> MOUNT\n",
                msgtype[int buf[0]], n);
    }
}

xfrm2e (export_pipe, mount_pipe : array of ref Sys->FD, sync : chan of int)
{
    sync <-= 1;

    buf := array [sys->ATOMICIO] of byte;

    while (1)
    {
            n := sys->read(mount_pipe[0], buf, len buf);
            sys->write(export_pipe[1], buf, n);
            sys->print("Message type [%s] length [%d] from MOUNT --> EXPORT\n",
                msgtype[int buf[0]], n);
    }
}
```

The interloper module as shown above will by default export the root filesystem and mount it in /n/remote. All accesses in /n/remote will lead to the generated Styx messages being printed out as shown below:

```
; interloper
Message type [Tattach] length [61] from MOUNT --> EXPORT
Message type [Rattach] length [13] from EXPORT --> MOUNT
; cd /n/remote
; pwd
Message type [Tclone] length [7] from MOUNT --> EXPORT
Message type [Rclone] length [5] from EXPORT --> MOUNT
Message type [Tstat] length [5] from MOUNT --> EXPORT
Message type [Rstat] length [121] from EXPORT --> MOUNT
Message type [Tclunk] length [5] from MOUNT --> EXPORT
```

```
Message type [Rclunk] length [5] from EXPORT --> MOUNT
Message type [Tclone] length [7] from MOUNT --> EXPORT
Message type [Tclunk] length [5] from MOUNT --> EXPORT
Message type [Rclone] length [5] from EXPORT --> MOUNT
/n/#/
; Message type [Rclunk] length [5] from EXPORT --> MOUNT
;
```

This simple application can be easily extended to yield a much more interesting one. As hinted at previously, the interloper could in theory modify the Styx messages being exchanged between the mount and export without either of those two knowing. A useful general-purpose application that builds on this idea is *Filterfs*.

8.7 Building Filesystem Filters: Filterfs

Filterfs is an infrastructure for building *filesystem filters*. It acts like the interloper, interposing between a server and the client mounting the server, and calling routines in an auxiliary module to filter the transpiring messages. Using this infrastructure, we can build filters as simple as the Interloper above, where the auxiliary module would just print out the messages supplied to it without modifying them. We could also construct a more complicated filter which, for example, replaces all whitespace in file names seen at the mount point with another character.

Filterfs makes it easy to write such filters. It does all the work of interposing in the stream of Styx messages between an export and mount point, and formats these messages in a structure that eases the difficulty of writing auxiliary modules. These modules, which Filterfs can load dynamically, must conform to the module interface shown below:

```
# File : filter.m

Filter : module
{
    filtername : string;

    Filtermsg : adt
    {
        styxmsg        : ref Styx->Smsg;
        isdirread : int;
        dirlist        : list of ref Sys->Dir;
    };

    rewrite   : fn(msg : ref Filtermsg);
    init : fn(exportfd, mountfd : array of ref Sys->FD);
};
```

Each auxiliary module has type `Filter`. It must define two methods, `init` and `rewrite`, which will be called to initialize the module and supply it with Styx messages in transit between the export and mount points, respectively. The `rewrite` method will be called for both messages going from the mount point to the export point, and replies from the export to the mount. It may modify these messages or leave them intact. These messages are of the `Filtermsg` type.

The `Filtermsg` ADT contains a member with the entire Styx message and, if its `isdirread` member is set, also contains a list of `Dir` entries corresponding to the decoded payload of the Styx message for directory reads. This field is useful for filters that wish to change the appearance of directory listings, such as the one mentioned earlier, which replaces whitespace in filenames with some other character.

Before looking at the implementation of the Filterfs module itself, let us look at re-implementing the functionality of the interloper in a Filterfs auxiliary module.

8.7.1 Printfilter

Let us call this module *Printfilter*. It must provide the appropriate methods `init` and `rewrite`. The `init` function will be used to load the Sys module (for printing messages). The rewrite method simply prints out the type of the message, which is encapsulated in the `styxmsg` field of the `Filtermsg` ADT it receives as its argument. In fact, since the `Styx->Smsg` ADT already provides a routine for printing out useful information about the Styx message it represents, we can call that routine, making our job even easier. The implementation of Printfilter is thus very simple, as shown below:

```
# File : printfilter.b

implement Filter;

include "sys.m";
include "styx.m";
include "filter.m";

sys : Sys;
styx : Styx;
Smsg : import styx;

init(nil, nil : array of ref Sys->FD)
{
    sys = load Sys Sys->PATH;

    styx = load Styx Styx->PATH;
    if (styx == nil)
    {
        sys->raise(sys->sprint("fail:Could not load %s : %r", Styx->PATH));
    }

    filtername = "Print Filter : Print Styx messages in filter pipeline.";
    sys->print("Filter module \"%s\" initialized.\n", filtername);
}
```

```
rewrite(fmsg : ref Filtermsg)
{
    sys->print("%s\n", fmsg.styxmsg.print());
}
```

The implementation of the Printfilter is simple, as it leaves all the work to be done by the Filterfs module. We use the module definition from `filter.m`, and implement the `Filter` interface, providing a `rewrite` function that prints out information on each Styx message received.

8.7.2 Canonfilter

It is easy to build more sophisticated filters, such as one that modifies the names of files in directories, as seen at the mount point. The complete implementation of such a filter is shown below:

```
# File : canonfilter.b

implement Filter;

include "sys.m";
include "string.m";
include "styx.m";
include "filter.m";

sys : Sys;
styx : Styx;
str : String;
Smsg : import styx;

init(nil, nil : array of ref Sys->FD)
{
    sys = load Sys Sys->PATH;

    styx = load Styx Styx->PATH;
    if (styx == nil)
    {
        sys->raise(sys->sprint("fail:Could not load %s : %r",
                Styx->PATH));
    }

    str = load String String->PATH;
    if (styx == nil)
    {
        sys->raise(sys->sprint("fail:Could not load %s : %r",
                String->PATH));
    }

    filtername = "Canon Filter : Canonicalizes file names with whitespace.";
}
```

```
rewrite(fmsg : ref Filtermsg)
{
    newlist : list of ref Sys->Dir;

    if (fmsg.styxmsg.mtype == Styx->Rstat)
    {
        direntry := styx->convM2D(fmsg.styxmsg.stat);
        canondir(direntry);
        fmsg.styxmsg.stat = styx->convD2M(direntry);
    }

    if (fmsg.styxmsg.mtype == Styx->Twalk)
    {
        fmsg.styxmsg.name = decanon(fmsg.styxmsg.name);
    }

    if (fmsg.isdirread && (len fmsg.dirlist > 0))
    {
        while (fmsg.dirlist != nil)
        {
            item := hd fmsg.dirlist;
            canondir(item);
            newlist = item :: newlist;

            fmsg.dirlist = tl fmsg.dirlist;
        }

        fmsg.dirlist = newlist;
    }
}

canondir(item : ref Sys->Dir)
{
    #   BUG : should also cater for long filenames,
    #   with possible identical stems
    for (i := 0; i < len (*item).name; i++)
    {
        if ((*item).name[i] == ' ')
        {
            (*item).name[i] = '?';
        }
    }
}

decanon(name : string) : string
{
    #   BUG : this reversion should only happen for
    #   files that we canonicalized in the first place
    for (i := 0; i < len name; i++)
    {
        if (name[i] == '?')
        {
            name[i] = ' ';
        }
    }
```

```
        return name;
}
```

The `rewrite` method in the above works as follows. If the message received is a directory read, then Filterfs would have set the `isdirread` field of the message, and would have decoded the payload of the Styx message into a list of `Dir` ADTs. The `Dir` ADT (defined in the `Sys` module) is used to represent a directory entry, which may either be a file or itself a directory. For a directory read, the function `canondir` is called on all the directory entries, appropriately modifying the directory entry names.

If the message delivered to `rewrite` is a Styx `Rstat` message, then it must similarly be modified so that the mount point sees the directory entry's name modified.

The above two message types will both be originating from the export point and going to the mount point.

Lastly, since the mount point now knows the directory entries by their modified names, Styx `Twalk` messages, which will reference the modified names, must be appropriately reverted to the original names known by the server at the export end.

The above implementation is simplistic in some respects, as it does not cater for file names on the export end which already use the character used for replacement ('?' in this case). In such a case, the `decanon` function will incorrectly 'revert' them to names unknown by the export point.

8.7.3 Implementation of Filterfs

We have left the discussion of the implementation of Filterfs itself until this point, since it is not a prerequisite to implementing filters that can be loaded from it.

The construction of Filterfs is very similar to the Interloper discussed in Section 8.6. It performs encoding of the intercepted Styx messages to the `Filtermsg` ADT, calls the `rewrite` method of a loaded `Filter` module, and then decodes the possibly modified message and passes it along. The implementation of Filterfs is shown below:

```
# File : filterfs.b

implement FilterFS;

include "sys.m";
include "draw.m";
include "styx.m";
include "filter.m";
include "cachelib.m";

sys : Sys;
styx : Styx;
filter : Filter;
cachelib : CacheLib;

Smsg : import styx;
Cache : import cachelib;
```

```
Filtermsg : import filter;

CACHESIZE : con 64;
fidcache : ref Cache;

FilterFS : module
{
    init : fn(nil : ref Draw->Context, nil : list of string);
};

init(nil : ref Draw->Context, nil : list of string)
{
    sync := chan of int;
    filterpath := "printfilter.dis";


        sys = load Sys Sys->PATH;
    styx = load Styx Styx->PATH;
    cachelib = load CacheLib CacheLib->PATH;
    filter = load Filter filterpath;

    fidcache = Cache.allocate(CACHESIZE);

        sys->bind("#|", "/chan", sys->MBEFORE);
    export_pipe := array [2] of ref Sys->FD;
    mount_pipe := array [2] of ref Sys->FD;

    sys->pipe(export_pipe);
    sys->pipe(mount_pipe);

    filter->init(export_pipe, mount_pipe);

        spawn xfre2m(export_pipe, mount_pipe, sync);
        spawn xfrm2e(export_pipe, mount_pipe, sync);

    <- sync;
    <- sync;

    if (sys->export(export_pipe[0], sys->EXPASYNC))
    {
        sys->print("Error - Could not export : %r\n");
            exit;
    }

    if (sys->mount(mount_pipe[1], "/n/filterfs", sys->MREPL, nil) == -1)
    {
        sys->print("FilterFS : mount failed");
    }
}

xfre2m (export_pipe, mount_pipe : array of ref Sys->FD, sync : chan of int)
{
    sync <-= 1;

    buf := array [sys->ATOMICIO] of byte;
    while (1)
```

```
    {
          n := sys->read(export_pipe[1], buf, len buf);

          msg := data2fmsg(buf[:n]);
          filter->rewrite(msg);

          if (msg != nil)
          {
               sys->write(mount_pipe[0], fmsg2data(msg), n);
          }
    }
}

xfrm2e (export_pipe, mount_pipe : array of ref Sys->FD, sync : chan of int)
{
     sync <-= 1;

     buf := array [sys->ATOMICIO] of byte;
     while (1)
     {
          n := sys->read(mount_pipe[0], buf, len buf);

          msg := data2fmsg(buf[:n]);
          filter->rewrite(msg);

          if (msg != nil)
          {
               sys->write(export_pipe[1], fmsg2data(msg), n);
          }
     }
}

fmsg2data(fmsg : ref Filtermsg) : array of byte
{
     nentries := len fmsg.dirlist;
     for (i := 0; i < (Styx->DIRLEN*nentries); i += Styx->DIRLEN)
     {
          fmsg.styxmsg.data[i:] = styx->convD2M(hd fmsg.dirlist);
          fmsg.dirlist = tl fmsg.dirlist;
     }

     return fmsg.styxmsg.convS2M();
}

data2fmsg(buf : array of byte) : ref Filtermsg
{
     msg := ref Filtermsg;

     (n, styxmsg) := styx->convM2S(buf);
     if (n < 0)
     {
          return nil;
     }

     if ((styxmsg.mtype == Styx->Rattach)||
         (styxmsg.mtype == Styx->Rwalk)||
```

```
                (styxmsg.mtype == Styx->Ropen)||
                (styxmsg.mtype == Styx->Rcreate))
        {
                if (styxmsg.qid.path & Sys->CHDIR)
                {
                        fidcache.addtocache(styxmsg.fid);
                }
        }

        if ((styxmsg.mtype == Styx->Tclone) &&
                fidcache.isincache(styxmsg.fid))
        {
                fidcache.addtocache(styxmsg.newfid);
        }

        if ((styxmsg.mtype == Styx->Tclunk) ||
                ((styxmsg.mtype == Styx->Rwalk) &&
                        !(styxmsg.qid.path & Sys->CHDIR)))
        {
                fidcache.delfromcache(styxmsg.fid);
        }

        msg.styxmsg = styxmsg;

        if (styxmsg.mtype == Styx->Rread)
        {
                if (fidcache.isincache(msg.styxmsg.fid))
                {
                        msg.isdirread = 1;
                        msg.dirlist = data2dirlist(styxmsg.data);
                }
        }

        return msg;
}

data2dirlist(buf : array of byte) : list of ref Sys->Dir
{
        dirlist : list of ref Sys->Dir;

        if (len buf % Styx->DIRLEN)
        {
                sys->print("Weird read from directory, data length [%d]\n",
                        len buf);
                return nil;
        }

        for (i := 0; i < len buf; i += Styx->DIRLEN)
        {
                direntry := styx->convM2D(buf[i:i+116]);
                dirlist = direntry :: dirlist;
        }

        return dirlist;
}
```

Filterfs uses the CacheLib module (from Chapter 3) to construct a cache of fids which point to directories, enabling it to distinguish between reads of files and those of directories. The filter module to use for rewriting messages is hard-coded in the above example for brevity—a more useful interface for Filterfs would be to have it provide a file interface, into which commands to load new filters could be passed, enabling dynamic filtering of a name space as the needs of the user change. Such a file interface would be implemented using the *file2chan* facility described in Chapter 7, or it could also be implemented using *Styxlib*, which we describe next.

8.8   Implementing a Styx Server with the Styxlib Module

The Interloper and Filterfs modules discussed above gave examples of the basic way to construct an application that handles raw Styx messages. In the Interloper module, and to a lesser extent in Filterfs, the messages are not actually interpreted, but it is easy to see how it could be extended to implement a general-purpose file server that served an arbitrary name space. As the Styx messages are received from the mount point, rather than passing them to the listening `export`, the messages could be interpreted and responded to by the application.

Building a Styx server in this manner is not too difficult, and there is a module provided with the Inferno distribution to make writing Styx servers significantly easier. This module is the *Styxlib* module.

The basic idea behind using Styxlib to build a Limbo filesystem server is very similar to the ideas used in the Interloper module. A pipe is created, one end of the pipe is fitted to our fileserver and the other end is mounted into a mount point. Subsequently, all accesses in the mount point will cause the delivery of Styx messages to the other end of the pipe. The Styxlib module provides a set of routines for receiving these Styx messages and generating replies to them. The simplest form of such a server that serves a single file is shown below:

```
# File : styxserver.b

implement StyxServer;

include "sys.m";
include "draw.m";
include "arg.m";
include "styx.m";
include   "styxlib.m";

sys  : Sys;
arg  : Arg;
styx : Styx;
styxlib   : Styxlib;

Styxserver, Rmsg, Tmsg, Dirtab, Chan: import styxlib;

mntflg     := Sys->MREPL;
```

```
mntpt     := "/n/remote/";
Qpath     : con 1;
Qvers     : con 0;

dirtab := array [] of
     {
          Dirtab("dynamic.dis", (Qpath, Qvers), big 0, 8r755)
     };

StyxServer : module
{
     init : fn(nil : ref Draw->Context, args : list of string);
};

init(nil : ref Draw->Context, args : list of string)
{
     sys = load Sys Sys->PATH;
     styxlib = load Styxlib Styxlib->PATH;
     styx = load Styx Styx->PATH;
     arg = load Arg Arg->PATH;
     arg->init(args);

     while((c := arg->opt()) != 0)
     {
          case c
          {
               'b' => mntflg = Sys->MBEFORE;
               'a' => mntflg = Sys->MAFTER;
               'r' => mntflg = Sys->MREPL;
               'c' => mntflg |= Sys->MCREATE;
                  *    =>
                  {
                       sys->print("Usage : styxserver [-rabc] <mount point>\n");
                       exit;
                  }
          }
     }
     args = arg->argv();

     if (len args != 1)
     {
          sys->print("Usage : styxserver [-rabc] <mount point>\n");
          exit;
     }
     mntpt = hd args;

     styxpipe := array [2] of ref Sys->FD;
     sys->pipe(styxpipe);

     (tmsgchan, srv) := Styxserver.new(styxpipe[0]);

     sync := chan of int;
     spawn server(tmsgchan, srv, sync);
     <-sync;

     if (sys->mount(styxpipe[1], mntpt, mntflg, nil) < 0)
```

```
        {
                sys->raise(sys->sprint("fail:StyxServer mount failed : %r"));
        }
}

server(tmsgchan : chan of ref Styxlib->Tmsg, srv : ref Styxserver,
        sync : chan of int)
{
        devgen := styxlib->dirgenmodule();

        sync <-= 0;

        while ()
        {
                msg := <-tmsgchan;
                if (msg == nil)
                {
                        exit;
                }

                pick m := msg
                {
                        Readerror =>    sys->raise(sys->sprint(
                                        "fail:Styxserver error reading Styx pipe : %r"));

                        Nop =>          srv.reply(ref Rmsg.Nop(m.tag));

                        Attach => srv.devattach(m);

                        Clone =>  srv.devclone(m);

                        Clunk =>  srv.devclunk(m);

                        Create => srv.reply(ref Rmsg.Error(m.tag, Styxlib->Eperm));

                        Flush =>  srv.devflush(m);

                        Open =>         srv.devopen(m, devgen, dirtab);

                        Read =>
                        {
                                c := srv.fidtochan(m.fid);
                                if (c == nil)
                                {
                                        srv.reply(ref Rmsg.Error(m.tag, Styxlib->Eperm));
                                        break;
                                }

                                if (c.isdir())
                                {
                                        srv.devdirread(m, devgen, dirtab);
                                        break;
                                }

                                srv.reply(ref Rmsg.Error(m.tag, Styxlib->Eperm));
```

```
            }

        Remove => srv.reply(ref Rmsg.Error(m.tag, Styxlib->Eperm));

        Stat =>         srv.devstat(m, devgen, dirtab);

        Walk =>         srv.devwalk(m, devgen, dirtab);

        Write => srv.reply(ref Rmsg.Error(m.tag, Styxlib->Eperm));

        Wstat => srv.reply(ref Rmsg.Error(m.tag, Styxlib->Eperm));
        }
    }
}
```

In a manner similar to what was done for the interloper, the above example constructs a pipe and mounts one end in a name space. Reads from the other end of the pipe will therefore see Styx messages generated by accesses to the mount point.

A new Styx server is constructed by calling the new method of the Styxserver ADT, which returns a reference to a newly initialized instance of Styxserver, and a channel on which Styx T-messages from the mount point can be received:

```
(tmsgchan, srv) := Styxserver.new(styxpipe[0]);
```

We then spawn a thread that will read off this channel, tmsgchan, and perform the appropriate responses to be delivered to the client at the mount point. Once this server has begun listening for messages, we mount the other end of the pipe on which the server is listening into our name space, at the mount point.

The job of the server thread, server, is to provide appropriate replies to incoming Styx messages. Recalling our discussion of the Styx protocol in Section 8.3, some of the messages received by a Styx server do not elicit much action. For example, if a server receives a Tnop, it will always send back an Rnop with a tag being that of the Tnop. Since we can in many cases settle for some form of 'default behavior', the Styxserver ADT provides several default methods that a server can invoke to perform the necessary default replies.

The main loop of the server thread reads messages off the channel of incoming T-messages. The messages on this channel are encoded into Tmsg pick ADT types, defined in the Styxlib module. By performing a pick on the received ADT, the type of the message is ascertained, and an appropriate reply made. For example, for incoming Tattach, Tclone, Tclunk and Tflush messages, we can simply call the default methods in our Styxserver ADT instance to perform the replies for us. In the case of directory reads, we would like to make a file visible, so we must do a little more work.

So, how does a server know, for example, which file is being read when it receives a Tread message, since such a message does not explicitly reference a complete file path?

A Styx server maintains some structure about all the entries in the name space it serves. Each of these entries has a unique identifier, *qid*, as described in Section 8.4. On the initial connection, a client provides the server with another identifier, called a *fid*, which the client uses to refer to the root of the server. The client traverses the name space of the server by sending Twalk Styx messages to 'walk' a given fid to an entry in the current directory with a new qid. Thus, a fid held by a client always points at some qid on the server. Each qid on the server corresponds to a unique entry, such as a file or directory.

The mapping of fids to qids is of course dynamic as we traverse the filesystem. The mapping of qids to entries in the name space is, however, usually fixed[1], and this mapping is what is implemented in the above example by the dirtab structure and the devgen instance of the Dirgenmod module.

The Dirgenmod module provides a function, dirgen, which will return the ith member of a directory, or an error if the directory has fewer entries. In the above example, our directory structure is simple, a single file, and described in the dirtab structure supplied to dirgen (we supply references to devgen and dirtab to the appropriate reply methods of Styxserver, and the calling of dirgen happens behind the scenes).

8.9 Summary

This chapter provided an introduction to the Styx protocol. The nature of Styx transactions and the format of Styx messages, client *fids* and server *qids* were explained. The construction of applications dealing directly with Styx was illustrated, ranging from a simple interloper to transparently monitor Styx transactions resulting from filesystem accesses to more interesting applications such as filesystem filters. The use of the Styxlib module to build user-level filesystem servers was also introduced.

Bibliographic Notes

The Styx protocol is described in [65]. Styx is descended from the 9P protocol of the Plan 9 operating system [53], which has evolved to further to what is now sometimes referred to as *9P2000* [56]. Styx, 9P and 9P2000 are in essence remote procedure call protocols, and bear some similarity to the NFS RPC protocol [69]. Unlike NFS RPC, Styx is intended for, and well suited to distribution of resources in a network.

---

[1]In the chapter example, we will see a case in which the filesystem is dynamic, with new qids being created, but the mapping of qids to entries remaining fixed.

8.10 Chapter Example: Dynamic User-Level Filesystems

As the concluding example of this chapter, we will look at the construction of a dynamic user-level filesystem, in the spirit of the /net/tcp filesystem, where reading a file named clone causes the synthesis of a new directory, populated with a number of entries.

To achieve this, we will use the Styxlib module. The primary extension from the example in Section 8.8 is that we will not use a fixed table to represent the filesystem, as was done with the dirtab structure in that example, but will rather create our own dirgen function, which will manage qids and create new entries in the name space dynamically. The implementation of the server is shown below:

```
# File : orangefs.b

implement StyxServer;

include "sys.m";
include "draw.m";
include "arg.m";
include "styx.m";
include "styxlib.m";

sys          : Sys;
arg          : Arg;
styx         : Styx;
styxlib      : Styxlib;

Styxserver, Rmsg, Tmsg, Dirtab, Chan: import styxlib;

mntflg       := Sys->MREPL;
mntpt        := "/n/remote/";
numoranges   : int;
Qmax         : con 1024;
QSHIFT       : con 4;
Qroot, Qorange, Qnew, Qctl, Qdate, Qtime, Qline : con iota;
perms        := array [Qmax] of {Qnew to Qtime => 8r400, * => 8r755};
mtimes       := array [Qmax] of int;
atimes       := array [Qmax] of int;
lengths      := array [Qmax] of int;

StyxServer : module
{
    init : fn(nil : ref Draw->Context, args : list of string);

    dirgen: fn(srv: ref Styxlib->Styxserver, c: ref Styxlib->Chan,
        tab: array of Styxlib->Dirtab, i: int): (int, Sys->Dir);
};

init(nil : ref Draw->Context, args : list of string)
{
    sys = load Sys Sys->PATH;
    styxlib = load Styxlib Styxlib->PATH;
    styx = load Styx Styx->PATH;
    arg = load Arg Arg->PATH;
```

```
    arg->init(args);

    while((c := arg->opt()) != 0)
    {
        case c
        {
            'b' => mntflg = Sys->MBEFORE;
            'a' => mntflg = Sys->MAFTER;
            'r' => mntflg = Sys->MREPL;
            'c' => mntflg |= Sys->MCREATE;
                   *   =>
            {
                sys->print("Usage : styxserver [-rabc] <mount point>\n");
                exit;
            }
        }
    }
    args = arg->argv();

    if (len args != 1)
    {
        sys->print("Usage : styxserver [-rabc] <mount point>\n");
        exit;
    }
    mntpt = hd args;

    styxpipe := array [2] of ref Sys->FD;
    sys->pipe(styxpipe);
    (tmsgchan, srv) := Styxserver.new(styxpipe[0]);

    sync := chan of int;
    spawn server(tmsgchan, srv, sync);
    <-sync;

    if (sys->mount(styxpipe[1], mntpt, mntflg, nil) < 0)
    {
        sys->raise(sys->sprint("fail:StyxServer mount failed : %r"));
    }
}

server(tmsgchan : chan of ref Styxlib->Tmsg, srv : ref Styxserver,
    sync : chan of int)
{
    devgen := load Dirgenmod "$self";

    sync <-= 0;
    while ()
    {
        msg := <-tmsgchan;
        if (msg == nil)
        {
            exit;
        }

        pick m := msg
        {
```

```
        Readerror =>
        {
            sys->raise(sys->sprint(
                "fail:Styxserver error reading Styx pipe : %r"));
        }

        Nop     =>  srv.reply(ref Rmsg.Nop(m.tag));
        Attach  =>  srv.devattach(m);
        Clone   =>  srv.devclone(m);
        Clunk   =>  srv.devclunk(m);
        Create  =>  srv.reply(ref Rmsg.Error(m.tag,Styxlib->Eperm));
        Flush   =>  srv.devflush(m);
        Open    =>  srv.devopen(m, devgen, nil);

        Read    =>
        {
            c := srv.fidtochan(m.fid);

            if (c == nil)
            {
                srv.reply(ref Rmsg.Error(m.tag,Styxlib->Eperm));
                break;
            }

            if (c.isdir())
            {
                srv.devdirread(m, devgen, nil);
                break;
            }

            if (c.qid.path == Qnew)
            {
                if (((numoranges << QSHIFT) + Qline) < Qmax)
                {
                    numoranges++;
                }

                srv.reply(ref Rmsg.Read(m.tag, m.fid, nil));

                break;
            }

            srv.reply(ref Rmsg.Error(m.tag,Styxlib->Eperm));
        }

        Remove  =>  srv.reply(ref Rmsg.Error(m.tag,Styxlib->Eperm));
        Stat    =>  srv.devstat(m, devgen, nil);
        Walk    =>  srv.devwalk(m, devgen, nil);
        Write   =>  srv.reply(ref Rmsg.Error(m.tag,Styxlib->Eperm));
        Wstat   =>  srv.reply(ref Rmsg.Error(m.tag,Styxlib->Eperm));
        }
    }
}

dirgen(nil : ref Styxserver, c : ref Chan, nil : array of Dirtab,
    entry : int) : (int, Sys->Dir)
```

```
{
    level := c.qid.path & ((1 << QSHIFT) - 1);

    #   Top level directory, say /n
    if (level == Qroot)
    {
        if (entry == 0)
        {
            return (1, packdir("orange", Qorange, Sys->CHDIR, 0));
        }
    }

    #   Second level directory, say, /n/orange
    if (level == Qorange)
    {
        if (entry == 0)
        {
            return (1, packdir("new", Qnew, 0, 0));
        }
        else if (entry <= numoranges)
        {
            which := entry - 1;
            return (1, packdir(sys->sprint("%d", which),
                    Qline|(which<<QSHIFT), Sys->CHDIR, 0));
        }
    }

    #   Third level directory, say, /n/orange/5
    if (level == Qline)
    {
        line := (c.qid.path&~Sys->CHDIR) >> QSHIFT;

        case(entry)
        {
            0 =>    return (1, packdir("ctl", Qctl, 0, line));
            1 =>    return (1, packdir("date", Qdate, 0, line));
            2 =>    return (1, packdir("time", Qtime, 0, line));
        }
    }

    return (-1, packdir(nil, 0, 0, 0));
}

packdir(name : string, Q, dirflag, line : int) : Sys->Dir
{
    qid : Sys->Qid;

    qid.vers = 0;
    qid.path = Q;
    qid.path |= line << QSHIFT;
    qid.path |= dirflag;

    return Sys->Dir (name,
            "pip",
            "pip",
            qid,
```

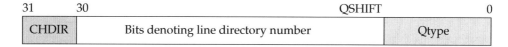

31	30	QSHIFT	0
CHDIR	Bits denoting line directory number		Qtype

Figure 8.2 Layout of qid for our dynamic name space server.

```
        perms[Q] | (qid.path & Sys->CHDIR),
        atimes[Q],
        mtimes[Q],
        lengths[Q],
        '0',
        '0');
}
```

Discussion   Rather than using the `dirgen` module function provided by Styxlib and providing it with a fixed directory structure, `dirtab`, as was done in the example in Section 8.8, we provide a custom `dirgen` function which tracks accesses to the name space and creates directory entries appropriately.

The primary job of `dirgen` is to manage qids. Each time `dirgen` is called, it is supplied with the qid of a directory, and an index, `entry`, into the directory, it must return the qid for the `entry` element of the directory.

To achieve this, `dirgen` encodes the name space structure in the qid. The server root directory is named `orange`. Within the server root is a file named `new`, which is read to create new *line directories*, each with name being a number counting from 0. Each of these line directories contains three files, `ctl`, `date` and `time`, which can neither be read from nor written to. Besides the line directory names, there is a fixed number of unique names in the name space of the server. Each of these unique names is encoded in the lower QSHIFT bits of the qid. The line directory number is encoded in the more significant (31 - QSHIFT) bit positions. The most significant bit encodes whether the qid represents a directory. This layout of the qid is illustrated in Figure 8.2.

Given a qid, `dirgen` can thus determine which level in the hierarchy is being read, and will appropriately construct and return a new qid for the requested entry in the directory. The construction of the new qid is performed by the `packdir` function.

A transcript of an interaction with the server is shown below:

```
; lc /n/remote
CVS/
; server /n/remote
; lc /n/remote
orange/
; cd /n/remote/orange
; lc
new
; cat new
; lc
0/ new
```

```
; lc 0
ctl date time
; cat new
; lc
0/ 1/ new
; ls -ls 0
-r-------- M 14 pip pip 0 Jan 01 1970 0/ctl
-r-------- M 14 pip pip 0 Jan 01 1970 0/date
-r-------- M 14 pip pip 0 Jan 01 1970 0/time
; ls -q 0
00000003.0 0/ctl
00000004.0 0/date
00000005.0 0/time
```

In the above, `ls -q` shows the qids for each directory entry in the form *qid-path.qidversion*. The qid path for the `ctl`, `date` and `time` entries are 3, 4 and 5, respectively, corresponding to the constants `Qctl`, `Qdate` and `Qtime` defined in the example.

Problems

8.1 Extend the filter in Section 8.7.2 to handle long file names which have identical stems.

8.2 Extend Filterfs to provide a filesystem interface, say in `/chan/filterfs`. Filterfs should accept commands to load new filters through this file interface.

8.3 What is the easiest way to support multiple concurrent filters with Filterfs? Can this be implemented without substantially modifying the architecture of Filterfs?

8.4 Modify the end-of-chapter example to return the new line allocated whenever the file `new` is read.

8.5 The chapter example does not permit reads of any of the files it serves except `new`. Try your hand at providing data for reads of the `ctl`, `date` and `time` files, with information specific to their *line*, i.e. say `/n/remote/orange/5/data` is regarded as *line 5*.

8.6 The end-of-chapter example does not handle '..'. Implement this.

8.7 Is it possible to implement *lexical names* [52] in a user-level file server? What changes would be required?

9
Networking

The entire network protocol stack of Inferno is accessible directly through entries in the name space. Connections to remote machines and acceptance and control of both incoming and outgoing connections can be performed entirely by manipulating entries in the name space, writing to and reading from them. The #I device in Inferno, the IP device, implements the Internet Protocol version 4. In typical use, the #I device is bound into the /net/ directory. The IP device serves a filesystem that contains interfaces to the implemented protocol stacks as subdirectories. Through the entries contained in each directory, each corresponding network protocol can be completely exercised and controlled.

The design of Inferno makes it very easy to write networked applications. Inferno provides two interfaces through which an application that wishes to communicate over a network may establish connections and transmit or receive data. The first interface, which is described in more detail in the next section, is through a filesystem interface, the /net/ filesystem, served by the #I device. The second equivalent interface is through method calls in the Sys module, and is described later in this chapter. It is chosen to describe the filesystem interface first since this provides an opportunity to describe configuring Inferno hosts connected to a network.

9.1 The /net/ Filesystem

The Inferno network stack is presented to the user as a filesystem, typically bound to /net/ through an operation such as:

```
/net/arp
/net/cs
/net/tcp/0/ctl
/net/tcp/0/data
/net/tcp/0/listen
/net/tcp/0/local
/net/tcp/0/remote
/net/tcp/0/status
/net/tcp/clone
/net/udp/0/ctl
/net/udp/0/data
/net/udp/0/listen
/net/udp/0/local
/net/udp/0/remote
/net/udp/0/status
/net/udp/clone
```

Figure 9.1 A typical /net/ filesystem on the emulated version of Inferno.

```
bind -a '#I' /net
```

This is typically performed automatically by either your startup shell or the network services, described further below. All network operations—such as receiving incoming connections, initiating outgoing connections or controlling open connections—may be performed by manipulating files in the /net/ filesystem. Applications are, however, not restricted to this interface, and Inferno provides system calls through Limbo modules, which applications may invoke, rather than manipulating the /net/ filesystem manually.

9.1.1 Protocol Directory Example: TCP

Inferno's implementation of the Transport Control Protocol (TCP) is accessible through the /net/tcp/ filesystem. The /net/tcp/ directory contains a single file clone and zero or more directories. The clone file is read to reserve a new TCP network connection. Reading the clone file returns an integer greater than or equal to zero, and a new directory entry in /net/tcp/ with the name corresponding to the number is generated.

9.2 Configuring the Network on the Inferno Emulator

The network stack in the Inferno emulator is a much simplified version of that available in native Inferno. The networking facilities in the emulator are interfaces to the facilities provided by the underlying system. The emulator provides support for two inter-networking protocols, TCP/IP and UDP/IP, as well as address resolution, ARP. A typical default emulator /net/ filesystem is shown in Figure 9.1.

There is no explicit configuration necessary for inter-networking in the emulator, beyond setting up the network services, as discussed in Chapter 1.

9.3   Configuring the Network in Native Inferno

The networking capabilities provided by native Inferno are significantly more extensive than for the emulator. The native Inferno kernel supports a wide variety of Inter-networking protocols—TCP/IP, UDP/IP, ICMP, RUDP, ESP and GRE, to name a few—and support for new protocols is easily added, and frequently is.

A single host may have multiple network stacks, each of which is independent of the other, with no implicit transfer of information between stacks. Each stack may be thought of as a collection of state information related to all the supported networking protocols. This state information may be network connections and interfaces for manipulating them, statistics, relations between physical network media and network interface configurations, etc. Multiple protocol stacks are disjoint only in the state they maintain, and they share the same implementation code within the kernel. The network stacks generally have names of the form #In, such as #I0. The integer n following the letter I specifies which network stack is being referred to: #I0 refers to the first, #I3 refers to the fourth, etc. The number specifier may be omitted, as in #I, in which case it is assumed that the stack being referred to is the first one, #I0.

A network stack is typically bound to a location in the filesystem, as in the following:

```
bind -a '#I' /net
```

A network stack is made up of two parts: interfaces and media. Media are devices which can be the source of network data. A typical medium is Ethernet, but there are also media such as the *ppp medium*, which permits configuring an asynchronous serial device as a source and sink of network traffic, and the generic *packet medium*, which allows user-level applications to source network data. Interfaces are front ends to media and have properties such as IP addresses (none, one or more).

Media are generally bound to interfaces, acting as sources of network data for the interfaces, while the interfaces provide a means of configuration. For example, one might bind an Ethernet medium corresponding to an Ethernet network adapter in a computer to an interface, which is then subsequently configured with a specific IP address.

To set up an IP address for an Ethernet controller in your computer, the steps involved are (1) to make the Ethernet medium visible under /net/ in your current name space, (2) to obtain a new interface, (3) to bind the Ethernet medium to the obtained interface, and (4) to configure the Ethernet with an IP address by configuring

(1) *Bind Ethernet medium to appropriate location in name space:*
```
Bind a '#l0' /net
```

(2) *Obtain a new interface:*
```
cat /net/ipifc/clone
```

(3) *Establish a relation between the Ethernet medium and the interface:*
```
echo n 'bind ether ether0' > /net/ipifc/0/ctl
```

(4) *Configure the interface with an IP address and network mask:*
```
echo n 'add 192.168.0.3 255.255.255.0' > /net/ipifc/0/ctl
```

(5) *Add an entry in routing tables for the default route:*
```
echo n 'add 0.0.0.0 0.0.0.0 192.168.0.1' > /net/iproute
```

Figure 9.2 Basic network configuration of an Ethernet interface under native Inferno.

the interface to which it is bound. In general, you will also possibly need a fifth step, to set up a *default route* in the kernel's routing table to indicate where all packets which are not destined for your local network should be forwarded. Figure 9.2 illustrates these five steps.

As a further illustration of setting up networking, consider a more complicated scenario: a machine with two Ethernet media and which straddles two networks, as depicted in Figure 9.3. If this machine forwarded packets between the two networks, it would be referred to as a router. In the following, it is assumed that such packet forwarding is neither required nor performed, but applications running on this host should be able to access both networks. The process is similar to the previous example. The steps are to make both Ethernet media visible in the current name space, to create two new interfaces, one for each Ethernet medium, to bind each Ethernet medium to one of these interfaces, to configure each interface bound to an Ethernet medium with an IP address and network mask appropriate for the network to which it is connected, and to create an entry in the routing table for the default route. Figure 9.3 illustrates these steps.

As shown in Figure 9.3, such a machine could act as a network gateway between a local Inferno network and the Internet. Machines in the local network (the 192.168.1.0 network, connected to the Ethernet switch) could mount the network stack of the gateway into their local name space, and bind that stack over their local network stack. Applications accessing the network on these machines subsequent to this operation would now be using the network stack of the gateway.

Accesses to the gateway's network stack occur through Styx messages sent over the 192.168.1.0 network to the gateway through its medium ether0. Data may then be read or written via the network interfaces connected to either the 10.0.0.0 network or the 192.168.1.0 network.

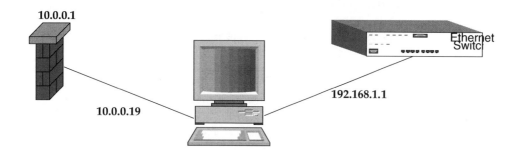

For the network interface connected to the switch, on the 192.168.1.0 network:

(1) *Bind Ethernet medium to appropriate location in name space:*
```
Bind a '#l0' /net
```

(2) *Obtain a new interface:*
```
cat /net/ipifc/clone
```

(3) *Establish a relation between the Ethernet medium and the interface:*
```
echo n 'bind ether ether0' > /net/ipifc/0/ctl
```

(4) *Configure the interface with an IP address and network mask:*
```
echo n 'add 192.168.1.1 255.255.255.0' > /net/ipifc/0/ctl
```

For the network interface connected to the firewall, on the 10.0.0.0 network:

(5) *Bind Ethernet medium to appropriate location in name space:*
```
Bind a '#l1' /net
```

(6) *Obtain a new interface:*
```
cat /net/ipifc/clone
```

(7) *Establish a relation between the Ethernet medium and the interface:*
```
echo n 'bind ether ether1' > /net/ipifc/1/ctl
```

(8) *Configure the interface with an IP address and network mask:*
```
echo n 'add 10.0.0.19 255.255.0.0' > /net/ipifc/1/ctl
```

(9) *Add an entry in routing tables for the default route:*
```
echo n 'add 0.0.0.0 0.0.0.0 10.0.0.1' > /net/iproute
```

Figure 9.3 Network configuration of an Inferno gateway.

9.4 Networking Through Sys Module Calls

There are four methods within the Sys module which enable the establishment of network connections: dial, announce, export and listen.

The dial method is used to initiate a new connection to a server over a network. Executing a dial call is equivalent to writing a 'dial net!addr!service' into the ctl file of a protocol line directory. An application that wishes to receive connections on a port uses announce to reserve the port for subsequent connections. After an announce, the application performs a listen on the announced port, which blocks until a new incoming connection is received.

```
Connection: adt
{
    dfd:    ref FD;   # data file
    cfd:    ref FD;   # control file
    dir:    string;   # pathname of line directory
};
```

The dial, announce and listen methods each return a tuple consisting of a success indicator and a Connection ADT. The Connection ADT represents a protocol line directory, and file descriptors open on the ctl and data files in that line directory.

The dial and announce methods take address parameters addr and local, which may take one of the following forms.

1. *network!netaddr!service*

2. *network!netaddr*

3. *netaddr*

4. "*"

The *network* field denotes the transport protocol to use. It may take the name of any of the protocol directories in the /net/ hierarchy, for example, tcp or udp. It may also be net, in which case the default transport (usually TCP) is used. The *netaddr* field is a name to be resolved by the connection server, *cs*. The *service* parameter is either a port number or a service name that will also be looked up by the connection server.

9.4.1 dial

Synopsis : dial: fn(addr, local:string):(int, Connection);

Dial is used to make a new connection to an address *addr*, with the local address and port set by *local*. The parameter *addr* is translated by the connection server, detailed in the manual pages for *cs(8)*. The translation may result in several addresses, in which case dial will try all of these addresses until one succeeds.

The dial call returns a tuple consisting of the success status and a Connection ADT. The dir field of the Connection ADT is a string naming the path of the line directory created for this connection. The cfd and dfd fields are file descriptors open on the ctl and data files in that line directory, respectively.

9.4.2 announce

Synopsis : announce: fn(addr:string):(int, Connection);

The announce function, together with the listen function described further below, permit Limbo applications to accept connections on supported protocols and addresses. Announce creates a new line directory in the corresponding protocol directory of the /net/ hierarchy, and is equivalent to opening /net/<proto>/clone and reading to obtain the number of a new line directory, and writing the string "announce net!<proto>!service" into its ctl file. The *service* field of the addr argument specifies the service port on which to listen for the specified protocol, or it may be '*' to listen on all ports.

The returned connection ADT has its cfd file descriptor entry open on the ctl file of the reserved line directory. The data file must be separately opened and read from by a *listen* call.

An Inferno host may have several network interfaces, each with a different IP address associated with it, or each interface may have more than one IP address associated with it, as described at the beginning of this chapter. There is usually only one interface to which an IP address is bound. Before accepting connections, it is therefore necessary to specify which address an application wishes to receive connections on, and this is what the announce call facilitates. For example, to announce a service on port 6670 of the interface which has the IP address corresponding to www.gemusehaken.org bound to it:

```
(err, conn) := sys->announce("net!www.gemusehaken.org!6670");
```

The service is announced on port 6670 of the default transport for the IP address that the name www.gemusehaken.org resolves to (say, 192.168.1.1). Since a service name may be used instead of the port number, and one may also explicitly specify the transport protocol to use, the above is therefore equivalent to:

```
(err, conn) := sys->announce("tcp!www.gemusehaken.org!infweb");
```

9.4.3 listen

Synopsis : listen: fn(c:Connection):(int, Connection);

The listen call is used in conjunction with announce. Announce reserves a line directory for use in receiving connections, and returns a Connection ADT with the cfd entry open on the ctl file of the reserved line directory. This is then used in a listen call, which then returns a Connection ADT with the cfd member open on the ctl file and the dfd open on the data file.

After a listen call, new connections may be made to the address and port specified in the announce, and an application waits for incoming connections by blocking on a read of the dfd.

9.4.4   Example: A Simple HTTP Server

```
# File : simplehttpd.b

implement SimpleHTTPD;

include "sys.m";
include "draw.m";

sys   : Sys;
Connection : import Sys;

SimpleHTTPD : module
{
    init : fn(nil : ref Draw->Context, nil : list of string);
};

init(nil : ref Draw->Context, nil : list of string)
{
    sys = load Sys Sys->PATH;

    #    First, announce the service. This creates a line directory
    #    and conn.cfd will be open on the ctl file
    (n, conn) := sys->announce("tcp!*!1984");
    if (n < 0)
    {
        sys->print("SimpleHTTPD - announce failed : %r\n");
        exit;
    }

    #    Now, listen for incoming connections, spawn new thread
    #    for each incoming connection.
    while (1)
    {
        listen(conn);
    }
}
```

```
listen(conn : Connection)
{
    buf := array [sys->ATOMICIO] of byte;

    (ok, c) := sys->listen(conn);
    if (ok < 0)
    {
        sys->print("SimpleHTTPD - listen failed : %r\n");
        exit;
    }

    #    Create a new thread to handle this connection
    rfd := sys->open(conn.dir + "/remote", Sys->OREAD);

    #    The client IP is not yet set at this point. The following will
    #    therefore show the client IP as 0.0.0.0!0:
    n := sys->read(rfd, buf, len buf);
    sys->print("SimpleHTTPD : Got new connection from (incomplete) %s\n",
            string buf[:n]);

    spawn hdlrthread(c);
}

hdlrthread(conn : Connection)
{
    buf := array [sys->ATOMICIO] of byte;

    #    The connections data file is not opened by default,
    #    must explicitly do so to accept the new connection
    rdfd := sys->open(conn.dir + "/data", Sys->OREAD);
    wdfd := sys->open(conn.dir + "/data", Sys->OWRITE);
    rfd := sys->open(conn.dir + "/remote", Sys->OREAD);

    #    The client IP is now available, once we have accepted connection.
    #    The following will print the actual client IP address:
    n := sys->read(rfd, buf, len buf);
    sys->print("SimpleHTTPD : Got new connection from %s\n",
            string buf[:n]);

    while (sys->read(rdfd, buf, len buf) >= 0)
    {
        sys->write(wdfd,
                array of byte "<HTML><BODY>Hello!</BODY></HTML>\n",
                len "<HTML><BODY>Hello!</BODY></HTML>\n");

        return;
    }
}
```

Once a new connection is received, the connection's data file is not opened by default, rather, applications must explicitly open it to accept the new connection. Once opened, it can then be written to, to provide data to the client. The simple server above always prints the string "Hello!" wrapped in HTML tags to any client that accesses it.

9.5 Dealing with HTML: The Webgrab, Url and HTML Modules

Retrieving content from the Web is becoming an increasingly popular part of many applications written today.

There are two modules available to make such tasks trivial. The first, the Webgrab module, provides an interface for applications to make HTTP requests. The applications do not have to deal with any of the details of the HTTP protocol. The module interface for the Webgrab module is shown below:

```
Webgrab: module
{
    init: fn(ctxt: ref Draw->Context, argl: list of string);
    httpget : fn(u: ref Url->ParsedUrl) :
        (string, array of byte, ref Sys->FD, ref Url->ParsedUrl);
    readconfig : fn();
};
```

Webgrab is actually an Inferno command-line utility for retrieving Web content. It exports functionality to allow other applications to use it to retrieve data off the Web.

Like all Limbo modules that wish to be run from the shell, the Webgrab module has an init function that has the now familiar function signature. In order to use Webgrab, calling modules must first initialize its internal data structures. This is performed by calling Webgrab's init function with a nil graphics context and an argument list consisting of the single list item "init", subsequent to loading the module:

```
webgrab = load Webgrab "/dis/webgrab.dis";
if (webgrab == nil)
{
    sys->raise(sys->sprint("fail:Could not load /dis/webgrab.dis: %r"));
}

webgrab->init(nil, "init"::nil);
webgrab->readconfig();
```

The first item in the argument list of programs executed from the shell is usually the program's own name. The Webgrab module interprets a single first argument of "init" to indicate that it is being used as a helper module, not being run from the shell. Subsequent to calling the init method, the httpget method can now be called to retrieve data off the Web.

URLs are specified as ParsedUrl ADTs, defined by the Url module, listed in Appendix B.8 and repeated below:

```
Url: module
```

```
{
  PATH : con "/dis/lib/url.dis";

  #    Scheme IDs
  NOSCHEME, HTTP, HTTPS, FTP, FILE, GOPHER, MAILTO, NEWS,
  NNTP, TELNET, WAIS, PROSPERO, JAVASCRIPT, UNKNOWN: con iota;

  #    General url syntax:
  #      <scheme>://<user>:<passwd>@<host>:<port>/<path>?<query>#<fragment>
  #
  #    Relative urls might omit some prefix of the above
  ParsedUrl: adt
  {
      scheme:      int;
      utf8:        int;
      user:        string;
      passwd:      string;
      host:        string;
      port:        string;
      pstart:      string;
      path:        string;
      query:       string;
      frag:        string;

      makeabsolute: fn(url: self ref ParsedUrl, base: ref ParsedUrl);
      tostring: fn(url: self ref ParsedUrl) : string;
  };

  schemes: array of string;
  init: fn();
  makeurl: fn(s: string) : ref ParsedUrl;
};
```

A new `ParsedUrl` can be constructed (in this case, we need to construct one to pass to Webgrab) by calling the `makeurl` method:

```
u := url->makeurl("http://www.gemusehaken.org");
(err, bytes, fd, realurl) := webgrab->httpget(u);
```

In the above, the return value of Webgrab's `httpget` method is a tuple containing the following (as per the Webgrab module definition previously listed).

- `err`   A string stating the error status of the request.

- `bytes`   An array of bytes with the leading bytes read from the URL. The remainder of the data must be obtained by reading the returned `fd` descriptor.

- `fd`   A file descriptor which should be read to obtain the remainder of the data from the URL, trailing those bytes supplied in the `bytes` field.

- `realurl`   The URL from which the data were actually retrieved, after possibly being redirected by the remote Web server.

That is indeed all an application needs to do to retrieve data from a URL. Parsing the retrieved HTML can also be simplified using the HTML module, whose module definition is listed in Appendix B.7 and repeated below. The HTML module provides data structures and methods for parsing HTML documents:

```
HTML: module
{
    PATH:        con "/dis/lib/html.dis";

    Lex: adt
    {
        tag:     int;
        text:    string; # text in Data, attribute text in tag
        attr:    list of Attr;
    };

    Attr: adt
    {
        name:    string;
        value:   string;
    };

    #    Sorted in lexical order; used as array indices
    Notfound,
    Ta, Taddress, Tapplet, Tarea, Tatt_footer, Tb, Tbase,
    Tbasefont, Tbig, Tblink, Tblockquote, Tbody, Tbq, Tbr,
    Tcaption, Tcenter, Tcite, Tcode, Tcol, Tcolgroup, Tdd,
    Tdfn, Tdir, Tdiv, Tdl, Tdt, Tem, Tfont, Tform, Tframe,
    Tframeset, Th1, Th2, Th3, Th4, Th5, Th6, Thead, Thr, Thtml,
    Ti, Timg, Tinput, Tisindex, Titem, Tkbd, Tli, Tlink, Tmap,
    Tmenu, Tmeta, Tnobr, Tnoframes, Tol, Toption, Tp, Tparam,
    Tpre, Tq, Tsamp, Tscript, Tselect, Tsmall, Tstrike, Tstrong,
    Tstyle, Tsub, Tsup, Tt, Ttable, Ttbody, Ttd, Ttextarea,
    Ttextflow, Ttfoot, Tth, Tthead, Ttitle, Ttr, Ttt, Tu, Tul,
    Tvar: con iota;

    RBRA: con 1000;
    Data: con 2000;

    #    Character sets
    Latin1, UTF8: con iota;

    lex:         fn(b: array of byte, charset: int, keepnls: int) :
                 array of ref Lex;
    attrvalue:   fn(attr: list of Attr, name: string): (int, string);
    globalattr:  fn(html: array of ref Lex, tag: int, attr: string) :
                 (int, string);
    isbreak:     fn(h: array of ref Lex, i: int): int;
    lex2string:  fn(l: ref Lex): string;
};
```

The lex method takes as arguments an array of bytes, such as the raw data read from a URL, and returns an array of Lex items. This array is in essence the raw HTML data converted to an array of attribute/value pairs. The `tag` field of each `Lex` item specifies the type of the item, so, for example, an HTML `<IMAGE>` tag will become one item in the returned array, with its `tag` field having the value `Timg` (defined in the enumeration in the Url module). Any attributes of the tag, for example, `src=banner.gif width=50` for the `<IMG>` tag, will be accessible in the `attr` field as a list of `Attr` items.

The remaining methods are used to obtain the value of a specified attribute string from a list of `Attr` items (`attrvalue`), retrieve global document attributes such as background color (`globalattr`), determine if a `Lex` item is a tag that causes a break, such as `<BR>`, `<HR>` or even `<PRE>` tags (`isbreak`), and convert a `Lex` item into a string (`lex2string`). The following code fragments illustrates some of these methods:

```
tokens := html->lex(array of byte s, HTML->Latin1, 0);
for (i := 0; i < len tokens; i++)
{
    sys->print("Tag = [%d], Text = [%s], Attrs = [",
            tokens[i].tag, tokens[i].text);
    attrs := tokens[i].attr;
    while (attrs!= nil)
    {
        sys->print("(name=%s, value=%s) ",
            (hd attrs).name, (hd attrs).value);
        attrs = tl attrs;
    }
    sys->print("]\n");
}
```

We will now look at a complete example that integrates many of the ideas presented in this section.

9.5.1   Example: A Simple 'Web Service', Webdict

The example application we consider is *Webdict*. It is a simple program that queries an online dictionary service with a word, extracts the relevant portion of the received HTML containing the dictionary lookup, and attempts to format this received text for display on the console. This methodology is certainly not the most elegant or robust, and is sometimes referred to as 'screen scraping'. A more preferable method might be to query a service that provided the data in XML format, but that is beyond the scope of this book. The complete source listing for the application follows:

```
# File : simplewebdict.b

implement WebDict;

include "sys.m";
include "draw.m";
include "url.m";
include "html.m";
```

```
include "arg.m";
include "string.m";

ParsedUrl : import url;

sys : Sys;
webgrab : Webgrab;
url : Url;
str : String;
html    : HTML;
arg : Arg;

verbose : int;
FMTWIDTH: con 60;

WebDict : module
{
    init : fn(nil : ref Draw->Context, args : list of string);
};

Webgrab : module
{
    init : fn(ctxt : ref Draw->Context, args : list of string);
    httpget : fn(u: ref Url->ParsedUrl) :
        (string, array of byte, ref Sys->FD, ref Url->ParsedUrl);
    readconfig : fn();
};

init(nil : ref Draw->Context, args : list of string)
{
    body : string;


    sys = load Sys Sys->PATH;

    (there, nil) := sys->stat("/net/cs");
    if (there == -1)
    {
        cs := load WebDict "/dis/lib/cs.dis";
        cs->init(nil, nil);
    }

    webgrab = load Webgrab "/dis/webgrab.dis";
    if (webgrab == nil)
    {
        sys->print("Could not load /dis/webgrab.dis : %r");
        exit;
    }

    webgrab->init(nil, "init"::nil);
    webgrab->readconfig();

    str = load String String->PATH;
    html = load HTML HTML->PATH;

    url = load Url Url->PATH;
```

```
    url->init();

    arg = load Arg Arg->PATH;
    arg->init(args);

    while((c := arg->opt()) != 0)
    {
        case c
        {
            'v' => verbose = 1;
                *   =>
            {
                sys->print("Usage : webdict [-v] <list of words>\n");
                exit;
            }
        }
    }
    args = arg->argv();

    while (args != nil)
    {
        u := url->makeurl(
            "http://www.gemusehaken.org/cgi-bin/dict.pl?term="+
            hd args);

        (err, bytes, fd, realurl) := webgrab->httpget(u);

        if (fd != nil)
        {
            buf := array[Sys->ATOMICIO] of byte;
            while((n := sys->read(fd, buf, len buf)) > 0)
            {
                body = body + string buf[:n];
            }
        }

        munch((string bytes)+body);

        args = tl args;
        body = nil;
    }
}

munch(body : string)
{
    nrecords : int = 1;
    block : string;

    (nlines, lines) := sys->tokenize(sys->sprint("%s", body), "\n");

    while (lines != nil)
    {
        sys->print("\n");

        while ((lines != nil) && (hd lines != "<!-- resultItemStart -->"))
        {
```

```
                lines = tl lines;
        }

        if (lines != nil)
            lines = tl lines;

        while ((lines != nil) && (hd lines != "<!-- resultItemEnd -->"))
        {
            block = block + hd lines;
            lines = tl lines;
        }

        htmltxtprint(block);
        block = nil;

        if (!verbose)
            break;
    }

    sys->print("\n");
}

htmltxtprint(s : string)
{
    index   := 0;
    inli    := 0;

    tokens := html->lex(array of byte s, HTML->Latin1, 0);
    for (i := 0; i < len tokens; i++)
    {
        text := tokens[i].text;

        if (tokens[i].tag == HTML->Data)
        {
            strlen := len text;
            if ((index + strlen) >= FMTWIDTH)
            {
                (n, sl) := sys->tokenize(text, " \t");
                while (sl != nil)
                {
                    index += len (hd sl);
                    if (index >= FMTWIDTH)
                    {
                        sys->print("\n");
                        if (inli)
                            sys->print("\t");

                        index = 0;
                    }

                    sys->print("%s ", hd sl);
                    sl = tl sl;
                }

                sys->print("\n");
                if (inli)
```

```
                              sys->print("\t");

                     index = 0;
              }
              else
              {
                     sys->print("%s ", text);

                     index += len text;
                     if (index >= FMTWIDTH)
                     {
                              sys->print("\n");

                              if (inli)
                                    sys->print("\t");

                              index = 0;
                     }
              }
       }

       if (tokens[i].tag == HTML->Tli)
       {
              sys->print("\n\n\t");
              index = 0;
              inli = 1;
       }
       else if(tokens[i].tag == HTML->Tli+HTML->RBRA)
       {
              inli = 0;
       }
       else if (html->isbreak(tokens[i:i+1], 0))
       {
              sys->print("\n");
              index = 0;
       }
   }
}
```

Webdict uses the Webgrab module to query an online dictionary, and receives the reply of the query as raw HTML. It first isolates the portion of the returned Web page containing the query responses, then uses the facilities of the HTML module to format this data for output on the console.

9.6 Summary

This chapter provided an overview of networking in Inferno, configuration of Inferno hosts in both the emulated and native versions of Inferno, and the interface provided to Limbo programs for constructing networked applications.

Bibliographic Notes

The networking facilities in Inferno are very similar to those in the Plan 9 operating system [53]. The networking facilities in Plan 9 are described in [59]. Many reference texts on data networking exist, such as as [10, 11, 12]. A thorough coverage of the Secure Sockets Layer (SSL) and Transport Layer Security (TLS) protocols are provided in [63].

9.7   Chapter Example: Tunneling Styx Traffic over HTTP

This example builds upon the concepts introduced in both this chapter and the previous one. We will look at a pair of applications, a client and a server, for tunneling Styx traffic over HTTP. In case you might be wondering, possible uses of this would be to enable a user behind a firewall that only passes HTTP traffic to disguise all its network traffic as HTTP requests and replies. The user runs an application program that mounts a remote name space to use its network stack in /net/. The client encapsulates the Styx messages resulting from the mount and subsequent name space accesses at the mount point into HTTP requests to the server, which in turn converts those requests into Styx messages to be delivered to its exported name space. The Styx responses from the exported name space are also encapsulated in HTTP responses and delivered to the client, which extracts the Styx message data and delivers them to the mount point.

For example, the use of the client and server might be as follows:

```
(On the server)
; shtun &
27
;




(On the client, with server running on www.gemusehaken.org port 80)
; shtunclient -m /n/remote -s www.gemusehaken.org -p 80
Remote name space mounted in /n/remote
; lc /n/remote/net
arp      cs      tcp/     udp/
; bind /n/remote/net /net
;
```

Shared module definitions used by both the client and the server:

```
# File : shtun.m

SRVPORT        : con "8080";
SRVADDR        : con "localhost";

StyxHTTPtunnel : module
{
    init : fn(ctxt : ref Draw->Context, args : list of string);

    REPLYHDPAD     : con 10;
    REPLYTLPAD     : con 10;

    QUERYHDPAD     : con 37;
    QUERYTLPAD     : con 4;
};
```

The source for the client:

```
# File : shtunclient.b
implement StyxHTTPtunnelClient;

include "sys.m";
include "draw.m";
include "arg.m";
include "shtun.m";

arg : Arg;
sys : Sys;

srvaddr, srvport, mntdir    : string;
INITSYNC                : con 1;

StyxHTTPtunnelClient : module
{
    init : fn(nil : ref Draw->Context, args : list of string);
};

init(nil : ref Draw->Context, args : list of string)
{
    sys = load Sys Sys->PATH;
    arg = load Arg Arg->PATH;
    arg->init(args);

    #    Defaults
    mntdir = "/n/remote";
    srvport = SRVPORT;
    srvaddr = SRVADDR;
    while((c := arg->opt()) != 0)
    {
        case c
        {
            's' => srvaddr = arg->arg();
            'p' => srvport = arg->arg();
            'm' => mntdir = arg->arg();
            *   =>
            {
                usage();
                exit;
            }
        }
    }
    if (arg->argv() != nil)
    {
        usage();
        exit;
    }

    (there, nil) := sys->stat("/net/cs");
    if (there == -1)
    {
        cs := load StyxHTTPtunnelClient "/dis/lib/cs.dis";
        if (cs == nil)
```

```
        {
            sys->raise(sys->sprint(
                "fail:Could not load /dis/lib/cs.dis : %r"));
        }
        cs->init(nil, nil);
    }

    sys->bind("#|", "/chan", sys->MBEFORE);
    mount_pipe := array [2] of ref Sys->FD;
    sys->pipe(mount_pipe);

    #   Mount will block if it can't send Tattach
    sync := chan of int;
    spawn xfrm2web(mount_pipe[0], sync);

    <- sync;

    spawn mountthread(mount_pipe[1]);
}

usage()
{
    sys->print(
        "Usage: shtunclient [-s <server addr>][-p port][-m mountpoint]\n");
}

mountthread(mountfd : ref Sys->FD)
{
    if (sys->mount(mountfd, mntdir, sys->MREPL, nil) == -1)
    {
        sys->print("Shtunclient : mount failed : [%r]\n");
        exit;
    }

    sys->print(
        "ShtunClient : Remote end of tunnel mounted in %s\n", mntdir);
}

xfrm2web(mountfd : ref Sys->FD, sync : chan of int)
{
    #   We must fork namespace so that if after running,
    #   say, user binds /n/remote/net to /net, we can
    #   still maintain tunnel.
    sys->pctl(Sys->FORKNS, nil);

    sync <-= INITSYNC;

    dialaddr := "tcp!" + srvaddr + "!" + srvport;

    #   We could be reading Sys->ATOMICIO + Styx headers + HTML headers
    buf := array [2*Sys->ATOMICIO] of byte;
    while (1)
    {
        n := sys->read(mountfd, buf, len buf);
        if (n < 1)
        {
```

```
            sys->print(
                "mount->web: Empty read from rdfd: %r.\n");

            return;
        }

        (ok, net) := sys->dial(dialaddr, nil);
        if (ok < 0)
        {
            sys->print("Could not dial %s: %r\n", dialaddr);
            exit;
        }

        (requestlen, request) := webfmt(buf[:n], n);
        if (sys->write(net.dfd, request, requestlen) != requestlen)
        {
            sys->print("Could not write to net.dfd : %r\n");
            exit;
        }

        n = sys->read(net.dfd, buf, len buf);

        #   We need at least the header, which encodes the length
        #   that must be read. Yuck : implement a mechanism to
        #   recover from such a runt read.
        if (n < StyxHTTPtunnel->REPLYHDPAD)
        {
            sys->sprint("xfrweb2m : could short read from webfd : %r\n");

            #   Yuck : we shouldnt just bail out like this:
            exit;
        }

        encodedlen := int buf[StyxHTTPtunnel->REPLYHDPAD-2] +
                ((int buf[StyxHTTPtunnel->REPLYHDPAD-1]) << 8);

        while (n < encodedlen)
        {
            n += sys->read(net.dfd, buf[n:], len buf);
        }

        (styxlen, styxdata) := webdecode(buf[:n], n);

        if (sys->write(mountfd, styxdata, styxlen) != styxlen)
        {
            sys->print("xfrweb2m : could not write to mountfd : %r\n");
        }
    }
}

webfmt(buf : array of byte, nbytes : int) : (int, array of byte)
{
    a := StyxHTTPtunnel->QUERYHDPAD;
    b := StyxHTTPtunnel->QUERYTLPAD;

    query := array [nbytes + a + b] of byte;
```

```
    query[0:] = array of byte
        ("GET / HTTP/1.0\r\nHost: none\r\nAccept: ");

    query[a:] = buf[:nbytes];
    query[a+nbytes:] = array of byte "\r\n\r\n";

    return (len query, query);
}

webdecode(buf : array of byte, nbytes : int) : (int, array of byte)
{
    a := StyxHTTPtunnel->REPLYHDPAD;
    c := StyxHTTPtunnel->REPLYTLPAD;

    return (nbytes - (a+c), buf[a: nbytes - c]);
}
```

The implementation of the server:

```
# File : shtun.b

implement StyxHTTPtunnel;

include "sys.m";
include "draw.m";
include "string.m";
include "shtun.m";

sys        : Sys;
str        : String;

Connection     : import Sys;
export_pipe    : array of ref Sys->FD;
StyxMAX        : con 29;


init(nil : ref Draw->Context, nil : list of string)
{
    sys = load Sys Sys->PATH;
    str = load String String->PATH;

        sys->bind("#|", "/chan", sys->MBEFORE);
    export_pipe = array [2] of ref Sys->FD;
    sys->pipe(export_pipe);

    if (sys->export(export_pipe[0], sys->EXPASYNC))
    {
        sys->print("Error - Could not export : %r\n");
                exit;
    }

    (n, conn) := sys->announce("tcp!*!"+SRVPORT);
    if (n < 0)
    {
```

```
            sys->print("StyxHTTPtunnel - announce failed : %r\n");
            exit;
    }

    while (1)
    {
            listen(conn);
    }
}

listen(conn : Connection)
{
    (ok, c) := sys->listen(conn);
    if (ok < 0)
    {
            sys->print("StyxHTTPtunnel - listen failed : %r\n");
            exit;
    }

    spawn hdlrthread(c);
}

hdlrthread(conn : Connection)
{
    #    At most, we have a full Styx message encap. in padding HTML
    buf := array [2*Sys->ATOMICIO] of byte;
    n : int = 0;


    #    The connections data file is not opened by default,
    #    must explicitly do so to accept the new connection
    rdfd := sys->open(conn.dir + "/data", Sys->OREAD);
    wdfd := sys->open(conn.dir + "/data", Sys->OWRITE);
    rfd := sys->open(conn.dir + "/remote", Sys->OREAD);

    n = sys->read(rfd, buf, len buf);
    sys->print("\nStyxHTTPtunnel : Got new connection from %s",
            string buf[:n]);

    n = sys->read(rdfd, buf, len buf);
    if (n < 1)
    {
        sys->print("Received empty request, discarding...\n");
        return;
    }

    #    Get the request from the client and deliver it to the Export
    (clientdatalen, clientdata) := requestdecode(buf[:n]);
    if (int clientdata[0] > StyxMAX)
    {
        sys->print("Bad msgtype [%d] from client", int clientdata[0]);
        return;
    }

    if (sys->write(export_pipe[1], clientdata, clientdatalen) !=
        clientdatalen)
```

```
        {
            sys->print("Could not write to export_pipe : %r");
        }

        #    Get the response from the Export and deliver it to the client
        n = sys->read(export_pipe[1], buf, len buf);
        if (n < 1)
        {
            sys->print("Empty read from export pipe\n");
            return;
        }

        if (int buf[0] > StyxMAX)
        {
            sys->raise(sys->sprint(
                "fail:Bad msgtype [%d] from Export",int buf[0]));
        }

        (n, buf) = clientfmt(buf, n);

        if (sys->write(wdfd, buf[:n], n) != n)
        {
            sys->raise(sys->sprint("fail:Could not write to wfd : %r"));
        }
}

clientfmt(buf : array of byte, size : int) : (int, array of byte)
{
    a := StyxHTTPtunnel->REPLYHDPAD;
    b := StyxHTTPtunnel->REPLYTLPAD;

    bytes := array [size+a+b] of byte;
    numbytes := len bytes;

    bytes[0:] = array of byte "<HTML><!";
    bytes[a-2] = byte (numbytes & 16rFF);
    bytes[a-1] = byte ((numbytes >> 8) & 16rFF);
    bytes[a:] = buf[:size];
    bytes[a+size:] = array of byte "></HTML>\r\n";

    return (numbytes, bytes);
}

requestdecode(body : array of byte) : (int, array of byte)
{
    a := StyxHTTPtunnel->QUERYHDPAD;
    b := StyxHTTPtunnel->QUERYTLPAD;

    return (len body - (a+b), body[a: len body - b]);
}
```

Discussion   Shtun and Shtunclient perform a crude tunneling of Styx traffic over HTTP. Shtun is the server, and it receives HTTP GET requests with an Accept: field containing the raw bytes of a Styx message. It responds with <HTML><!...></HTML>, where the ellipsis denotes a sequence of raw bytes of the Styx response.

Shtun client encapsulates attempts to mount the default filesystem on the server, encapsulating its Styx requests in HTML as described above. It reads back HTML replies from server and extracts the raw data. Given a server running shtun, shtun-client will mount the server's default served name space.

Problems

9.1 Try your hand at implementing a 'chat' application.

9.2 The chapter example, Shtun, should prune the name space appropriately before exporting. It might even serve different name spaces based on the requested URL. Try implementing these extensions.

10
Cryptographic Facilities

In a networked environment, applications and their users must be protected from the modification and interception of sensitive data. Protection against such acts is not a singular act, but rather a process that makes use of several facilities. Communicating entities must be able to verify the identity of the parties they are in communication with, using techniques for *mutual authentication*. It must be ensured that once the authenticity of the parties involved in communication has been established, the communications between them are neither tampered with nor is their content disclosed. These threats can be addressed using *message digests* and *encryption*, respectively.

Inferno provides cryptographic facilities to aid in building secure applications. The facilities provided by Inferno include those for *mutual authentication, message digests* and *encryption*. Inferno applications may choose whether or not to take advantage of these facilities.

Before describing the interfaces available to Limbo applications for taking advantage of these facilities, it is instructive to understand the role played by these facilities in an Inferno system. To that end, the next two sections describe the process of configuring Inferno systems to act as authentication servers, and the process of utilizing the cryptographic facilities within the Inferno environment to make secure connections between hosts.

10.1 Setting Up an Authentication Server

Authentication servers are required to perform mutual authentication between users. A *signer key* is a public/private key pair for the authentication server. This will be used

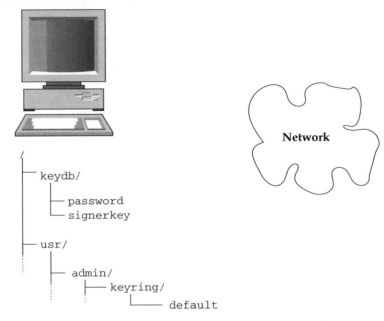

Figure 10.1 An Inferno host acting as its own certificate authority.

by the authentication server to generate certificates, for users, vouching for the authenticity of their identity, and enabling those users to initiate secure communications with other Inferno systems in a network.

Figure 10.1 shows the layout of a simple Inferno network consisting of a single machine which acts as the solitary host, file server and certifying authority. The connection server configuration file for such a system will have entries which all point to the local machine. Such a machine would maintain its own `/keydb/passwd` file for user account information, and would be responsible for vouching for the authenticity of its own identity. This may be acceptable for a non-networked setup.

In reality, networks consist of large numbers of hosts, all potentially malicious. Hosts that wish to communicate securely need assurance that their communications are indeed occurring with the intended destination: the communication must be *authenticated*. Once a host has assurance of the authenticity of the party they are communicating with, they require assurance that their messages will not be eavesdropped upon by a third party, and this may be achieved through *encryption*. Other issues exist, such as guaranteeing that messages are not inserted in the communication stream of an authenticated connection, or that the order of messages is not changed, or even that a prior authenticated and encrypted communication is not replayed to gain access to services.

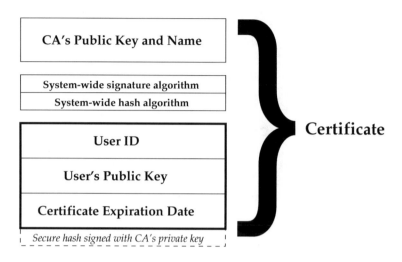

Figure 10.2 Components of a certificate generated by an Inferno certifying authority.

The *certificate authority* maintains a database of known users in the network. It maintains information on (1) the user ID of a user, a string such as 'pip', (2) the SHA (*keyring-sha(2)*) secure cryptographic hash of the user's password, (3) the expiration date of the password, and (4) other miscellaneous information about a user (full name, phone number, nickname, etc.). The certificate authority keeps this information in its /keydb/password file, which should be readable and writable only by its administrative user. In addition to user passwords, the certificate authority maintains a public/private key pair, in the file /keydb/signerkey. These are employed in generating certificates for users on hosts in the network. The certificate authority's public/private key pair is created by *createsignerkey(8)* .

Two hosts that wish to authenticate their identity to each other exchange certificates, which are essentially 'letters of introduction' from a third party that both hosts trust, this third party being the certifying authority (CA).

These certificates therefore contain the name of the third party (usually the symbolic host name of the certifying authority, the *signer ID* specified during the certifying authority's setup *createsignerkey* step), and proof that the certificate did actually come from that trusted third party. The proof that the certificate did actually come from the certifying authority is embodied in the components of the certificate itself: the certifying authority's public key, and its signature (by its private key) of (1) the user's name, (2) the certificate's expiration date (or the password's expiration date of the user in question on the certifying authority, whichever is sooner), and (3) the user's public key. The components of a certificate are shown in Figure 10.2.

The user contacts the CA for a certificate using the *getauthinfo(8)* command. This initiates the key exchange protocol based on the Diffie–Hellman [14] key exchange protocol. The details of this key exchange protocol are described in *login(6)*.

The result of the interaction (if successful) is (1) a secret key for the user, (2) a public key for the user, (3) a certificate which is as described above, (4) the public key of the certifying authority, and (5) the Diffie–Hellman parameters *base, α*, and *modulus, p*, which are used in mutual authentication.

10.2   Mutual Authentication

Mutual authentication of two hosts that wish to communicate occurs via the *Station to Station Protocol*, which works in the following manner.

The two hosts (say, a and b) must first have a common certificate authority. They each obtain a certificate from their common certifying authority before they commence communication. The common certifying authority defines the system-wide Diffie–Hellman parameters, the *base α* and *modulus p*.

Each host then generates a random number, say, r_a and r_b respectively, with magnitude less than, but in the range of, the system-wide modulus, p. The two hosts then each compute the value of the system-wide base raised to the power of this random number. Thus host a computes α^{r_a} and host b computes α^{r_b}, each computation being performed *modulo p*. These computed values, together with their public keys and certificates as obtained from the CA (Figure 10.2) are then exchanged. Each host then uses the CA's public key (obtained from the CA) to verify the public key sent in the exchange against that contained in the certificate, also sent in the exchange.

The use of the random numbers helps guard against *replay attacks*, in which an interloper records the sequence of messages interchanged, and, for example, *replays* the messages from one party going to another, feigning that party's identity.

The signing of the exchanged public key and computed exponents help guard against *man-in-the-middle attacks*. A man-in-the-middle attack entails a third party intercepting the keys sent by the two communicating parties and replacing them with his own. Thus each party receives the key of the attacker rather than that of the party they intend to communicate with. The attacker may then decrypt and re-encrypt the messages as they pass through him. With the signing of the exchanged public keys, an effective attack would entail forging the public key of one of the authentic communicating parties, which would require an effective attack on the key signature algorithm.

At this point, hosts a and b now know the quantities $\alpha^{r_b} \bmod p$ and $\alpha^{r_a} \bmod p$, respectively. They then each sign these quantities with their private keys and exchange the signed quantities. At this point, each host can thus verify that the other is really who they say they are. They can now calculate the shared secret, $\alpha^{r_a \cdot r_b} \bmod p$, and this shared secret will be used as a key to encrypt further communications. This process is illustrated in Figure 10.3.

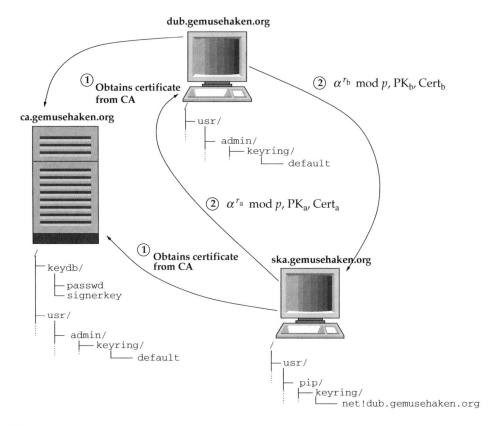

Figure 10.3   Steps in performing mutual authentication between two Inferno hosts. Both hosts obtain certificates from `ca.gemusehaken.org`.

10.2.1   Using Certificates

As previously mentioned, a certificate is like a letter of introduction. A user may want to gather several letters of introduction from third parties that are well trusted within certain circles to increase their chances of begin able to prove their authenticity during mutual authentication. Each such certificate can be thought of as a key on a key-ring: the more you have, the more doors you are likely to be able to open. During mutual authentication with a user on a remote host, a user will need to employ a certificate from the same certifying authority as the user at the remote end. It is therefore convention to store a certificate which is good for a connection to a remote host, say *remotehost*, in the file *keyring/net!remotehost* in the user's directory.

Each user may also maintain a default certificate which will be used in the absence of a more specific certificate for a remote host. This default certificate, stored in `keyring/default`, is also used as the server certificate for incoming requests.

Each server in a network must maintain a local certificate for mutual authentication during incoming connections; unlike the case described above, where a user (client) connects to a remote host (server), having previously obtained and saved a certificate to present to that host in a file named, say, *keyring/net!remotehost*, a server will have no *a priori* knowledge of what clients will be connecting to it. For this reason Inferno servers maintain a *default certificate*, stored in `keyring/default` of the administrative user (or whichever user it is that launches the actual server applications that will be serving incoming requests). This default certificate must be obtained from a certifying authority, and only incoming connections with certificates from the same certifying authority will be successful during mutual authentication.

Consider the example in Figure 10.4, which depicts a scenario in which mutual authentication between two hosts would fail. Two hosts on the network, `dub.gemusehaken.org` and `dub.gemusehaken.org`, wish to communicate securely. The communication is initiated by user 'pip' on `dub.gemusehaken.org`, with the connection being made to a service, the login daemon, running on `dub.gemusehaken.org`, which was started by the user 'admin' on `dub.gemusehaken.org`. All the system configuration files on `dub.gemusehaken.org` should be owned by the user 'admin'; in particular, the `/keydb/password` file will be readable and writable by 'admin' only. In the scenario depicted in Figure 10.4, user 'pip' obtains a certificate for `dub.gemusehaken.org` from his local machine, `dub.gemusehaken.org`, i.e. 'pip' acts as his own certifying authority. The user 'admin' on `dub.gemusehaken.org`, however, obtains a certificate from `ca.gemusehaken.org`. Mutual authentication of the connection between 'pip' and the login daemon will fail as shown in the figure.

10.3 Summary

This chapter briefly introduced the cryptographic facilities provided by Inferno for building secure systems. Inferno installations typically employ a central *certificate authority* (CA). The CA maintains a database of users and their passwords, and issues certificates for use in authentication procedures. The configuration and operation of the CA were described, and the protocol involved in mutual authentication between services and their clients was introduced.

Bibliographic Notes

An overview of Inferno's security model can be found in [58]. A good introduction to the principles of cryptography is [74]. A comprehensive coverage can also be found in [71]. The Diffie-Hellman key generation algorithm is described in [14], and its variant for performing key signatures, ElGamal, is described in [16]. The Secure Hash Algorithm (SHA-1) is described in [45]. SHA-1 is an update of the original description in [44]. The current Inferno security model will likely evolve to that in the fourth release of the Plan 9 operating system, which is described in [13]. Design and implementations of cryptographic filesystems can be found in [5, 6, 86].

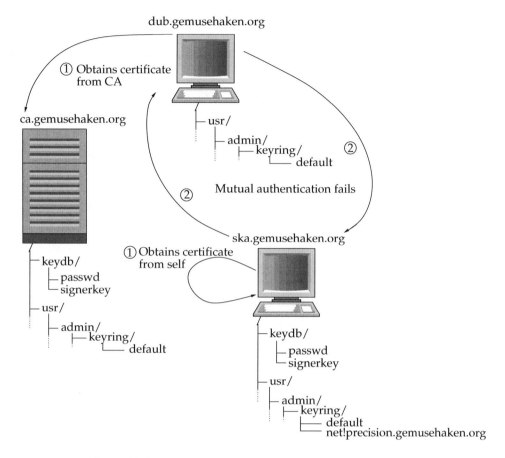

Figure 10.4   Failures to mutually authenticate in an Inferno network.

10.4   Chapter Example: Secure Hashes of Files

The following example implements a command-line utility for obtaining secure hashes of files using the SHA-1 algorithm:

```
# File : sha.b

implement SHA;

include "sys.m";
include "draw.m";
include "keyring.m";

sys : Sys;
keyring : Keyring;

stdin, stderr  : ref Sys->FD;
```

```
SHA : module
{
    init : fn(nil : ref Draw->Context, args : list of string);
};

init (nil : ref Draw->Context, args : list of string)
{
    sys = load Sys Sys->PATH;
    keyring = load Keyring Keyring->PATH;

    stdin = sys->fildes(0);
    stderr = sys->fildes(2);

    args = tl args;
    if (args == nil)
    {
        sha(nil);
    }
    else while (args != nil)
    {
        sha(hd args);

        args = tl args;
    }
}

sha(filename : string)
{
    cksum           : string;
    n           : int;
    nbytes          : big;
    fd        : ref Sys->FD;
    digeststate     : ref Keyring->DigestState;


    if (filename == nil)
    {
        fd = stdin;
        filename = "stdin";
    }
    else
    {
        fd = sys->open(filename, Sys->OREAD);
    }

    if (fd == nil)
    {
        sys->fprint(stderr, "SHA : Could not open input stream : %r\n");
        exit;
    }

    buf := array [Sys->ATOMICIO] of byte;
    while ((n = sys->read(fd, buf, len buf)) > 0)
    {
        digeststate = keyring->sha(buf[:n], n, nil, digeststate);
```

```
        nbytes += big n;
}
if (n < 0)
{
    sys->fprint(stderr, "SHA : Could not read input stream : %r\n");
    exit;
}

digest := array[Keyring->SHAdlen] of byte;
keyring->sha(buf[:n], n, digest, digeststate);

cksum += sys->sprint("SHA (%s) = ", filename);
for (i := 0; i < Keyring->SHAdlen; i++)
{
    cksum += sys->sprint("%2.2ux", int digest[i]);
}

sys->print("%s\n", cksum);
}
```

Discussion   The SHA module uses the facilities provided by the Keyring module to compute the SHA-1 secure hash of data in a file. The digest is computed by calling Keyring->sha(). The loop in which Keyring->sha() is first called computes and digests, maintaining state in the variable digeststate, and the call after the loop outputs the digest to the array digest.

Problems

10.1   Implement a *cryptographic filesystem filter* using FilterFS from Chapter 8. It should intercept all writes to disk and encrypt them, likewise intercepting reads, decrypting data read off the disk and forwarding the decrypted data.

11

Graphics

11.1 Introduction

Graphics in Inferno is facilitated by the Draw device. Like other devices in Inferno, it provides a filesystem interface (`/dev/draw`), but there is also a built-in module in the Limbo runtime system, Draw, which provides an easy means for Limbo programs to access the Draw device. This chapter describes the graphics system in Inferno release 3.0. Inferno's graphics subsystem is one area that is seeing exciting developments, and future releases will provide implementations of cutting-edge ideas from contemporary research in graphics.

The graphics system in Inferno was designed from the ground up to make it easy to build graphical applications in a networked environment, and on platforms with constrained memory and processing resources.

The filesystem interface to the Draw device (and all other devices for that matter), coupled with the use of a unifying protocol (Styx) for accessing devices be they local or remote, make it possible to build applications that seamlessly integrate accessing local and remote graphics hardware. The design of the graphics system reduces memory requirements of applications by allocating memory for graphics objects (images, fonts, the entire frame buffer, for that matter) only on the device with the physical display. Thus, for example, an application on a resource-limited computing device can display its output on another more capable device in a network, with all the memory for images, etc., on the remote device, and with any required image-manipulation operations performed by the hardware of the remote device.

The Inferno graphics model is built around eight primary structures: `Context`, `Display`, `Screen`, `Image`, `Rect`, `Point`, `Pointer` and `Font`. These structures are used

253

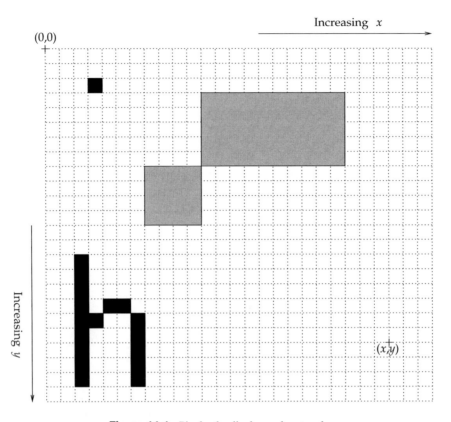

Figure 11.1 Pixels, the display and rectangles.

to represent information about the graphical device on which objects will be drawn, the location and nature of those objects, and facilities for interaction between screen objects and between a user and those objects. Each of these eight structures is represented by an ADT in the Draw module interface definition (located in /module/draw.m). They collectively define data structures and methods for operation on, and interaction between, these data structures.

Figure 11.1 illustrates the relation between some of these objects. The figure shows a physical display device (say, an LCD screen). The dotted grid lines demarcate the border between picture elements. Each pixel occupies a region of the physical display, its location being the grid point location of its upper left corner. The number of pixels in the horizontal and vertical extents are defined by the screen resolution (xresmax pixels in the horizontal extent by yresmax pixels in the vertical extent). The coordinate (0,0) is the location of the uppermost leftmost grid point, and the coordinate (xresmax,yresmax) is the location of the lowest rightmost grid point.

Since the location of a pixel is defined by the coordinates of the grid point to its upper left, the black pixel in Figure 11.1 is considered to be at location (3,2).

In terms of the eight structures previously mentioned, the entire grid of pixels is the `Display`, and it constitutes a new attachment to a draw device, which may be local or located elsewhere in the network. This is an important point to keep in mind. All the structures we will deal with are relative to a specific display.

Before any instances of these structures can be created, we must first have a reference or handle or *attachment* to a draw device. This means each `Display` ADT instance is related to a specific `/dev/draw` instance, and we must specify an instance of a `draw` device interface in the name space when allocating a new display. For example, we might allocate a new display specifying our local draw device in `/dev/draw`, or might specify one on a remote machine, bound at some location in the name space (say `/n/remote/dev/draw`).

A `Rect` is a region (rectangle) defined by two pixels, one at its upper left and the other *just beyond* its lower right-hand corner. Thus, for example, the two shaded rectangles in Figure 11.1 are specified by `((7,8),(11,12))` and `((11,3),(21,8))`. Images are made up of groups of pixels, whose individual locations are each specified by a `Point`, and regions are demarcated by a `Rect`. Windows are a special type of `Image`. One or more windows may be managed together and form a `Screen`.

A special case of such images is text, which is represented in a `Font`. Fonts can be thought of as *masks* or 'stencils' for transferring one image onto another. The shape of the mask describes the individual glyphs and the image in question describes the text color. The manner in which Inferno manages fonts is described in the manual pages *draw-font(2)* and *font(6)*. Colors in Inferno are represented as `Images`; thus the image for which a font acts as a mask need not be a fixed color, but could be any graphic, such as a picture of a mountain lion, or polar bear, or a meerkat.

Figure 11.2 shows a blowup of a region of an Inferno display. The individual colored boxes represent pixels. The figure shows both text and graphics, all being just a collection of pixels, and part of an `Image`. This `Image` may in fact be a window, and may be part of a collection of `Images` represented in a `Screen` and all these are by definition associated with some `Display`.

Screens and images are associated with a display. This is an important relation that underlies the organization of the Inferno graphics system. The display is the lowest-level entity, and corresponds directly to an actual physical display device and its associated memory. When screens and images are allocated, they are allocated out of the memory of the display device with which they are associated. If an application is connected to a display on its local computing device, the images, etc., that it will allocate are allocated from local memory. If on the other hand an application is connected to a remote display device, these images will be allocated from the memory of the remote device.

Let us say we have a Limbo program that wishes to draw an image on a screen. As has been discussed thus far, a connection would first have to be made to a display device. Once the application has a handle to the display, it may allocate screens, windows, images and fonts. All the storage for these allocated entities reside on the device with the display. If, for example, the display the application is connected to is a remote display on a different computing device, the allocated images reside on *that* remote device, with the associated display. Operations on these objects all occur on

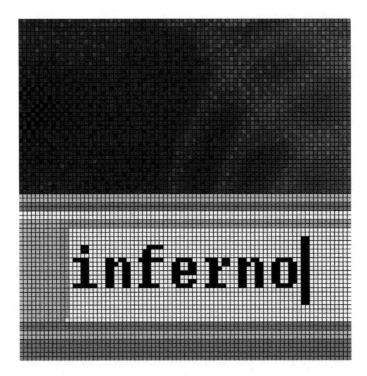

Figure 11.2 Fonts and graphics.

references to them; thus when an application manipulates objects on a remote display, these objects are not transferred over the network—the application essentially just issues commands to the remote display on how to manipulate the objects.

The following sections describe the different structures, detailing the data structures and methods accessible to Limbo programs, and also the interface through the /dev/draw filesystem where appropriate. Fundamental to all these structures is the Point and Rect. These two structures are used to define individual pixels and operations on them, as well as regions of the display and operations on these regions. Although it is easier to grasp the functioning of the graphics system by delving into the behavior of the Display and Screen structures, we will first look at Point and Rect, since they show up everywhere.

11.2   Point

```
Point: adt
{
    x:  int;
```

```
    y:  int;

    add:     fn(p: self Point, q: Point): Point;
    sub:     fn(p: self Point, q: Point): Point;
    mul:     fn(p: self Point, i: int): Point;
    div:     fn(p: self Point, i: int): Point;
    eq: fn(p: self Point, q: Point): int;
    in: fn(p: self Point, r: Rect): int;
};
```

Points represent locations on a display. They are usually manipulated by value, as opposed to most of the other objects we will discuss, which are manipulated by reference. Also unlike those objects, a Point is not associated with a Display.

The Point ADT captures the location of the pixel of interest in its two data fields, x and y, and provides methods for manipulating instances of its type.

All the methods of the Point ADT have as an implicit first argument the particular instance of the ADT (more on this type of construction in Chapter 4). The methods add, sub, mul and div are used to perform the obvious operations between a Point instance and another, and return a new Point that is the sum, difference, product or quotient, respectively.

The method eq returns a non-zero value if the two pixels are *equal* (i.e. have the same coordinates). The method in returns a non-zero value if the Point is contained within the specified region defined by the rectangle r of type Rect. This behavior is illustrated in the following examples:

```
#    Declare three Points, one at coordinates (0,0)
#    and a third at (640, 480):
a := Point(0,0);
b := Point(320, 240);
c := Point(640,480);

#    a = (a.x + b.x, a.y + b.y)
a = a.add(b);

#    b = (b.x - a.x, b.y - a.y)
b = b.sub(a);

#    a = (a.x*2, a.y*2)
a = a.mul(2);

#    c = (c.x/2, c.y/2)
c = c.div(2);

if (c.eq(a))
{
    sys->print("Points a and c are at the same location\n");
}

if (a.in(Rect(b, a)))
{
```

```
        sys->print("The Point at location (%d, %d) is defined to be
            within the Rect bounded by (%d, %d) and (%d, %d)\n",
            a.x, a.y, b.x, b.y, a.x, a.y);
    }
```

The above example hints at how a `Rect` is constructed out of two `Point`s. In the example, it was desired to ascertain whether the point a was within the region defined by a rectangle whose upper left vertex was defined by b and whose lower left vertex was defined by a. In the above, b and a, at the point of construction of the `Rect`, have the values (0,0) and (640,480), respectively.

The rectangle defined by `Rect(b,a)` is thus what we might refer to as a *well-formed* rectangle. What would it mean to define a rectangle (a,b) in this case? As we shall see in the next section, such a rectangle can be transformed to a canonical representation by methods in the `Rect` ADT.

11.3   Rect

```
Rect: adt
{
    min:        Point;
    max:        Point;

    canon:      fn(r: self Rect): Rect;
    dx:     fn(r: self Rect): int;
    dy:     fn(r: self Rect): int;
    eq:     fn(r: self Rect, s: Rect): int;
    Xrect:      fn(r: self Rect, s: Rect): int;
    inrect:     fn(r: self Rect, s: Rect): int;
    clip:       fn(r: self Rect, s: Rect): (Rect, int);
    contains:   fn(r: self Rect, p: Point): int;
    addpt:      fn(r: self Rect, p: Point): Rect;
    subpt:      fn(r: self Rect, p: Point): Rect;
    inset:      fn(r: self Rect, n: int): Rect;
};
```

A `Rect` defines a region on a display and is defined by the coordinates of its upper left (`min`) and lower right (`max`) pixels.

The `Rect` ADT, like the `Point` ADT discussed in the previous section, contains both data items representing the extent of the rectangle (`min` and `max`) and methods for operating on the rectangle.

The `canon` method puts a `Rect` in *canonical form*, i.e. if the location of the `min` and `max` fields is such that `min` is not located to the left and above of `max` or identical to it, the contents of `min` and `max` are swapped.

The `dx` and `dy` methods return the horizontal and vertical extents of the rectangle defined by the `Rect`, in pixels. The methods `eq` and `Xrect` return non-zero if the two rectangles in question are equal or intersecting, respectively. Whether a given rectangle is completely *within* another can be ascertained by calling the inrect method of the Rect instance with the potential container Rect as an argument.

While the Xrect method only specifies whether two rectangles intersect, the actual intersection (if any)—itself a rectangle—can be determined by the clip method. The clip method returns a tuple containing the resulting rectangle of the intersection, and an integer which is non-zero if the two rectangles actually intersect. If they do not, the returned Rect is that of the calling Rect instance. The method contains returns a non-zero value if the instance contains the pixel specified as an argument.

Translation of Rects can be achieved by the addpt and subpt methods. In these methods, the value of the argument point is added and subtracted, respectively, from both the min and max fields of the Rect instance.

Rectangles may be uniformly grown or shrunk with the inset method. Calling the inset method of a Rect instance with a positive integer n will return a new Rect whose min.x and max.y are smaller than the original rectangle by n pixels. Likewise, calling inset with a negative integer can be used to grow a rectangle.

11.4   Context

```
Context: adt
{
    screen:      ref Screen;
    display:     ref Display;
    cir:         chan of int;
    ckbd:        chan of int;
    cptr:        chan of ref Pointer;
    ctoappl:     chan of int;
    ctomux:      chan of int;
};
```

The graphics Context maintains a state pertaining to an attachment to a draw device, and provides a means for a higher-level application such as a window manager to make resources (the display, keyboard and mouse events) accessible to applications. It is the highest-level structure in the hierarchy of information pertaining to a graphical display.

The screen member is used to manage a collection of windows, and the display member represents an allocated display and the attendant memory for holding images—a frame buffer. Applications also receive keyboard and mouse events through the graphics Context. Thus far we have seen many references to this structure. All applications that will be run from the shell have as their first parameter a reference to a Context. For the non-graphical applications that we have looked at in previous chapters, it was not necessary to worry about the validity of the supplied

Context, since our applications did not draw on the screen. The next three sections describe the Display, Screen and Image structures in more detail.

The first application starting a graphical environment must construct a new context. As an example, by default, the Inferno login program or window manager allocates an initial Context, and applications launched from them will inherit this Context.

A new connection to the draw device must be made to allocate a new frame buffer, which will subsequently be referenced through the display field. Once a display has been allocated, it can be drawn upon directly through its image field, which is of type Image, using any of the methods of the Image ADT.

The display image is, however, not usually directly drawn upon, and is rather managed as a collection of screens, each screen being a collection of windows. The following program provides an example of the initialization of a Context, as would be performed by, say, a window manager. Stand-alone graphical applications are not required to craft a valid Context.

```
# File : drawcontext.b

implement DrawContext;

include "sys.m";
include "draw.m";

sys : Sys;
draw : Draw;
Screen, Display : import draw;

DrawContext : module
{
    init : fn(ctxt : ref Draw->Context, args : list of string);
};

init (ctxt : ref Draw->Context, nil : list of string)
{
    sys = load Sys Sys->PATH;
    draw = load Draw Draw->PATH;

    if (ctxt == nil)
    {
        sys->print("No valid graphics Context, allocating a new one...\n");

        #   First, allocate a new Display, then allocate a screen to
        #   manage windows on that Display. We set the screen fill
        #   to gray (RGB 99 99 99):
        display := Display.allocate(nil);
        screen := Screen.allocate(display.image, display.rgb(99,99,99), 1);

        #   We may now also want to allocate the appropriate event
        #   channels for I/O devices such as mice, keyboards, etc.,
        #   then construct a new ctxt:

        #   ...

        ctxt = ref (screen, display, nil, nil, nil, nil, nil);
```

```
        }
}
```

The first step in creating a valid graphics context is to allocate a new display or frame buffer to hold images. In the above example, that step is followed by the allocation of a *screen*, which is used to manage the display—a display may be managed as a collection of screens (it can be thought of as a collection of *display images*), each of which is usually a collection of windows.

Now a display has been allocated and can be referenced through `ctxt.display`, we may draw directly upon a display or manage the display using `ctxt.screen`.

11.5   Display and /dev/draw

```
Display: adt
{
  image:   ref Image;
  ones:    ref Image;
  zeros:   ref Image;

  #   Allocate and start refresh slave
  allocate:     fn(dev: string): ref Display;
  startrefresh: fn(d: self ref Display);

  #   Attach to existing Screen
  publicscreen:   fn(d: self ref Display, id: int): ref Screen;

  #   Image creation
  newimage:   fn(d: self ref Display, r: Rect, ldepth, repl, color: int):
              ref Image;
  color:      fn(d: self ref Display, color: int): ref Image;
  rgb:        fn(d: self ref Display, r, g, b: int): ref Image;

  #   I/O to files
  open:       fn(d: self ref Display, name: string): ref Image;
  readimage:  fn(d: self ref Display, fd: ref Sys->FD): ref Image;
  writeimage: fn(d: self ref Display, fd: ref Sys->FD, i: ref Image):
              int;

  #   Color map
  rgb2cmap:   fn(d: self ref Display, r, g, b: int): int;
  cmap2rgb:   fn(d: self ref Display, c: int): (int, int, int);
  cursor:     fn(d: self ref Display, i: ref Image, p: ref Point): int;
  cursorset:  fn(d: self ref Display, p : Point);
};
```

The `Display` ADT is used to manage an attachment to a *draw(3)* device. The draw device serves a filesystem in `/dev/draw`. This hierarchy initially contains the solitary file new. Reading new will allocate a new display. The data for images drawn by an application are stored in a display which is allocated from the draw device. As a consequence, when an application is drawing on a remote display, all the storage for images being drawn will be allocated from the memory of the remote device, and in performing operations on images on the display it is not necessary to move the corresponding image data across the network.

Reading /dev/draw/new will allocate a new display and create a new entry in the name space served by the draw device as /dev/draw/n^1, where n is the ID of the newly allocated Display. This directory corresponding to a new display is populated with three files: *ctl*, *data* and *refresh*. These can be used by applications to interact with the display; however, most applications will most likely use the equivalent procedural interface provided by the methods in the Display ADT of the Draw module (the allocate method of the Display ADT performs the equivalent function of reading /dev/draw/new).

Besides providing functionality for allocating new connections to the draw device, Display provides methods for the handling of images: methods for allocating memory for images, creating images of a particular color to be used to paint other images, methods for reading images from a file and writing images to files, manipulating the cursor and managing color maps.

In the previous section, we created a new graphics context by allocating a new Display using Display.allocate, and subsequently creating a new Screen to manage the display image. In creating the new screen, the rgb method of Display was used to create an image to provide the default background of the screen. Alternatively, any of the other methods in Display for creating images could have been used to create an image for the default background. For example, the following example uses Display.readimage to create an Image from a file and for use as the default background:

```
init (ctxt : ref Draw->Context, args : list of string)
{
    sys = load Sys Sys->PATH;
    draw = load Draw Draw->PATH;

    if (ctxt == nil)
    {
        imgfd := sys->open("/icons/inferno.bit", sys->OREAD);

        display := Display.allocate(nil);
        if (display == nil)
        {
            sys->print("Cannot initialize display : %r\n");
            exit;
        }

        screen := Screen.allocate(display.image,
```

---

[1]This entry in the name space will persist only as long as the client remains attached: the file new or one of the created subdirectories must be kept open.

```
            display.readimage(imgfd), 1);
        if (screen == nil)
        {
            sys->print("Cannot allocate screen on display : %r\n");
            exit;
        }

        display.image.draw(display.image.r, screen.fill,
                display.ones, display.image.r.min);
    }
}
```

11.6 Screen

```
Screen: adt
{
    id:         int;
    image:      ref Image;
    fill:       ref Image;
    display:    ref Display;

    #   Create new screen
    allocate:   fn(image, fill: ref Image, public: int):
                ref Screen;

    #   Allocate a new window
    newwindow:  fn(screen: self ref Screen, r: Rect, color: int):
                ref Image;

    #   Make group of windows visible
    top:        fn(screen: self ref Screen, wins: array of ref Image);
};
```

As mentioned previously, *screens* are generally used to manage displays, rather than operating on the displays directly. Like a Display, a Screen holds an Image which can be drawn upon. The Screen ADT provides methods for creating windows within this Image, Screen.newwindow, and managing these windows, Screen.top. Screens are allocated by calling the allocate method of the Screen ADT:

```
screen := Screen.allocate(display.image, display.readimage(imgfd), 1);
```

Note that the allocate method of the ADT *type* was called to yield an *instance* of the ADT.

Each Screen has a unique id, assigned at the time of allocation. A screen may be defined to be *public* at the time of allocation, such that it may be manipulated by any process with access to its associated `Display`. This is achieved when the process calls the `Display.publicscreen` method after attaching to a display.

The `image` member of a `Screen` ADT is that object on which actual drawing occurs, or on which new windows are allocated. It can be thought of as the top of the hierarchy of windows on a screen. Windows allocated on a screen will appear on top of this image. The actual color or graphic to be used to fill this image is determined by the `fill` parameter to `Screen.allocate` and is referenced in the `fill` member of the allocated entry. When windows on a screen are deleted, this image is used to repaint the underlying screen.

11.7   Image

```
Image: adt
{
    #   These data are local copies, but repl and clipr are
    #   monitored by the runtime and may be modified as desired.
    r:          Rect;
    clipr:      Rect;
    ldepth:     int;
    repl:       int;
    display:    ref Display;
    screen:     ref Screen;

    #   Graphics operators
    draw:       fn(dst: self ref Image, r: Rect, src: ref Image,
                mask: ref Image, p: Point);
    gendraw:        fn(dst: self ref Image, r: Rect, src: ref Image,
                p0: Point, mask: ref Image, p1: Point);
    line:       fn(dst: self ref Image, p0,p1: Point, end0,end1,
                radius: int, src: ref Image, sp: Point);
    poly:       fn(dst: self ref Image, p: array of Point, end0,
                end1,radius: int, src: ref Image, sp: Point);
    bezspline:  fn(dst: self ref Image, p: array of Point, end0,
                end1,radius: int, src: ref Image, sp: Point);
    fillpoly:       fn(dst: self ref Image, p: array of Point, wind: int,
                src: ref Image, sp: Point);
    fillbezspline:  fn(dst: self ref Image, p: array of Point, wind: int,
                src: ref Image, sp: Point);
    ellipse:        fn(dst: self ref Image, c: Point, a, b, thick: int,
                src: ref Image, sp: Point);
    fillellipse:    fn(dst: self ref Image, c: Point, a, b: int,
                src: ref Image, sp: Point);
    arc:            fn(dst: self ref Image, c: Point, a, b, thick: int,
                src: ref Image, sp: Point, alpha, phi: int);
    fillarc:        fn(dst: self ref Image, c: Point, a, b: int,
                src: ref Image, sp: Point, alpha, phi: int);
    bezier:     fn(dst: self ref Image, a,b,c,d: Point, end0,end1,
                radius: int, src: ref Image, sp: Point);
    fillbezier: fn(dst: self ref Image, a,b,c,d: Point, wind:int,
```

```
                 src: ref Image, sp: Point);
    text:        fn(dst: self ref Image, p: Point, src: ref Image,
                 sp: Point, font: ref Font, str: string): Point;
    arrow:       fn(a,b,c: int): int;

    #   Direct access to pixels
    readpixels: fn(src: self ref Image, r: Rect, data: array of byte):
                 int;
    writepixels:    fn(dst: self ref Image, r: Rect, data: array of byte):
                 int;

    #   Windowing
    top:         fn(win: self ref Image);
    bottom:      fn(win: self ref Image);
    flush:       fn(win: self ref Image, func: int);
    origin:      fn(win: self ref Image, log, scr: Point): int;
};
```

Images, represented by the Image ADT, form the core type of objects that are drawn on a display device. The pixels of a display are an image, as are windows (windows are Images with a few restrictions enforced), fonts, colors or generic pictures to be drawn on the screen.

Images are defined by the `Image` ADT in the Draw module. We have already encountered one of the methods of Images, `Image.draw`, that was used in previous discussions to effect the drawing of images on screens and displays subsequent to allocating them. Rather than diving into the details of the individual methods of the Image ADT, their use will be exposited through the examples in the remainder of the chapter.

11.8 Example: Pong

So, here we are. What should we do? What components do we need? We certainly need a reference to some physical display which will hold the images and display them to a happy gamer. There will be three primary objects that we will be dealing with on top of this display: two paddles and a ball. To satisfy the human urge to somehow *win something*, let's also throw in a scoreboard.

Now, on to the details of the design. Based on our discussion thus far, we can imagine the following data items as being the core of our game.

`display:Draw->Display.`	Our physical display device, frame buffer.
`scoreboard:Draw->Image.`	The scoreboard.
`gamescreen:Draw->Screen.`	The playground.
`ball:Draw->Image.`	The unfortunate ball.
`leftpaddle:Draw->Image.`	The paddle on the left-hand side of the screen.
`rightpaddle:Draw->Image.`	The paddle on the right-hand side of the screen.

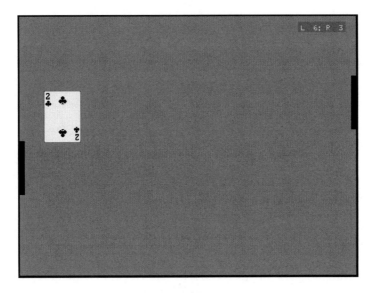

Figure 11.3 Pong.

The organization of these structures will be as follows. The display, `display`, is the top of the hierarchy. On the `display` is allocated a toplevel screen, `gamescreen`. The `scoreboard` is allocated as a window on `gamescreen` and will be drawn with text representing the current score of each player. The objects `ball`, `leftpaddle` and `rightpaddle` will be drawn on the `gamescreen`, allocated as windows thereupon. Figure 11.3 shows a screen capture of the game in play, and the complete implementation is listed below:

```
# File : pong.b
implement Pong;

include "sys.m";
include "draw.m";
include "keyring.m";
include "security.m";
include "daytime.m";
include "rand.m";

sys : Sys;
draw : Draw;
rand : Rand;
daytime : Daytime;

Display, Screen, Image, Rect, Point, Font: import draw;

MAXSPEED    : con 3;
INITGAMEDELAY  : con 30;

ZP         := (0,0);
```

```
gamedelay : int = INITGAMEDELAY;
gameover  : int = 0;
leftscore, rightscore : int = 0;
leftpaddlerect : Rect;
rightpaddlerect        : Rect;
scoreboxrect   : Rect;
ballimage : ref Image;
ballwin          : ref Image;
ballrect   : ref Rect;
scorebox  : ref Image;
font       : ref Font;
kbdpid          : int;

Pong : module
{
    init : fn(ctxt : ref Draw->Context, args : list of string);
};

init(ctxt : ref Draw->Context, nil : list of string)
{
    kbdchan          := chan of int;
    cmdchan          := chan of int;
    paddlespeed    := 10;
    display    : ref Display;
    gamescreen     : ref Screen;
    leftpaddle     : ref Image;
    rightpaddle    : ref Image;


    sys = load Sys Sys->PATH;
    draw = load Draw Draw->PATH;
    daytime = load Daytime Daytime->PATH;
    random := load Random Random->PATH;
    rand = load Rand Rand->PATH;
    rand->init(random->randomint(Random->ReallyRandom));

    if (ctxt == nil)
    {
        display = Display.allocate(nil);
        if (display == nil)
        {
            sys->raise(sys->sprint(
                "fail:Cannot initialize display : %r"));
        }
    }
    else
    {
        display = ctxt.display;
    }

    ballimage = display.open("ball.bit");
    if (ballimage == nil)
    {
        sys->print("Cannot read ball.bit : %r");
        exit;
```

```
}

spawn kbd(kbdchan);

font = Font.open(display, "*default*");
leftpaddlerect = Rect((0, 0), (10, 100));
rightpaddlerect = Rect((display.image.r.dx() - 10, 0),
               (display.image.r.dx(), 100));
scoreboxrect = Rect((display.image.r.dx() - 110, 10),
               (display.image.r.dx() - 20, 30));

#    The game screen is a public screen
gamescreen = Screen.allocate(display.image,
        display.rgb(147, 221, 0), 1);
if (gamescreen == nil)
{
    sys->raise(sys->sprint(
        "fail:Cannot allocate gamescreen on display : %r"));
}

#    Paint the display black
display.image.draw(display.image.r, display.rgb(147, 221, 0),
    display.ones, display.image.r.min);

#    Draw the scorebox
scorebox = gamescreen.newwindow(scoreboxrect, Draw->Red);
scorebox.draw(scoreboxrect, scorebox, scorebox,
        scoreboxrect.min);

#    Draw the paddles
leftpaddle = gamescreen.newwindow(leftpaddlerect, Draw->Black);
rightpaddle = gamescreen.newwindow(rightpaddlerect, Draw->Black);

leftpaddle.draw(leftpaddlerect, leftpaddle, leftpaddle,
        leftpaddlerect.min);
rightpaddle.draw(rightpaddlerect, rightpaddle, rightpaddle,
        rightpaddlerect.min);

#    Initial score
updatescore();

#    Spawn a new thread to handle ball
spawn    pongball(gamescreen, cmdchan);

while (!gameover)
{
    case (c := <- kbdchan)
    {
        'q'  =>
        {
            gameover = 1;
            cmdchan <- = 'q';
            endsplash(display);

            exit;
        }
```

```
        'x'   =>
        {
            leftpaddlerect = leftpaddlerect.addpt(
                (0, paddlespeed));
            leftpaddle.origin(ZP, leftpaddlerect.min);
        }
        'c'   =>
        {
            leftpaddlerect = leftpaddlerect.subpt(
                    (0, paddlespeed));
            leftpaddle.origin(ZP, leftpaddlerect.min);
        }
        'a'   =>
        {
            rightpaddlerect = rightpaddlerect.addpt(
                    (0, paddlespeed));
            rightpaddle.origin(ZP, rightpaddlerect.min);
        }
        's'   =>
        {
            rightpaddlerect = rightpaddlerect.subpt(
                    (0, paddlespeed));
            rightpaddle.origin(ZP, rightpaddlerect.min);
        }
        }
    }
}

pongball(gamescreen : ref Screen, cmdchan : chan of int)
{
    vector        : ref Point;
    midx       : int = 0;


    midx = gamescreen.image.r.dx()/2;
    ballrect = ref Rect((midx, 0),
            (midx+ballimage.r.dx(), ballimage.r.dy()));
    ballwin = gamescreen.newwindow(*ballrect,
            Draw->Yellow);
    ballwin.draw(ballwin.r, ballimage,
            nil, ballimage.r.min);
    vector = ref Point(rand->rand(MAXSPEED)+1,
            rand->rand(MAXSPEED)+1);

top: while (1)
    alt
    {
        cmd := <-cmdchan =>
        {
            break top;
        }

        * =>
        if (!(sys->millisec() % gamedelay))
        {
            if ((leftscore == 100) || (rightscore == 100))
```

```
                        {
                                endsplash(scorebox.display);
                                gameover = 1;

                                break top;
                        }
                        moveball(gamescreen, vector);
                        ballwin.origin(ZP, ballrect.min);
                }
        }
}

moveball(gamescreen : ref Screen, vector : ref Point)
{
        *ballrect = (*ballrect).addpt(*vector);

        #    If we hit bottom or top, reflect y-axis
        if ((ballrect.max.y >= gamescreen.image.r.max.y) ||
            (ballrect.min.y <= gamescreen.image.r.min.y))
        {
                *vector = (vector.x, -vector.y);
                return;
        }

        #    If we hit a paddle, reflect y-axis
        if (((*ballrect).Xrect(leftpaddlerect)) ||
            ((*ballrect).Xrect(rightpaddlerect)))
        {
                *vector = (-vector.x, vector.y);
                return;
        }

        if (ballrect.max.x >= gamescreen.image.r.max.x)
        {
                leftscore++;
                updatescore();
                resetball(gamescreen, vector);
        }
        else if (ballrect.min.x <= gamescreen.image.r.min.x)
        {
                rightscore++;
                updatescore();
                resetball(gamescreen, vector);
        }
}

resetball(gamescreen : ref Screen, vector : ref Point)
{
        midx := gamescreen.image.r.dx()/2;
        ballrect = ref Rect((midx, 0),
                (midx+ballimage.r.dx(), ballimage.r.dy()));

        ballwin.origin(ZP, ballrect.min);

        invert := 1;
        if (rand->rand(2))
```

```
        {
            invert = -1;
        }

        *vector = Point(invert*(rand->rand(MAXSPEED)+1),
                rand->rand(MAXSPEED)+1);
}

updatescore()
{
        scorestring := sys->sprint("L %2d: R %2d",
                leftscore, rightscore);
        textbox := scorebox.r.inset(5);

        #       Wipe the scoreboard
        scorebox.draw(scorebox.r, scorebox.display.color(Draw->Red),
                scorebox.display.ones, scorebox.r.min);

        #       Re-draw
        scorebox.text(textbox.min, scorebox.display.color(Draw->White),
                (0, 0), font, scorestring);
        scorebox.draw(scorebox.r, scorebox, scorebox.display.ones,
                scorebox.r.min);
}

endsplash(display : ref Display)
{
        font = Font.open(display, "/fonts/lucida/unicode.32.font");
        if (font == nil)
        {
            sys->print("Could not load font : %r");
            return;
        }

        display.image.text(display.image.r.inset(display.image.r.dx()/3).min,
                display.color(Draw->Green),
                (0, 0), font, "Game Over");

        display.image.draw(display.image.r, display.image,
                display.ones, display.image.r.min);

        fd := sys->open("#p/"+string kbdpid+"/ctl", sys->OWRITE);
        if (fd != nil)
        {
            sys->fprint(fd, "kill");
        }
}

kbd(kbdchan : chan of int)
{
        buf := array [1] of byte;

        #       Since this thread blocks on sys calls to read(), we will
        #       have to kill it forcefully when the game ends:
        kbdpid = sys->pctl(0,nil);
```

```
    kfd := sys->open("/dev/keyboard", sys->OREAD);
    if (kfd == nil)
    {
        sys->raise(sys->sprint("fail:Could not open /dev/cons : %r"));
    }

    while (sys->read(kfd, buf, 1) == 1)
    {
        kbdchan <-= int buf[0];
    }
    sys->raise(sys->sprint(
        "fail:Could not read from /dev/cons or ctxt.ckbd: %r"));
}
```

11.9 The Tk and Wmlib Modules

In addition to the facilities provided by the Draw module, Inferno provides higher-level means of constructing graphical user interfaces through the Tk module. The Tk module implements a significant portion of the popular graphical toolkit. Instead of having bindings to Tcl, the command language usually used to provide the glue for Tk applications in other systems, the Inferno Tk module provides a means for binding Tk events to Limbo channels. This section provides a brief overview of the interaction between Inferno's implementation of Tk and Limbo applications. Tk is best described elsewhere, for example, in [48], and the peculiarities of Inferno's implementation of Tk are described in [32] and in the manual pages *tk(2)* and *wmlib(2)*.

The module interface definition for the Tk module is shown below:

```
Tk: module
{
    PATH:    con      "$Tk";

    Tki:     type ref Draw->Image;

    Toplevel: adt
    {
        id:      int;
        image:   Tki;
    };

    toplevel:  fn(screen: ref Draw->Screen, arg: string): ref Toplevel;
    intop:     fn(screen: ref Draw->Screen, x, y: int): ref Toplevel;
    windows:   fn(screen: ref Draw->Screen): list of ref Toplevel;
    namechan:  fn(t: ref Toplevel, c: chan of string, n: string): string;
    cmd:       fn(t: ref Toplevel, arg: string): string;
    mouse:     fn(screen: ref Draw->Screen, x, y, button: int);
    keyboard:  fn(screen: ref Draw->Screen, key: int);
    imageput:  fn(t: ref Toplevel, name: string, i, m: Tki): string;
    imageget:  fn(t: ref Toplevel, name: string) : (Tki, Tki, string);
```

```
};
```

Widgets are constructed by passing textual Tk command strings to the Tk module using the cmd function of the Tk module. The namechan function is used to bind event channel names in the Tk command strings to Limbo channels.

The first step in constructing a GUI using the Tk module is to create a 'toplevel' entity on which individual widgets will be created. This is done with the toplevel function, which returns a reference to a Toplevel ADT instance. This instance contains an ID for the toplevel widget, as well as a reference to the Image that represents the pixels of the toplevel widget.

After creating the toplevel widget, Tk widgets are created by calling the cmd function with a reference to the toplevel widget and a Tk command string, e.g. to create a button widget. These Tk command strings are mostly identical to those used in Tcl/Tk. The peculiarities of Limbo/Tk are described in [32]. There is a command-line utility, *tkcmd(1)*, similar to the *wish* utility in implementations of Tcl/Tk, for interactively building Tk widgets. It is useful in prototyping Tk widgets before they are implemented in Limbo applications.

Events on such a widget can be specified in Tk to be sent on a Tk event name. In order to make such events available to a Limbo program for possible actions, Tk event names can be bound to Limbo channels using the namechan function.

The following example creates a simple Tk widget, a solitary button on the screen. Pressing the button causes a string to be sent on a channel:

```
# File : simple-tk.b

implement SimpleTk;

include "sys.m";
include "draw.m";
include "tk.m";

draw : Draw;
sys  : Sys;
tk   : Tk;

SimpleTk : module
{
    init : fn(ctxt : ref Draw->Context, nil : list of string);
};

init(ctxt : ref Draw->Context, nil : list of string)
{
    sys = load Sys Sys->PATH;
    draw = load Draw Draw->PATH;
    tk = load Tk Tk->PATH;

    #    Create a top level Tk widget:
    t := tk->toplevel(ctxt.screen, "");

    #    Create channel on which Tk events will be sent and
```

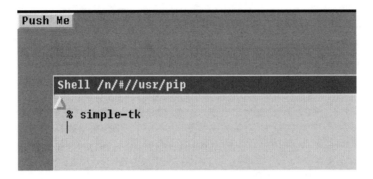

Figure 11.4   A simple button widget using the Tk module.

```
#    associate the channel with the Tk event name 'cmd':
cmdchan := chan of string;
tk->namechan(t, cmdchan, "cmd");

#    Send literal strings to Tk to create a button with the
#    text 'Push Me'. Pushing it sends the string 'pressed'
#    on the channel associated with Tk name 'cmd':
tk->cmd(t, "button .b -text {Push Me} -command {send cmd pressed}");
tk->cmd(t, "pack .b");
tk->cmd(t, "update");

#    Wait for events on the channel 'cmdchan' and service them:
for (;;)
alt
{
    c := <- cmdchan =>
    {
        if (c == "pressed")
        {
            sys->print("... catch you later!\n");
            exit;
        }
    }
}
}
```

The example above creates a solitary button on the screen, as shown in Figure 11.4. Usually, however, we want to build GUIs complete with title bars. The Wmlib module interacts with the *wm(1)* window manager to provide such functionality.

Wmlib provides a function, `titlebar`, for creating a toplevel Tk widget and associating it with a titlebar. It takes as arguments a reference to a display `Screen` and a name for the toplevel widget (just as in `tk->toplevel`), as well as a string to be displayed on the title bar and buttons to be placed on the title bar.

A call to the `titlebar` function returns a tuple consisting of a reference to a Tk `Toplevel` and a channel on which events from the titlebar buttons will be sent. For example, the following shows how one would allocate a new Tk `Toplevel` instance with an attached title bar:

```
(toplevel,menubut) := wmlib->titlebar(ctxt.screen, "","My GUI",Wmlib->Hide);
```

The above will create a new Tk toplevel, with a title bar reading 'My GUI', and a title bar button to hide the application window. Clicking on this button will cause an event (the string 'task') to be sent on the `menubut` channel that is returned by `titlebar`. The application window is automatically minimized by the window manager when the 'hide' button is pressed. Title bars created by the Wmlib `titlebar` function by default have a button for closing the window, and when pressed, this button causes the string 'exit' to be sent on the title bar's event channel.

The Wmlib module provides a function, `cmds`, analogous to the `cmd` function of the Tk module, which takes an array of strings. It is therefore often convenient to define the Tk widget as an array of string, and to pass this to `cmds`. The following example illustrates these concepts. It implements three slider widgets which are used to control the color of a frame area, as shown in Figure 11.5. Note that the `init` function of the Wmlib module must be called to initialize the module before calling any other Wmlib functions.

```
# File : rgbsliders.b

implement RGBSliders;

include "sys.m";
include "draw.m";
include "tk.m";
include   "wmlib.m";

sys  : Sys;
draw : Draw;
tk   : Tk;
wmlib     : Wmlib;

RGBSliders: module
{
    init : fn(ctxt: ref Draw->Context, nil: list of string);
};

sliders_cfg := array[] of
{
    "frame .f2",
    "frame .f2.c -bg black -width 100 -height 100",
    "label .f2.l -text {#000000}",
    "frame .f",
    "scale .f.r -from 0 -to 255 -height 100 -orient vertical "+
        "-showvalue 1 -command {send cmd r}",
    "scale .f.g -from 0 -to 255 -height 100 -orient vertical "+
        "-showvalue 1 -command {send cmd g}",
    "scale .f.b -from 0 -to 255 -height 100 -orient vertical "+
```

```
            "-showvalue 1 -command {send cmd b}",
    ".f.r set 0",
    ".f.g set 0",
    ".f.b set 0",
    "pack .f.r .f.g .f.b -side left",
    "pack .f2.l .f2.c -side top",
    "pack .f .f2 -side left",
    "pack propagate . 0",
    "focus .f2",
    "update",
};

init(ctxt: ref Draw->Context, nil: list of string)
{
    red   := 0;
    green    := 0;
    blue := 0;

    sys = load Sys Sys->PATH;
    draw = load Draw Draw->PATH;
    tk = load Tk Tk->PATH;
    wmlib = load Wmlib Wmlib->PATH;

    wmlib->init();
    (toplevel, menubut) := wmlib->titlebar(ctxt.screen, "",
                "RGB Sliders", Wmlib->Hide);

    cmd := chan of string;
    tk->namechan(toplevel, cmd, "cmd");
    wmlib->tkcmds(toplevel, sliders_cfg);

    for(;;)
    alt
    {
        s := <- menubut =>
            if (s == "exit")
            {
                return;
            }
            wmlib->titlectl(toplevel, s);

        s := <- cmd =>
            c : string;
            (n, word) := sys->tokenize(s, " \t");
            case (hd word)
            {
                "r" => red = int hd tl word;
                "g" => green = int hd tl word;
                "b" => blue = int hd tl word;
            }

            c = sys->sprint("%2x%2x%2x", red, green, blue);
            for (i := 0; i < len c; i++)
            {
                if (c[i] == ' ')
                {
```

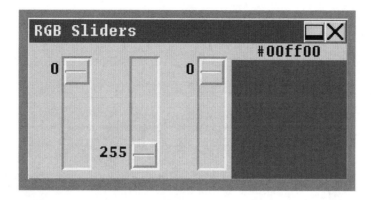

Figure 11.5 A Tk GUI using the Wmlib module to provide a title bar.

```
                    c[i] = '0';
            }
    }

    tk->cmd(toplevel, ".f2.l configure -text {#" + c + "}");
    tk->cmd(toplevel, ".f2.c configure -bg #" + c);
    tk->cmd(toplevel, "focus .f2");
    tk->cmd(toplevel, "update");
    }
}
```

11.10 Summary

This chapter introduced the graphics facilities provided by Inferno. Underlying the graphics subsystem of Inferno is the *draw* device. Like all other devices in Inferno, it is accessible through a filesystem interface, usually bound to /dev/draw. Through this interface, applications, be they local or remote, may access the graphics capabilities of a device. Limbo applications may access the draw device of their local host or that of a remote host over the network, and in either case the resources, such as memory for storing images, fonts and the like, are stored on the device with the actual physical display device. This makes it inexpensive to perform graphics operations distributed across a network, since the actual computation on graphics objects is performed at the site of display—applications simply send control messages to drive a remote display.

The *Draw* module provides a Limbo module interface to the resources of a local or remote graphics display, and removes the need for Limbo applications to drive the draw devices with control messages directly.

The Tk and Wmlib modules build on the functionality of the draw device, to provide higher-level constructs for building graphical user interfaces, such as title bars, pull-down menus, sliders, etc. The Tk module implements the popular Tk graphics toolkit, with glue provided by Limbo rather than Tcl (thus Limbo/Tk as opposed to Tcl/Tk).

Bibliographic Notes

Inferno's graphics system is described in more detail in the manual pages *draw-intro(2)*, *tk(2)*, *image(6)* and *font(6)* [79]. There are many texts that provide an introduction to interactive computer graphics, such as [17, 21, 73]. Inferno's graphics system will be evolving to something along the lines of the current graphics model in the Plan 9 operating system. The theoretical foundation for this is provided in [57]. A good reference text on Tk is [48]. Inferno's Tk implementation is described in [32]. Cellular automata or cellular arrays (CAs) were first proposed by John von Neumann [46]. John Conway's *Game of Life* [4], is one of the most popular CA rules. Norm Margolus and Tommaso Toffoli have built hardware CA machines, which are described in [35, 78]. The ancestors of the game *Pong* are games developed by Ralph H. Baer *circa* 1966 [3, 67] and Nolan Bushnell (of Atari) [8].

11.10.1 Chapter Example: Conway's Game of Life

The following is an implementation of Conway's Game of Life.

```
# File : gameoflife-wm.b
implement GameOfLife;

include "sys.m";
include "draw.m";
include "tk.m";
include "wmlib.m";
include "rand.m";
include "keyring.m";
include "security.m";

draw    : Draw;
rand    : Rand;
sys : Sys;
tk  : Tk;
wmlib   : Wmlib;

BOXSIZE     := 3;
CELLDENSITY := 5;
LDEPTH      := 8;
GENERATIONS := 1000;
ZP      := (0,0);
generation  := 0;

Display, Screen, Image, Rect, Point, Font: import draw;

Cell : adt
{
    boxarray    : array of Point;
    boxrect     : Rect;
    image       : ref Draw->Image;
    oldstate, state : int;
};

ca      : array of array of Cell;
gamewinbuf  : ref Image;
gamewinrect : Rect;
toplevel    : ref Tk->Toplevel;

GameOfLife : module
{
    init : fn(ctxt : ref Draw->Context, nil : list of string);
};

init(ctxt : ref Draw->Context, nil : list of string)
{
    LDEPTH = ctxt.display.image.ldepth;
    menubutton := chan of string;

    sys = load Sys Sys->PATH;
    tk = load Tk Tk->PATH;
    draw = load Draw Draw->PATH;
```

```
random := load Random Random->PATH;

rand = load Rand Rand->PATH;
rand->init(random->randomint(Random->ReallyRandom));

wmlib = load Wmlib Wmlib->PATH;
wmlib->init();

(toplevel, menubutton) = wmlib->titlebar(ctxt.screen, "",
                "gameoflife", Wmlib->Hide);

#   An off screen image to buffer the window updates
gamewinrect = ((0, 0), (300, 300));
gamewinbuf = ctxt.display.newimage(gamewinrect, LDEPTH,
            0, Draw->Black);

dx := gamewinrect.dx();
dy := gamewinrect.dy();

tk->cmd(toplevel, sys->sprint(
    "canvas .c -height %d -width %d -background white", dx, dy));
tk->cmd(toplevel, "image create bitmap gamewin");
tk->cmd(toplevel,
    ".c create image 0 0 -image gamewin -anchor nw -tags gamewin");
tk->cmd(toplevel, "pack .c -side bottom -fill both");
    tk->cmd(toplevel, "focus .c");
tk->cmd(toplevel, "update");

ca = array [dx/BOXSIZE + 1] of {* => array [dy/BOXSIZE + 1] of Cell};

xi := 0;
yi := 0;

#   Allocate images for each grid location, draw offscreen
for (y := 0; y < dy; y += BOXSIZE)
{
    xi = 0;
    for (x := 0; x < dx; x += BOXSIZE)
    {
        #   Roll dice to set state
        ca[xi][yi].state = Draw->White;
        ca[xi][yi].oldstate = Draw->White;

        if (!rand->rand(CELLDENSITY))
        {
            ca[xi][yi].state = Draw->Red;
            ca[xi][yi].oldstate = Draw->Red;
        }

        #   Draw an off-screen bordered box
        ca[xi][yi].boxrect = Rect((x,y), (x+BOXSIZE,y+BOXSIZE));
        ca[xi][yi].boxarray = array [] of {(x,y), (x+BOXSIZE,y),
            (x+BOXSIZE,y+BOXSIZE), (x,y+BOXSIZE), (x,y)};
        ca[xi][yi].image = ctxt.display.newimage(ca[xi][yi].boxrect,
                LDEPTH, 0, ca[xi][yi].state);
```

```
            #   Could alternatively be done using the clipr
            ca[xi][yi].image.poly(ca[xi][yi].boxarray, Draw->Endsquare,
                Draw->Endsquare, 0, ctxt.display.color(Draw->Black), ZP);
            gamewinbuf.draw(gamewinrect, ca[xi][yi].image, nil, ZP);

            xi++;
        }
        yi++;
    }

    #   Draw the buffered offscreen image in one go onto the screen
    tk->imageput(toplevel, "gamewin", gamewinbuf, nil);
    tk->cmd(toplevel, ".c coords gamewin 0 0");
    tk->cmd(toplevel, "update");

    cmd := chan of string;
    spawn update(xi, yi, ctxt, cmd);

    for (;;)
    {
        case (menu := <-menubutton)
        {
            "exit" =>
                cmd <-= "quit";
                exit;

            * =>
                tk->cmd(toplevel, "focus .c");
                wmlib->titlectl(toplevel, menu);
        }
    }
}

update(xmax, ymax : int, ctxt : ref Draw->Context, quit : chan of string)
{
    x, y : int = 0;

    while ()
    alt
    {
        <-quit => exit;

        * =>
        if (generation++ == GENERATIONS)
        {
            reset(xmax, ymax, ctxt);
            generation = 0;
        }

        for (y = 0; y < ymax; y++)
        {
            for (x = 0; x < xmax; x++)
            {
                neighbors := 0;

                xtop := x-1;
```

```
ytop := y-1;
xbottom := x+1;
ybottom := y+1;

if (x == 0)
    xtop = x+xmax-1;
if (x == xmax-1)
    xbottom = 0;
if (y == 0)
    ytop = y+ymax-1;
if (y == ymax-1)
    ybottom = 0;

neighbors += (ca[xtop][ytop].oldstate == Draw->Red);
neighbors += (ca[x][ytop].oldstate == Draw->Red);
neighbors += (ca[xbottom][ytop].oldstate == Draw->Red);
neighbors += (ca[xbottom][y].oldstate == Draw->Red);
neighbors += (ca[xbottom][ybottom].oldstate == Draw->Red);
neighbors += (ca[x][ybottom].oldstate == Draw->Red);
neighbors += (ca[xtop][ybottom].oldstate == Draw->Red);
neighbors += (ca[xtop][y].oldstate == Draw->Red);


if (ca[x][y].oldstate == Draw->Red)
{
    if ((neighbors == 2)||(neighbors == 3))
        ca[x][y].state = Draw->Red;
    else
        ca[x][y].state = Draw->White;
}
else if (ca[x][y].oldstate == Draw->White)
{
    if (neighbors == 3)
        ca[x][y].state = Draw->Red;
    else
        ca[x][y].state = Draw->White;
}

if (ca[x][y].oldstate == ca[x][y].state)
{
    continue;
}

ca[x][y].image.draw(ca[x][y].boxrect,
    ctxt.display.color(ca[x][y].state), nil, ZP);

#   Could alternatively be done using the clipr
ca[x][y].image.poly(ca[x][y].boxarray,
    Draw->Endsquare, Draw->Endsquare, 0,
    ctxt.display.color(Draw->Black),
    ca[x][y].boxrect.min);

gamewinbuf.draw(gamewinrect, ca[x][y].image,
    nil, (0, 0));
    }
}
```

```
        for (y = 0; y < ymax; y++)
        {
            for (x = 0; x < xmax; x++)
            {
                ca[x][y].oldstate = ca[x][y].state;
            }
        }

        #   Draw the buffered offscreen image in one go
        tk->imageput(toplevel, "gamewin", gamewinbuf, nil);
        tk->cmd(toplevel, ".c coords gamewin 0 0");
        tk->cmd(toplevel, "update");
    }
}

reset(xmax, ymax : int, ctxt : ref Draw->Context)
{
    for (y := 0; y < ymax; y++)
    {
        for (x := 0; x < xmax; x++)
        {
            if (!rand->rand(CELLDENSITY))
            {
                ca[x][y].state = Draw->Red;
                ca[x][y].oldstate = Draw->Red;
            }
            else
            {
                ca[x][y].state = Draw->White;
                ca[x][y].oldstate = Draw->White;
            }

            ca[x][y].image.draw(ca[x][y].boxrect,
                ctxt.display.color(ca[x][y].state), nil, ZP);

            ca[x][y].image.poly(ca[x][y].boxarray,
                Draw->Endsquare, Draw->Endsquare, 0,
                ctxt.display.color(Draw->Black), ca[x][y].boxrect.min);

            gamewinbuf.draw(gamewinrect, ca[x][y].image, nil, (0, 0));
        }
    }

    #   Draw the buffered offscreen image in one go onto the screen
    tk->imageput(toplevel, "gamewin", gamewinbuf, nil);
    tk->cmd(toplevel, ".c coords gamewin 0 0");
    tk->cmd(toplevel, "update");

    #   Wait two seconds before restarting
    sys->sleep(2000);
}
```

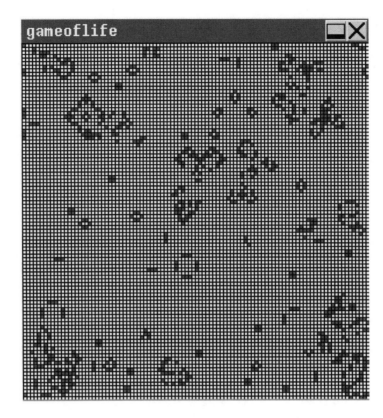

Figure 11.6   Screenshot of the Game of Life in progress.

Discussion   A screenshot from the execution of the Game of Life is shown in Figure 11.6.

Problems

11.1   Implement a graphing utility that permits the plotting of data and output to Inferno bit images or encapsulated postscript (using the *pslib(2)* module).

11.2   Implement a simple 'sketch' program using the facilities provided by the Draw module.

Appendix A
Limbo Language Grammar

A.1 Limbo Language Grammar

```
program:
        implement identifier ; top-declaration-sequence

top-declaration-sequence:
        top-declaration
        top-declaration-sequence top-declaration

top-declaration:
        declaration
        identifier-list := expression ;
        identifier-list = expression ;
        ( identifier-list ) := expression ;
        module-declaration
        function-definition
        adt-declaration

declaration:
        identifier-list : type ;
        identifier-list : type = expression ;
        identifier-list : con expression ;
        identifier-list : import identifier ;
        identifier-list : type type ;
        include string-constant ;

identifier-list:
        identifier
        identifier-list , identifier
```

```
expression-list:
      expression
      expression-list , expression

type:
      data-type
      function-type

data-type:
      byte
      int
      big
      real
      string
      tuple-type
      array of data-type
      list of data-type
      chan of data-type
      adt-type
      ref adt-type
      module-type
      module-qualified-type
      type-name

tuple-type:
      ( data-type-list )

data-type-list:
      data-type
      data-type-list , data-type

adt-type:
      identifier
      module-qualified-type

module-type:
      identifier

module-qualified-type:
      identifier -> identifier

type-name:
      identifier

function-type:
      fn function-arg-ret

function-arg-ret:
      ( formal-arg-listopt )
      ( formal-arg-listopt ) : data-type

formal-arg-list:
      formal-arg
      formal-arg-list , formal-arg

formal-arg:
      nil-or-D-list : type
      nil-or-D : self refopt identifier
      nil-or-D : self identifier
      *

nil-or-D-list:
      nil-or-D
      nil-or-D-list , nil-or-D
```

```
nil-or-D:
        identifier
        nil

module-declaration:
        identifier : module { mod-member-listopt } ;

mod-member-list:
        mod-member
        mod-member-list mod-member

mod-member:
        identifier-list : function-type ;
        identifier-list : data-type ;
        adt-declaration ;
        identifier-list : con expression ;
        identifier-list : type type ;

adt-declaration:
        identifier : adt { adt-member-listopt } ;

adt-member-list:
        adt-member
        adt-member-list adt-member

adt-member:
        identifier-list : cyclicopt  data-type ;
        identifier-list : function-type ;

function-definition:
        function-name-part function-arg-ret { statements }

function-name-part:
        identifier
        function-name-part . identifier

statements:
        (empty)
        statements declaration
        statements statement

statement:
        expression ;
        ;
        { statements }
        if ( expression ) statement
        if ( expression ) statement else statement
        labelopt  while ( expressionopt ) statement
        labelopt  do statement while ( expressionopt ) ;
        labelopt  for ( expressionopt ; expressionopt ; expressionopt ) statement
        labelopt  case expression { qual-statement-sequence }
        labelopt  alt { qual-statement-sequence }
        break identifieropt ;
        continue identifieropt ;
        return expressionopt ;
        spawn term ( expression-listopt ) ;
        exit ;

label:
        identifier :

qual-statement-sequence:
        qual-list =>
        qual-statement-sequence qual-list =>
        qual-statement-sequence statement
        qual-statement-sequence declaration
```

```
qual-list:
        qualifier
        qual-list or qualifier

qualifier:
        expression
        expression to expression
        *

expression:
        binary-expression
        lvalue-expression assignment-operator expression
        ( lvalue-expression-list ) = expression
        send-expression
        declare-expression
        load-expression

binary-expression:
        monadic-expression
        binary-expression binary-operator binary-expression

binary-operator: one of
        * / % + - << >> < > <= >= == != & ^ | :: && ||

assignment-operator: one of
        = &= |= ^= <<= >>= += -= *= /= %=

lvalue-expression:
        identifier
        nil
        term [ expression ]
        term [ expression : ]
        term . identifier
        ( lvalue-expression-list )
        * monadic-expression

lvalue-expression-list:
        lvalue
        lvalue-expression-list , lvalue

expression:
        term
        monadic-operator monadic-expression
        array [ expression ] of data-type
        array [ expressionopt ] of { init-list }
        list of { expression-list }
        chan of data-type
        data-type monadic-expression

term:
        identifier
        constant
        real-constant
        string-constant
        nil
        ( expression-list )
        term . identifier
        term -> term
        term ( expression-listopt )
        term [ expression ]
        term [ expression : expression ]
        term [ expression : ]
        term ++
        term --

monadic-operator: one of
        + -! ~ ref * <- hd tl len
```

```
init-list:
        element
        init-list , element

element:
        expression
        expression => expression
        * => expression

send-expression:
        lvalue-expression <- = expression

declare-expression:
        lvalue-expression := expression

load-expression:
        load identifier expression
```

Appendix B
Module Reference

B.1 The Bufio Module Interface

```
Bufio: module
{
    PATH:       con "/dis/lib/bufio.dis";

    SEEKSTART:  con Sys->SEEKSTART;
    SEEKRELA:   con Sys->SEEKRELA;
    SEEKEND:    con Sys->SEEKEND;
    OREAD:      con Sys->OREAD;
    OWRITE:     con Sys->OWRITE;
    ORDWR:      con Sys->ORDWR;
    EOF:        con -1;
    ERROR:      con -2;

    Iobuf: adt
    {
        seek:       fn(b: self ref Iobuf, n, where: int): int;
        read:       fn(b: self ref Iobuf, a: array of byte, n: int): int;
        write:      fn(b: self ref Iobuf, a: array of byte, n: int): int;
        getb:       fn(b: self ref Iobuf): int;
        getc:       fn(b: self ref Iobuf): int;
        gets:       fn(b: self ref Iobuf, sep: int): string;
        gett:       fn(b: self ref Iobuf, sep: string): string;
        ungetb:     fn(b: self ref Iobuf): int;
        ungetc:     fn(b: self ref Iobuf): int;
        putb:       fn(b: self ref Iobuf, b: byte): int;
        putc:       fn(b: self ref Iobuf, c: int): int;
        puts:       fn(b: self ref Iobuf, s: string): int;
        flush:      fn(b: self ref Iobuf): int;
```

```
        close:      fn(b: self ref Iobuf);
        setfill:    fn(b: self ref Iobuf, f: BufioFill);

        #    Internal variables
        fd:         ref Sys->FD;     # the file
        buffer:     array of byte;  # the buffer
        index:      int;            # read/write pointer in buffer
        size:       int;            # characters remaining/written
        dirty:      int;            # needs flushing
        bufpos:     int;            # position in file of buf[0]
        filpos:     int;            # current file pointer
        lastop:     int;            # OREAD or OWRITE
        mode:       int;            # mode of open
    };

    open:       fn(name: string, mode: int): ref Iobuf;
    create:     fn(name: string, mode, perm: int): ref Iobuf;
    fopen:      fn(fd: ref Sys->FD, mode: int): ref Iobuf;
    sopen:      fn(input: string): ref Iobuf;
    flush:      fn();
};

BufioFill: module
{
    fill:   fn(b: ref Bufio->Iobuf): int;
};

ChanFill: module
{
    PATH:   con "/dis/lib/chanfill.dis";

    init:   fn(data: array of byte, fid: int, wc: Sys->Rwrite,
                r: ref Sys->FileIO, b: Bufio): ref Bufio->Iobuf;
    fill:   fn(b: ref Bufio->Iobuf): int;
};
```

B.2 The Draw Module

```
Draw: module
{
    PATH:    con "$Draw";

    #   predefined colors; pass to Display.color
    Black:  con 255;
    Blue:   con 201;
    Red:    con 15;
    Yellow: con 3;
    Green:  con 192;
    White:  con 0;

    #   end styles for line
    Endsquare:  con 0;
    Enddisc:    con 1;
    Endarrow:   con 2;

    #   flush control
    Flushoff:   con 0;
    Flushon:    con 1;
    Flushnow:   con 2;

    #   Coordinate of a pixel on display
    Point: adt
    {
        x:  int;
        y:  int;

        #   arithmetic
        add:    fn(p: self Point, q: Point): Point;
        sub:    fn(p: self Point, q: Point): Point;
        mul:    fn(p: self Point, i: int): Point;
        div:    fn(p: self Point, i: int): Point;

        #   equality
        eq: fn(p: self Point, q: Point): int;

        #   inside rectangle
        in: fn(p: self Point, r: Rect): int;
    };

    #   Rectangle of pixels on the display; min <= max
    Rect: adt
    {
        min:    Point;  # upper left corner
        max:    Point;  # lower right corner

        #   make sure min <= max
        canon:      fn(r: self Rect): Rect;

        #   extent
        dx:     fn(r: self Rect): int;
        dy:     fn(r: self Rect): int;

        #   equality
        eq:     fn(r: self Rect, s: Rect): int;

        #   intersection and clipping
        Xrect:      fn(r: self Rect, s: Rect): int;
        inrect:     fn(r: self Rect, s: Rect): int;
        clip:       fn(r: self Rect, s: Rect): (Rect, int);
        contains:   fn(r: self Rect, p: Point): int;
        combine:    fn(r: self Rect, s: Rect): Rect;
```

```
        #    arithmetic
        addpt:      fn(r: self Rect, p: Point): Rect;
        subpt:      fn(r: self Rect, p: Point): Rect;
        inset:      fn(r: self Rect, n: int): Rect;
};


#    a picture; if made by Screen.newwindow, a window.
#    always attached to a Display
Image: adt
{
        #    these data are local copies, but repl and clipr
        #    are monitored by the runtime and may be modified as desired.
        r:          Rect;   # rectangle in data area, local coords
        clipr:      Rect;   # clipping region
        ldepth:     int;    # log base 2 of number of bits per pixel
        repl:       int;    # whether data area replicates to tile the plane
        display:    ref Display;   # where Image resides
        screen:     ref Screen; # nil if not window

        #    graphics operators
        draw:       fn(dst: self ref Image, r: Rect, src: ref Image,
                         mask: ref Image, p: Point);
        gendraw:    fn(dst: self ref Image, r: Rect, src: ref Image,
                         p0: Point, mask: ref Image, p1: Point);
        line:       fn(dst: self ref Image, p0,p1: Point, end0,end1,
                         radius: int, src: ref Image, sp: Point);
        poly:       fn(dst: self ref Image, p: array of Point, end0,
                         end1,radius: int, src: ref Image, sp: Point);
        bezspline:  fn(dst: self ref Image, p: array of Point, end0,
                         end1, radius: int, src: ref Image, sp: Point);
        fillpoly:   fn(dst: self ref Image, p: array of Point,
                         wind: int, src: ref Image, sp: Point);
        fillbezspline:  fn(dst: self ref Image, p: array of Point,
                             wind: int, src: ref Image, sp: Point);
        ellipse:    fn(dst: self ref Image, c: Point, a, b, thick: int,
                         src: ref Image, sp: Point);
        fillellipse:   fn(dst: self ref Image, c: Point, a, b: int,
                            src: ref Image, sp: Point);
        arc:        fn(dst: self ref Image, c: Point, a, b, thick: int,
                         src: ref Image, sp: Point, alpha, phi: int);
        fillarc:    fn(dst: self ref Image, c: Point, a, b: int,
                         src: ref Image, sp: Point, alpha, phi: int);
        bezier:     fn(dst: self ref Image, a,b,c,d: Point, end0, end1,
                         radius: int, src: ref Image, sp: Point);
        fillbezier: fn(dst: self ref Image, a,b,c,d: Point,
                         wind:int, src: ref Image, sp: Point);
        text:       fn(dst: self ref Image, p: Point, src: ref Image,
                         sp: Point, font: ref Font, str: string): Point;
        arrow:      fn(a,b,c: int): int;

        #    direct access to pixels
        readpixels: fn(src: self ref Image, r: Rect,
                         data: array of byte): int;
        writepixels:    fn(dst: self ref Image, r: Rect,
                             data: array of byte): int;

        #    windowing
        top:        fn(win: self ref Image);
        bottom:     fn(win: self ref Image);
        flush:      fn(win: self ref Image, func: int);
        origin:     fn(win: self ref Image, log, scr: Point): int;
};

#    a frame buffer, holding a connection to /dev/draw
Display: adt
{
        image:  ref Image;  # holds the contents of the display
```

```
ones:   ref Image;  # predefined mask
zeros:  ref Image;  # predefined mask

#   allocate and start refresh slave
allocate:       fn(dev: string): ref Display;
startrefresh:   fn(d: self ref Display);

#   attach to existing Screen
publicscreen:   fn(d: self ref Display, id: int): ref Screen;

#   image creation
newimage:   fn(d: self ref Display, r: Rect, ldepth, repl,
                color: int): ref Image;
color:      fn(d: self ref Display, color: int): ref Image;
colormix:   fn(d: self ref Display, c1: int, c2: int): ref Image;
rgb:        fn(d: self ref Display, r, g, b: int): ref Image;

#   I/O to files
open:       fn(d: self ref Display, name: string): ref Image;
readimage:  fn(d: self ref Display, fd: ref Sys->FD): ref Image;
writeimage: fn(d: self ref Display, fd: ref Sys->FD,
                i: ref Image): int;
#   color map
rgb2cmap:   fn(d: self ref Display, r, g, b: int): int;
cmap2rgb:   fn(d: self ref Display, c: int): (int, int, int);
cursor:     fn(d: self ref Display, i: ref Image, p: ref Point): int;
cursorset:  fn(d: self ref Display, p : Point);
};

#   a mapping between characters and pictures; always attached to a Display
Font: adt
{
    name:       string; # *default* or a file name (this may change)
    height:     int;    # interline spacing of font
    ascent:     int;    # distance from baseline to top
    display:    ref Display;    # where Font resides

    #   read from file or construct from local description
    open:       fn(d: ref Display, name: string): ref Font;
    build:      fn(d: ref Display, name, desc: string): ref Font;

    #   string extents
    width:      fn(f: self ref Font, str: string): int;
    bbox:       fn(f: self ref Font, str: string): Rect;
};

#   a collection of windows; always attached to a Display
Screen: adt
{
    id:     int;        # for export when public
    image:      ref Image;  # root of window tree
    fill:       ref Image;  # picture to use when repainting
    display:    ref Display;    # where Screen resides

    #   create; see also Display.publicscreen
    allocate:   fn(image, fill: ref Image, public: int): ref Screen;

    #   allocate a new window
    newwindow:  fn(screen: self ref Screen, r: Rect,
                    color: int): ref Image;

    # make group of windows visible
    top:        fn(screen: self ref Screen, wins: array of ref Image);
};
```

```
#   the state of a pointer device, e.g. a mouse
Pointer: adt
{
    buttons:     int;     # bits 1 2 4 ... represent state of
                          # buttons left to right; 1 means pressed
    xy:          Point;   # position
};

#   From appl to mux
AMexit:     con 10; # application is exiting
AMstartir:  con 11; # application is ready to receive IR events
AMstartkbd: con 12; # application is ready to receive keyboard characters
AMstartptr: con 13; # application is ready to receive mouse events
AMnewpin:   con 14; # application needs a PIN

#   From mux to appl
MAtop:      con 20; # application should make all its windows visible

Context: adt
{
    screen:      ref Screen; # place to make windows
    display:     ref Display;     # frame buffer on which windows reside
    cir:         chan of int;     # incoming events from IR remote
    ckbd:        chan of int;     # incoming characters from keyboard
    cptr:        chan of ref Pointer; # incoming stream of mouse positions
    ctoappl:     chan of int;     # commands from mux to application
    ctomux:      chan of int;     # commands from application to mux
};
};
```

B.3 The Keyring Module

```
#
# security routines implemented in C
#
Keyring: module
{
    PATH:    con "$Keyring";

    #   infinite precision integers
    IPint: adt
    {
        x:       int;    # dummy for C compiler for runt.h

        #    conversions
        iptob64:     fn(i: self ref IPint): string;
        b64toip:     fn(str: string): ref IPint;
        iptobytes:   fn(i: self ref IPint): array of byte;
        iptobebytes:     fn(i: self ref IPint): array of byte;
        bytestoip:   fn(buf: array of byte): ref IPint;
        bebytestoip:     fn(mag: array of byte): ref IPint;
        inttoip:     fn(i: int): ref IPint;
        iptoint:     fn(i: self ref IPint): int;
        iptostr:     fn(i: self ref IPint, base: int): string;
        strtoip:     fn(str: string, base: int): ref IPint;

        #    create a random large integer using the accelerated generator
        random:      fn(minbits, maxbits: int): ref IPint;

        #    operations
        bits:        fn(i: self ref IPint): int;
        expmod:      fn(base: self ref IPint, exp, mod: ref IPint):
                        ref IPint;
        add:         fn(i1: self ref IPint, i2: ref IPint): ref IPint;
        sub:         fn(i1: self ref IPint, i2: ref IPint): ref IPint;
        neg:         fn(i: self ref IPint): ref IPint;
        mul:         fn(i1: self ref IPint, i2: ref IPint): ref IPint;
        div:         fn(i1: self ref IPint, i2: ref IPint):
                        (ref IPint, ref IPint);
        eq:          fn(i1: self ref IPint, i2: ref IPint): int;
        cmp:         fn(i1: self ref IPint, i2: ref IPint): int;
    };

    #   signature algorithm
    SigAlg: adt
    {
        name:    string;
        #    C function pointers are hidden
    };

    #   generic public key
    PK: adt
    {
        sa:      ref SigAlg; # signature algorithm
        owner:   string;     # owner's name
        #    key and system parameters are hidden
    };

    #   generic secret key
    SK: adt
    {
        sa:      ref SigAlg; # signature algorithm
        owner:   string;     # owner's name
        #    key and system parameters are hidden
    };
```

```
#   generic certificate
Certificate: adt
{
    sa:     ref SigAlg; # signature algorithm
    ha:     string;     # hash algorithm
    signer: string;     # name of signer
    exp:    int;        # expiration date
    #   actual signature is hidden
};

#   state held while creating digests
DigestState: adt
{
    x:  int;          # dummy for C compiler for runt.h
    #   all the state is hidden
};

#   expanded DES key + state for chaining
DESstate: adt
{
    x:  int;          # dummy for C compiler for runt.h
    #   all the state is hidden
};

#   expanded IDEA key + state for chaining
IDEAstate: adt
{
    x:  int;          # dummy for C compiler for runt.h
    #   all the state is hidden
};

#   authentication info
Authinfo: adt
{
    mysk:   ref SK;          # my private key
    mypk:   ref PK;          # my public key
    cert:   ref Certificate;    # signature of my public key
    spk:    ref PK;          # signers public key
    alpha:  ref IPint;       # Diffie-Helman parameters
    p:      ref IPint;
};

#   convert types to byte strings
certtostr:  fn (c: ref Certificate): string;
pktostr:    fn (pk: ref PK): string;
sktostr:    fn (sk: ref SK): string;

#   parse byte strings into types
strtocert:  fn (s: string): ref Certificate;
strtopk:    fn (s: string): ref PK;
strtosk:    fn (s: string): ref SK;

#   create and verify signatures
sign:       fn (sk: ref SK, exp: int, state: ref DigestState, ha: string):
                ref Certificate;
verify:     fn (pk: ref PK, cert: ref Certificate, state: ref DigestState):
                int;

#   generate keys
genSK:      fn (algname, owner: string, length: int): ref SK;
genSKfromPK:    fn (pk: ref PK, owner: string): ref SK;
sktopk:     fn (sk: ref SK): ref PK;

#   digests
cloneDigestState: fn(state: ref DigestState): ref DigestState;
sha:        fn(buf: array of byte, n: int, digest: array of byte,
                state: ref DigestState): ref DigestState;
```

```
sha1:       fn(buf: array of byte, n: int, digest: array of byte,
                state: ref DigestState): ref DigestState;
md4:        fn(buf: array of byte, n: int, digest: array of byte,
                state: ref DigestState): ref DigestState;
md5:        fn(buf: array of byte, n: int, digest: array of byte,
                state: ref DigestState): ref DigestState;

hmac_sha1:  fn(data: array of byte, n: int, key: array of byte,
                digest: array of byte, state: ref DigestState):
                ref DigestState;
hmac_md5:   fn(data: array of byte, n: int, key: array of byte,
                digest: array of byte, state: ref DigestState):
                ref DigestState;

#   DES/IDEA interfaces
Encrypt:    con 0;
Decrypt:    con 1;

dessetup:   fn(key: array of byte, ivec: array of byte): ref DESstate;
desecb:     fn(state: ref DESstate, buf: array of byte, n: int, direction: int);
descbc:     fn(state: ref DESstate, buf: array of byte, n: int, direction: int);

ideasetup:  fn(key: array of byte, ivec: array of byte): ref IDEAstate;
ideaecb:    fn(state: ref IDEAstate, buf: array of byte, n: int,
                direction: int);
ideacbc:    fn(state: ref IDEAstate, buf: array of byte, n: int,
                direction: int);

#   create an alpha and p for Diffie-Helman exchanges
dhparams:   fn(nbits: int): (ref IPint, ref IPint);

#   comm link authentication is symetric
auth:       fn(fd: ref Sys->FD, info: ref Authinfo, setid: int):
                (string, array of byte);

#   auth io
readauthinfo:   fn(filename: string): ref Authinfo;
writeauthinfo:  fn(filename: string, info: ref Authinfo): int;

#   message io on a delimited connection (ssl for example)
#   messages > 4096 bytes are truncated
#   errors > 64 bytes are truncated
#   getstring and getbytearray return (result, error).
getstring:      fn(fd: ref Sys->FD): (string, string);
putstring:      fn(fd: ref Sys->FD, s: string): int;
getbytearray:   fn(fd: ref Sys->FD): (array of byte, string);
putbytearray:   fn(fd: ref Sys->FD, a: array of byte, n: int): int;
puterror:   fn(fd: ref Sys->FD, s: string): int;

#   to send and receive messages when ssl isn't pushed
getmsg:     fn(fd: ref Sys->FD): array of byte;
sendmsg:    fn(fd: ref Sys->FD, buf: array of byte, n: int): int;

#   algorithms
DEScbc:     con 0;
DESecb:     con 1;
SHA:        con 2;
MD5:        con 3;
MD4:        con 4;
IDEAcbc:    con 5;
IDEAecb:    con 6;

SHAdlen:    con 20; # old name
SHA1dlen:   con 20;
MD5dlen:    con 16;
MD4dlen:    con 16;
};
```

B.4 The Styx Module

```
Styx: module
{
    PATH:         con "/dis/lib/styx.dis";

    init:         fn();
    convM2S:      fn(a: array of byte): (int, ref Smsg);
    convD2M:      fn(f: ref Sys->Dir): array of byte;
    convM2D:      fn(f: array of byte): ref Sys->Dir;

    MAXFDATA:     con 8192;
    MAXMSG:       con 160;      # max header sans data (actually 128)
    MAXRPC:       con MAXMSG+MAXFDATA;

    Tnop,         #  0
    Rnop,         #  1
    Terror,       #  2, illegal
    Rerror,       #  3
    Tflush,       #  4
    Rflush,       #  5
    Tclone,       #  6
    Rclone,       #  7
    Twalk,        #  8
    Rwalk,        #  9
    Topen,        # 10
    Ropen,        # 11
    Tcreate,      # 12
    Rcreate,      # 13
    Tread,        # 14
    Rread,        # 15
    Twrite,       # 16
    Rwrite,       # 17
    Tclunk,       # 18
    Rclunk,       # 19
    Tremove,      # 20
    Rremove,      # 21
    Tstat,        # 22
    Rstat,        # 23
    Twstat,       # 24
    Rwstat,       # 25
    Tsession,     # 26
    Rsession,     # 27
    Tattach,      # 28
    Rattach,      # 29
    Tmax          : con iota;

    NAMELEN:      con 28;
    DIRLEN:       con 116;
    ERRLEN:       con 64;

    OREAD:        con 0;  # open for read
    OWRITE:       con 1;  # write
    ORDWR:        con 2;  # read and write
    OEXEC:        con 3;  # execute, == read but check execute permission
    OTRUNC:       con 16; # or'ed in (except for exec), truncate file first
    OCEXEC:       con 32; # or'ed in, close on exec
    ORCLOSE:      con 64; # or'ed in, remove on close

    CHDIR:        con int 16r80000000;    # mode bit for directory
    CHAPPEND:     con 16r40000000;    # mode bit for append-only files
    CHEXCL:       con 16r20000000;    # mode bit for exclusive use files

    Smsg: adt
    {
        convS2M:    fn(s: self ref Smsg): array of byte;
```

```
        print:      fn(s: self ref Smsg): string;

        mtype:      int;
        tag:        int;
        fid:        int;
        oldtag:     int;        # T-Flush
        qid:        Sys->Qid;   # R-Attach, R-Walk, R-Open, R-Create
        uname:      string;     # T-Attach
        aname:      string;     # T-Attach
        ename:      string;     # R-Error
        perm:       int;        # T-Create
        newfid:     int;        # T-Clone
        name:       string;     # T-Walk, T-Create
        mode:       int;        # T-Create, T-Open
        offset:     big;        # T-Read, T-Write
        count:      int;        # T-Read, T-Write, R-Read
        data:       array of byte;  # T-Write, R-Read
        stat:       array of byte;  # T-Wstat, R-Stat
    };
};
```

B.5 The Sys Module

```
SELF:  con "$self";          # Language support for loading my instance

Sys: module
{
    PATH:   con "$Sys";

    #   Details on exception
    Exception: adt
    {
        name:    string;
        mod:     string;
        pc:      int;
    };

    #   Parameters to exception handlers
    HANDLER,
    EXCEPTION,
    ACTIVE,
    RAISE,
    EXIT,
    ONCE:   con iota;

    #   Unique file identifier for file objects
    Qid: adt
    {
        path:    int;
        vers:    int;
    };

    #   Return from stat and directory read
    Dir: adt
    {
        name:    string;
        uid:     string;
        gid:     string;
        qid:     Qid;
        mode:    int;
        atime:   int;
        mtime:   int;
        length:  int;
        dtype:   int;
        dev:     int;
    };

    #   File descriptor
    FD: adt
    {
        fd: int;
    };

    #   Network connection returned by dial
    Connection: adt
    {
        dfd:     ref FD;
        cfd:     ref FD;
        dir:     string;
    };

    #   File IO structures returned from file2chan
    #   read:  (offset, bytes, fid, chan)
    #   write: (offset, data, fid, chan)
    Rread:  type chan of (array of byte, string);
    Rwrite: type chan of (int, string);
    FileIO: adt
```

```
{
    read:    chan of (int, int, int, Rread);
    write:   chan of (int, array of byte, int, Rwrite);
};

#    Maximum read which will be completed atomically;
#    also the optimum block size
ATOMICIO:    con 8192;

NAMELEN:     con 28;

SEEKSTART:   con 0;
SEEKRELA:    con 1;
SEEKEND:     con 2;

ERRLEN:      con 64;
WAITLEN:     con ERRLEN;

OREAD:       con 0;
OWRITE:      con 1;
ORDWR:       con 2;
OTRUNC:      con 16;
ORCLOSE:     con 64;
CHDIR:       con int 16r80000000;

DMDIR:       con int 1<<31;
DMAPPEND:    con int 1<<30;
DMEXCL:      con int 1<<29;
DMAUTH:      con int 1<<27;

MREPL:       con 0;
MBEFORE:     con 1;
MAFTER:      con 2;
MCREATE:     con 4;

NEWFD:       con (1<<0);
FORKFD:      con (1<<1);
NEWNS:       con (1<<2);
FORKNS:      con (1<<3);
NEWPGRP:     con (1<<4);
NODEVS:      con (1<<5);
NEWENV:      con (1<<6);
FORKENV:     con (1<<7);

EXPWAIT:     con 0;
EXPASYNC:    con 1;

UTFmax:      con 3;
UTFerror:    con 16r80;

announce:    fn(addr: string): (int, Connection);
aprint:      fn(s: string, *): array of byte;
bind:        fn(s, on: string, flags: int): int;
byte2char:   fn(buf: array of byte, n: int): (int, int, int);
char2byte:   fn(c: int, buf: array of byte, n: int): int;
chdir:       fn(path: string): int;
create:      fn(s: string, mode, perm: int): ref FD;
dial:        fn(addr, local: string): (int, Connection);
dirread:     fn(fd: ref FD, dir: array of Dir): int;
dup:         fn(old, new: int): int;
export:      fn(c: ref FD, flag: int): int;
exportdir:   fn(c: ref FD, dir: string, flag: int): int;
fildes:      fn(fd: int): ref FD;
file2chan:   fn(dir, file: string): ref FileIO;
fprint:      fn(fd: ref FD, s: string, *): int;
fstat:       fn(fd: ref FD): (int, Dir);
fwstat:      fn(fd: ref FD, d: Dir): int;
```

```
	listen:		fn(c: Connection): (int, Connection);
	millisec:	fn(): int;
	mount:		fn(fd: ref FD, on: string, flags: int, spec: string): int;
	open:		fn(s: string, mode: int): ref FD;
	pctl:		fn(flags: int, movefd: list of int): int;
	pipe:		fn(fds: array of ref FD): int;
	print:		fn(s: string, *): int;
	raise:		fn(s: string);
	rescue:		fn(s: string, e: ref Exception): int;
	rescued:	fn(flag: int, s: string): int;
	read:		fn(fd: ref FD, buf: array of byte, n: int): int;
	remove:		fn(s: string): int;
	seek:		fn(fd: ref FD, off, start: int): int;
	sleep:		fn(period: int): int;
	sprint:		fn(s: string, *): string;
	stat:		fn(s: string): (int, Dir);
	stream:		fn(src, dst: ref FD, bufsiz: int): int;
	tokenize:	fn(s, delim: string): (int, list of string);
	unmount:	fn(s1: string, s2: string): int;
	unrescue:	fn();
	utfbytes:	fn(buf: array of byte, n: int): int;
	write:		fn(fd: ref FD, buf: array of byte, n: int): int;
	wstat:		fn(s: string, d: Dir): int;
};
```

B.6   The Tk Module

```
Tk: module
{
    PATH:    con "$Tk";

    Tki:     type ref Draw->Image;

    Toplevel: adt
    {
        id: int;
        image:  Tki;
    };

    toplevel:   fn(screen: ref Draw->Screen, arg: string): ref Toplevel;
    intop:      fn(screen: ref Draw->Screen, x, y: int): ref Toplevel;
    windows:    fn(screen: ref Draw->Screen): list of ref Toplevel;
    namechan:   fn(t: ref Toplevel, c: chan of string, n: string): string;
    cmd:        fn(t: ref Toplevel, arg: string): string;
    mouse:      fn(screen: ref Draw->Screen, x, y, button: int);
    keyboard:   fn(screen: ref Draw->Screen, key: int);
    imageput:   fn(t: ref Toplevel, name: string, i, m: Tki): string;
    imageget:   fn(t: ref Toplevel, name: string) : (Tki, Tki, string);
};
```

B.7 The HTML Module

```
HTML: module
{
    PATH:        con "/dis/lib/html.dis";

    Lex: adt
    {
        tag:    int;
        text:   string;      # text in Data, attribute text in tag
        attr:   list of Attr;
    };

    Attr: adt
    {
        name:   string;
        value:  string;
    };

    #    sorted in lexical order; used as array indices
    Notfound,
    Ta, Taddress, Tapplet, Tarea, Tatt_footer, Tb,
        Tbase, Tbasefont, Tbig, Tblink, Tblockquote, Tbody,
        Tbq, Tbr, Tcaption, Tcenter, Tcite, Tcode, Tcol, Tcolgroup,
        Tdd, Tdfn, Tdir, Tdiv, Tdl, Tdt, Tem,
        Tfont, Tform, Tframe, Tframeset,
        Th1, Th2, Th3, Th4, Th5, Th6, Thead, Thr, Thtml, Ti, Timg,
        Tinput, Tisindex, Titem, Tkbd, Tli, Tlink, Tmap, Tmenu,
        Tmeta, Tnobr, Tnoframes, Tol, Toption, Tp, Tparam, Tpre,
        Tq, Tsamp, Tscript, Tselect, Tsmall, Tstrike, Tstrong,
        Tstyle, Tsub, Tsup, Tt, Ttable, Ttbody, Ttd, Ttextarea,
        Ttextflow, Ttfoot, Tth,
        Tthead, Ttitle, Ttr, Ttt, Tu, Tul, Tvar
            : con iota;

    RBRA:            con 1000;
    Data:            con 2000;
    Latin1, UTF8:    con iota;    # charsets

    lex:         fn(b: array of byte, charset: int, keepnls: int):
                    array of ref Lex;
    attrvalue:   fn(attr: list of Attr, name: string): (int, string);
    globalattr:  fn(html: array of ref Lex, tag: int, attr: string):
                    (int, string);
    isbreak:     fn(h: array of ref Lex, i: int): int;
    lex2string:  fn(l: ref Lex): string;
};
```

B.8 The Url Module

```
Url: module
{
    PATH : con "/dis/lib/url.dis";

    #   scheme ids
    NOSCHEME, HTTP, HTTPS, FTP, FILE, GOPHER, MAILTO, NEWS,
        NNTP, TELNET, WAIS, PROSPERO, JAVASCRIPT, UNKNOWN: con iota;

    #   general url syntax:
    #   <scheme>://<user>:<passwd>@<host>:<port>/<path>?<query>#<fragment>
    #
    #   relative urls might omit some prefix of the above
    ParsedUrl: adt
    {
        scheme:     int;
        utf8:       int;    # strings not in us-ascii
        user:       string;
        passwd:     string;
        host:       string;
        port:       string;
        pstart:     string; # what precedes <path>: either "/" or ""
        path:       string;
        query:      string;
        frag:       string;

        makeabsolute:   fn(url: self ref ParsedUrl, base: ref ParsedUrl);
        tostring:   fn(url: self ref ParsedUrl) : string;
    };

    schemes:    array of string;

    init:       fn();   # call before anything else
    makeurl:    fn(s: string) : ref ParsedUrl;
};
```

B.9 The Wmlib Module

```
Wmlib: module
{
    PATH:        con "/dis/lib/wmlib.dis";

    Resize,
    Hide,
    Help,
    OK:       con 1 << iota;

    Appl:        con Resize | Hide;

    init:        fn();
    titlebar:    fn(scr: ref Draw->Screen, where, name: string,
                    buts: int): (ref Tk->Toplevel, chan of string);
    untaskbar:   fn();          # deprecated
    unhide:      fn();
    titlectl:    fn(t: ref Tk->Toplevel, request: string);
    taskbar:     fn(t: ref Tk->Toplevel, name: string): string;
    geom:        fn(t: ref Tk->Toplevel): string;
    snarfput:    fn(buf: string);
    snarfget:    fn(): string;

    tkquote:     fn(s: string): string;
    tkcmds:      fn(top: ref Tk->Toplevel, a: array of string);
    dialog:      fn(parent: ref Tk->Toplevel, ico, title, msg: string,
                    dflt: int, labs : list of string): int;
    getstring:   fn(parent: ref Tk->Toplevel, msg: string): string;

    filename:    fn(scr: ref Draw->Screen, top: ref Tk->Toplevel,
                    title: string,
                    pat: list of string,
                    dir: string): string;

    mktabs:      fn(t: ref Tk->Toplevel, dot: string,
                    tabs: array of (string, string),
                    dflt: int): chan of string;

    tabsctl:     fn(t: ref Tk->Toplevel,
                    dot: string,
                    tabs: array of (string, string),
                    id: int,
                    s: string): int;
};
```

Appendix C
Selected Manual Pages

C.1 The Inferno Emulator

NAME
      emu - Inferno emulator

SYNOPSIS
      emu [-gXsizexYsize] [-c[0-9]] [-d[012]] [-m[0-9]]
      [-s] [-ppool=maxsize] [-ffont] [-rrootpath] [-7] [-d]
      [cmd [arg ...]]

DESCRIPTION
      Emu provides the Inferno emulation environment. The emulator
      runs as an application under the machine's native operating
      system, and provides system services and a Dis virtual
      machine for Inferno applications.

      Emu starts an Inferno initialization program
      /dis/emuinit.dis, whose path name is interpreted in the
      Inferno file name space, not in the native operating
      system's name space. It in turn invokes the shell
      /dis/sh.dis by default or the optional cmd and its
      arguments. If the -d option is specified, emu instead
      invokes /dis/lib/srv.dis, turning the emu instance into an
      Inferno service process on the network (see srv(8)).

      The emulator supports the following options:

-cn   Unless specified otherwise by the module (see wm/rt in
      wm-misc(1)), emu uses an interpreter to execute Dis
      instructions. Setting n to 1 (the default value is 0)
      makes the default behaviour to compile Dis into native
      instructions when a module is loaded, resulting in
      faster execution but larger run-time size. Setting n to
      values larger than 1 enables increasingly detailed
      traces of the compiler.

-gXsizexYsize
      Define screen width and height in pixels. The default
      values are 640 and 480 respectively. Values smaller
      than the defaults are disallowed.

-ffont
      Specify the default font for the tk module. The path is
      interpreted in the Inferno name space. If unspecified,
      the font variable has value /fonts/lucm/unicode.9.font.

-rrootpath
      Specify the host system directory that emu will serve
      as its root. The default value is /usr/inferno on most
      systems, but \users\inferno on Windows.

-s   Specify how the emulator deals with traps reported by
      the operating system. By default, they suspend
      execution of the offending thread within the virtual
      machine abstraction. The -s option causes emu itself to
      trap, permitting debugging of the broken host operating
      system process that results when a trap occurs. (This
      is intended to allow debugging of emu, not Inferno
      applications.)

-ppool=maxsize
      Specify the maximum size in bytes of the named memory
      allocation pool. The pools are:

      main the general malloc arena

      heap the Dis virtual machine heap

      image
           image storage for the display

-7   When host graphics is provided by X11, request a 7-bit
      color map; use this option only if X11 refused to
      allow emu to configure the normal (default) 8-bit
      Inferno color map.

Options may also be set in the host operating system's
environment variable EMU; they are overridden by options
supplied on the command line.

EXAMPLE
      To start wm/logon directly:

          EMU='-g800x600 -c1'
          emu /wm/logon.dis -u inferno

FILES
     /dis/emuinit.dis The default initialization program.
     /dis/sh.dis   The default Inferno shell.
SOURCE
     /emu

SEE ALSO
     Limbo(1), wm-misc(1)

                        Inferno Manual

C.2 The Limbo Compiler

NAME
     limbo - Limbo compiler

SYNOPSIS
     limbo [option ...] [file ...]

DESCRIPTION
     Limbo compiles the named Limbo files into
     machine-independent object files for the Dis virtual
     machine. Depending on the options, the compiler may create
     output files or write information to its standard output.
     Conventional files and their extensions include the
     following.

     file.b   Limbo source file.

     file.dis   Object code for the Dis virtual machine.

     file.m   Limbo source file for module declarations.

     file.s   Assembly code.

     file.sbl   Symbolic debugging information.

     With no options, limbo produces a .dis file for each source file.

     The compiler options are:

     -a
      Print on standard output type definitions and call frames
      useful for writing C language implementations of Limbo
      modules. Suppresses normal output file generation.

     -C
      Mark the Dis object file to prevent run-time compilation.

     -c
      Mark the Dis object file to guarantee run-time compilation.

     -D flags
      Turn on debugging flags. Flags include A for arrays, a for
      alt statements, b for booleans, C for case body statements,
      c for case statements, D for use descriptors, d for
      declarations, e for expressions, E for extended
      expressions, F for function information, f for constant
      folding, m for modules, n for nil references, P for program
      counter manipulations, r for reference types, S for type
      signatures, s for a code generation summary, T for tuples,
      t for type checking, and v for variable initialization.

     -e
      Increase the number of errors the compiler will report
      before exiting.

     -G
      Annotate assembly language output with debugging
      information. A no-op unless -S is set.

     -g
      Generate debugging information for the input files and
      place it in a file named by stripping any trailing .b from
      the input file name and appending .sbl.

-I dir
     An include file whose name does not begin with slash is
     sought first relative to the working directory, regardless
     of the source file argument. If this fails, limbo sequences
     through directories named in -I options, then searches in
     /module. An include file contains Limbo source code,
     normally holding one or more module declarations.

-o obj
     Place output in file obj (allowed only if there is a single
     input file). The output file will hold either object or
     assembly code, depending on -S. Default is to take the last
     element of the input file name, strip any trailing .b, and
     append .dis for object code and .s for assembly code. Thus,
     the default output file for dir/mod.b would be mod.dis.

-S
     Create assembly language output instead of object code.

-T module
     Print on standard output C stub functions, useful for
     implementing Limbo modules in the C language for linkage
     with the interpreter.

-t module
     Print on standard output a table of runtime functions, to
     link C language implementations of modules with the Limbo
     interpreter. Suppresses normal output file generation.

-w
     Print warning messages about unused variables, etc. More
     w's (e.g. -ww) increase the pedantry of the checking.

FILES
     /module   directory for Limbo include modules
SOURCE
     /appl/limbo   compiler source in Limbo
     /limbo   compiler source in C for host
SEE ALSO
     asm(1), emu(1), mk(10.1), intro(2), sys-intro(2), tk(2)

     ``The Limbo Programming Language''
     ``Program Development in Inferno''
     ``A Descent into Limbo''
     in Volume 2.

                         Inferno Manual

C.3 Formatted Output

NAME
        print, fprint, sprint - print formatted output

SYNOPSIS
        include "sys.m";
        sys := load Sys Sys->PATH;

        fprint: fn(fd: ref FD, format: string, *): int;
        print: fn(format: string, *): int;
        sprint: fn(format: string, *): string;

DESCRIPTION
        These functions format and print their arguments as UTF
        text. Print writes text to the standard output. Fprint
        writes to the named output file descriptor. Sprint places
        text in a string, which it returns. Print and fprint return
        the number of bytes transmitted or a negative value if an
        error was encountered when writing the output.

        Each of these functions converts, formats, and prints its
        trailing arguments under control of a format string. The
        format contains two types of objects: plain characters,
        which are simply copied to the output stream, and conversion
        specifications, each of which results in fetching of zero or
        more arguments. The Limbo compiler recognizes calls to these
        functions and checks that the arguments match the format
        specifications in number and type.

        Each conversion specification has the following format:

            % [flags] verb

        The verb is a single character and each flag is a single
        character or a (decimal) numeric string. Up to two numeric
        strings may be used; the first is called f1, the second f2.
        They can be separated by '.', and if one is present, then f1
        and f2 are taken to be zero if missing, otherwise they are
        considered 'omitted'. Either or both of the numbers may be
        replaced with the character *, meaning that the actual
        number will be obtained from the argument list as an
        integer. The flags and numbers are arguments to the verb
        described below.

        d, o, x, X
            The numeric verbs d, o, and x format their int
            arguments in decimal, octal, and hexadecimal (with hex
            digits in lower-case). The flag b is required when the
            corresponding value is a Limbo big, not an int.
            Arguments are taken to be signed, unless the u flag is
            given, to force them to be treated as unsigned. Each
            interprets the flags # and - to mean alternative format
            and left justified. If f2 is not omitted, the number is
            padded on the left with zeros until at least f2 digits
            appear. Then, if alternative format is specified for x
            conversion, the number is preceded by 0x. Finally, if
            f1 is not omitted, the number is padded on the left (or
            right, if left justification is specified) with enough
            blanks to make the field at least f1 characters long.
            The verb X is similar to x, except that the hexadecimal
            digits are displayed in upper-case, and in alternative
            format, the number is preceded by 0X.

e, f, g

> The floating point verbs e, f, and g take a real argument. Each interprets the flags +, -, and # to mean always print a sign, left justified, and alternative format. F1 is the minimum field width and, if the converted value takes up less than f1 characters, it is padded on the left (or right, if 'left justified') with spaces. F2 is the number of digits that are converted after the decimal place for e and f conversions, and f2 is the maximum number of significant digits for g conversions. The f verb produces output of the form [-]\c digits[\c .digits]. The e conversion appends an exponent e[-]\c digits. The g verb will output the argument in either e or f with the goal of producing the smallest output. Also, trailing zeros are omitted from the fraction part of the output, and a trailing decimal point appears only if it is followed by a digit. When alternative format is specified, the result will always contain a decimal point, and for g conversions, trailing zeros are not removed.

E, G   These are the same as e and g respectively, but use E not e to specify an exponent when one appears.

c   The c verb converts a single Unicode character from an int argument to a UTF encoding, justified within a field of f1 characters as described above.

r   The r verb takes no arguments; it prints the error string associated with the most recent system error.

s   The s verb copies a string to the output. The number of characters copied (n) is the minimum of the size of the string and f2. These n characters are justified within a field of f1 characters as described above.

SOURCE
> /interp/runt.c:/^xprint
> /os/port/print.c
> /lib9/print.c

SEE ALSO
> sys-intro(2), sys-open(2)

BUGS
> The x verb does not apply the 0x prefix when f2 is present. The prefix should probably be 16r anyway.

Inferno Manual

C.4   Secure Sockets Layer Device

SSL(3)   SSL(3)

NAME
    ssl - secure sockets layer device

SYNOPSIS
    bind '#D' /n/ssl

    /n/ssl/clone
    /n/ssl/n
    /n/ssl/n/data
    /n/ssl/n/ctl
    /n/ssl/n/secretin
    /n/ssl/n/secretout

DESCRIPTION
    The ssl device provides access to a Secure Socket Layer that
    implements the record layer protocol of SSLv2. The device
    provides encrypting and digesting for many independent
    connections. Once associated with a network connection, the
    ssl device can be thought of as a filter for the connection.
    Ssl can send data in the clear, digested or encrypted. In
    all cases, if ssl is associated with both ends of a
    connection, all messages are delimited. As long as reads
    always specify buffers that are of equal or greater lengths
    than the writes at the other end of the connection, one
    write will correspond to one read.

    The top-level directory contains a clone file and numbered
    directories, each representing a connection. Opening the
    clone file reserves a connection; the file descriptor
    resulting from the \%sys-open(2) will be open on the control
    file, ctl, in the directory that represents the new
    connection. Reading the control file will return a text
    string giving the connection number (and thus the directory
    name).

    Writing to ctl controls the corresponding connection. The
    following control messages are possible:

    fd n Associate the network connection on file descriptor n
        with the ssl device.

    alg clear
        Allow data to pass in the clear with only message
        delimiters added. The device starts in this mode.

    alg sha
        Append a SHA digest to each buffer written to data. The
        digest covers the outgoing secret (written to secretout),
        the message, and a message number which starts at 0 and
        increments by one for each message. Messages read have
        their appended digests compared to a digest computed
        using the incoming secret (written to secretin).
        If the comparison fails, so will the read.

    alg md4
        Like sha but using the MD4 message digest algorithm.

    alg md5
        Like sha but using the MD5 message digest algorithm.

    alg rc4
    alg rc4_40

```
alg rc4_128
alg rc4_256
        RC4 encrypt each message written to data with the key
        written to secretout, using the key length as indicated
        (40-bit keys by default).

alg des_56_cbc
        Encrypt the stream using DES and Cipher Block Chaining
        (CBC)

alg des_56_ecb
        Encrypt the stream using DES and Electronic Code Book
        (ECB)

alg ideacbc
        Encrypt the stream using IDEA and CBC

alg ideaecb
        Encrypt the stream using IDEA and ECB

alg digest/crypt
        Combine the use of the given digest algorithm and the
        stream encryption algorithm crypt
```

Files secretin and secretout must be written before digesting or encryption is turned on. If only one is written, they are both assumed to be the same.

The mode may be changed at any time during a connection.

The list of algorithms supported by a given implementation of ssl may be read from the read-only text files encalgs (encryption algorithms) and hashalgs (hashing algorithms for digests). Each contains a space-separated list of algorithm names.

SEE ALSO
```
        security-ssl(2)
        B. Schneier, Applied Cryptography, 1996, John Wiley & Sons,
        Inc.
```

Inferno Manual

C.5 Secure Sockets Layer Limbo Interface

SECURITY-SSL(2)   SECURITY-SSL(2)

NAME
      ssl: connect, secret - interface to the Secure Sockets Layer

SYNOPSIS
      include "sys.m";
      include "security.m";
      ssl := load SSL SSL->PATH;

      connect: fn(fd: ref Sys->FD): (string, ref Sys->Connection);
      secret: fn(c: ref Sys->Connection, secretin,
                  secretout: array of byte): string;

DESCRIPTION
      SSL provides an interface to the secure sockets layer device
      ssl(3).

      Connect allocates a new ssl(3) connection directory. It
      pushes file descriptor fd into the data file of that
      connection, and if successful, returns a reference to a
      Connection adt describing the connection. The Connection adt
      has its members set as follows: dir names the resulting
      connection directory; cfd is open on the connection's
      control file; and dfd is open on the connection's data file,
      which is read and written to exchange data on the original
      fd using SSL.

      Secret writes secretin and secretout to c.dir/secretin and
      c.dir/secretout where n is obtained from the Connection adt
      c. The string returned describes errors encountered, if any;
      otherwise it is nil.

SOURCE
      /appl/lib/ssl.b

SEE ALSO
      security-auth(2), ssl(3)

DIAGNOSTICS
      Connect returns a tuple containing a string and a Connection
      reference. On success the string is nil, and the connection
      reference is not nil; on error, the string contains a
      diagnostic, and the connection reference is nil.

                        Inferno Manual

C.6   Draw Introduction

DRAW-INTRO(2)   DRAW-INTRO(2)

NAME
    draw - basic graphics facilities module

SYNOPSIS
    include "draw.m";
    draw := load Draw Draw->PATH;

DESCRIPTION
    Inferno's Draw module provides basic graphics facilities, defining
    drawing contexts, images, character fonts, and rectangular
    geometric operations. See prefab-intro(2) and tk (2) for
    higher level operations, such as windows and menu handling.

  Pixels
    Images are defined on a rectangular region of an integer
    plane with a picture element, or pixel, at each grid point.
    Pixel values are integers with 0, 1, 2, 4, or 8 bits per
    pixel, and all pixels in a given image have the same size,
    or depth. Some operations allow images with different depths
    to be combined, for example to do masking.

    When an image is displayed, the value of each pixel
    determines the color of the display. For color displays,
    Inferno uses a fixed color map for each display depth (see
    rgbv(6)) and the application is responsible for mapping its
    desired colors to the values available. Facilities exist to
    convert from (red, green, blue) triplets to pixel values.
    Note that the triplet (255, 255, 255) maps to a pixel with
    all bits zero.

  Terminology
    Point   The graphics plane is defined on an integer grid,
              with each (x, y) coordinate identifying the upper
              left corner of the corresponding pixel. The plane's
              origin, (0, 0), resides at the upper left corner of
              the screen; x and y coordinates increase to the
              right and down. The abstract data type, Point
              defines a coordinate position.

    Rect   The type Rect defines a rectangular region of the
              plane. It comprises two Points, min and max, and
              specifies the region defined by pixels with
              coordinates greater than or equal to min and
              strictly less than max, in both x and y. This
              half-open property allows rectangles that share an
              edge to have equal coordinates on the edge.

    Display   The type Display represents a physical display,
              corresponding to a single connection to a draw(3)
              device. Besides the image of the display itself,
              the Display type also stores references to
              off-screen images, fonts, and so on. The contents
              of such images are stored in the display device,
              not in the client of the display, which affects how
              they are allocated and used, see for example
              draw-image(2).

    Screen   The Screen type is used to manage a set of windows
              on an image, typically but not necessarily that of
              a display. Screens and hence windows may be built
              recursively upon windows for subwindowing or even
              on off-screen images.

Image The Image type provides basic operations on groups of pixels. Through a few simple operations, most importantly the draw image combination operator (see draw-image(2)), the Image type provides the building blocks for Display, Screen, and Font.

Font A Font defines which character image to draw for each character code value. Although all character drawing operations ultimately use the draw primitive on the underlying images, Fonts provide convenient and efficient management of display text. Inferno uses the 16-bit Unicode character encoding, so Fonts are managed hierarchically to control their size and to make common subsets such as ASCII or Greek efficient in practice. See draw-font(2), utf(6), and font(6).

Context A Context provides an interface to the system graphics and interactive devices. The system creates this context when it starts an application.

Pointer The Pointer type conveys information for pointing devices, such as mice or trackballs.

More about Images

An image occupies a rectangle, Image.r, of the graphics plane. A second rectangle, Image.clipr, defines a clipping region for the image. Typically, the clipping rectangle is the same as the basic image, but they may differ. For example, the clipping region may be made smaller and centered on the basic image to define a protected border.

The pixel depth of an Image is stored as a logarithm called Image.ldepth; pixels with 1, 2, 4, and 8 bits correspond to ldepth values 0, 1, 2, and 3. In future, other image depths may be supported.

An image may be marked for replication: when set, the boolean Image.repl causes the image to behave as if replicated across the entire integer plane, thus tiling the destination graphics area with copies of the source image. When replication is turned on, the clipping rectangle limits the extent of the replication and may even usefully be disjoint from Image.r. See draw-image(2) for examples.

The Image member functions provide facilities for drawing text and geometric objects, manipulating windows, and so on.

Objects of type Display, Font, Screen, and Image must be allocated by the member functions; if such objects are created with a regular Limbo definition, they will not behave properly and may generate run-time errors.

There are no ''free'' routines for graphics objects. Instead Limbo's garbage collection frees them automatically. As is generally so within Limbo, one can eliminate references by assigning nil to reference variables, returning from functions whose local variables hold references, etc.

RETURN VALUES

Most drawing operations operate asynchronously, so they have no error return. Functions that allocate objects return nil for failure; in such cases the system error string may be interrogated (such as by the %r format (see sys-print(2))) for more information.

SOURCE
     /interp/draw.c
     /image/*.c

SEE ALSO
     draw(3), ir(2), prefab-intro(2), tk(2), font(6), image(6)

C.7 The Draw Image ADT

NAME
      Image - pictures and drawing

SYNOPSIS
      include   "draw.m";
      draw := load Draw Draw->PATH;

      Image: adt
      {
            r: Rect;
            clipr: Rect;
            ldepth: int;
            repl: int;

            display: ref Display;
            screen: ref Screen;

            draw: fn(dst: self ref Image, r: Rect, src: ref Image,
                            mask: ref Image, p: Point);
            gendraw: fn(dst: self ref Image, r: Rect, src: ref Image,
                            p0: Point, mask: ref Image, p1: Point);
            line: fn(dst: self ref Image, p0,p1: Point,
                            end0,end1,thick: int, src: ref Image, sp: Point);
            poly: fn(dst: self ref Image, p: array of Point,
                            end0,end1,thick: int, src: ref Image, sp: Point);
            bezspline: fn(dst: self ref Image, p: array of Point,
                            end0,end1,thick: int, src: ref Image, sp: Point);
            fillpoly: fn(dst: self ref Image, p: array of Point,
                            wind: int, src: ref Image, sp: Point);
            fillbezspline: fn(dst: self ref Image, p: array of Point,
                            wind: int, src: ref Image, sp: Point);
            ellipse: fn(dst: self ref Image, c: Point, a, b,
                            thick: int, src: ref Image, sp: Point);
            fillellipse:fn(dst: self ref Image, c: Point, a, b: int,
                            src: ref Image, sp: Point);
            bezier: fn(dst: self ref Image, a,b,c,d: Point,
                            end0,end1,thick: int, src: ref Image, sp: Point);
            fillbezier: fn(dst: self ref Image, a,b,c,d: Point, wind:int,
                            src: ref Image, sp: Point);
            arrow: fn(a,b,c: int): int;
            text: fn(dst: self ref Image, p: Point, src: ref Image,
                            sp: Point, font: ref Font, str: string): Point;
            readpixels: fn(src: self ref Image, r: Rect,
                            data: array of byte): int;
            writepixels:fn(dst: self ref Image, r: Rect,
                            data: array of byte): int;
            top: fn(win: self ref Image);
            bottom: fn(win: self ref Image);
            flush: fn(win: self ref Image, func: int);
            origin: fn(win: self ref Image, log, scr: Point): int;
      };

DESCRIPTION
      The Image type defines rectangular pictures and the methods
      to draw upon them; it is also the building block for higher
      level objects such as windows and fonts. In particular, a
      window is represented as an Image; no special operators are
      needed to draw on a window.

      r   The coordinates of the rectangle in the plane for
                 which the Image has defined pixel values. It
                 should not be modified after the image is created.

clipr   The clipping rectangle: operations that read or
         write the image will not access pixels outside
         clipr. Frequently, clipr is the same as Image.r,
         but it may differ; see in particular the
         discussion of Image.repl. The clipping region may
         be modified dynamically.

ldepth   The log base 2 of the number of bits per pixel in
         the picture: 0 for one bit per pixel, 3 for eight
         bits per pixel, etc. The library supports
         Image.ldepth values 0, 1, 2, and 3 only. The value
         should not be modified after the image is created.

repl   A boolean value specifying whether the image is
         tiled to cover the plane when used as a source for
         a drawing operation. If Image.repl is zero,
         operations are restricted to the intersection of
         Image.r and Image.clipr. If Image.repl is set,
         Image.r defines the tile to be replicated and
         Image.clipr defines the portion of the plane
         covered by the tiling, in other words, Image.r is
         replicated to cover Image.clipr; in such cases
         Image.r and Image.clipr are independent.

         For example, a replicated image with Image.r set to
         ((0,0),(1,1)) and Image.clipr set to ((0,0),(100,100)),
         with the single pixel of Image.r set to blue,
         behaves identically to an image with Image.r and
         Image.clipr both set to ((0,0),(100,100)) and all
         pixels set to blue. However, the first image requires
         far less memory. The replication flag may be modified
         dynamically along with the clipping rectangle.

dst.draw(r, src, mask, p)
         Draw is the standard drawing function. Only those
         pixels within the intersection of dst.r and dst.clipr
         will be affected; draw ignores dst.repl. The operation
         proceeds as follows:

         1.   If repl is set in src or mask, replicate their
              contents to fill their clip rectangles.

         2.   Translate src and mask so p is aligned with r.min.

         3.   Set r to the intersection of r and dst.r.

         4.   Intersect r with src.clipr. If src.repl is false,
              also intersect r with src.r.

         5.   Intersect r with mask.clipr. If mask.repl is
              false, also intersect r with mask.r.

         6.   For each location in r for which the mask pixel is
              non-zero, set the dst pixel to be the value of the
              src pixel.

         The various ldepth values involved need not be
         identical. If the src or mask images are single
         replicated pixels, any ldepth is fine. Otherwise, if
         their ldepth is not the same as the destination, they
         must have ldepth value 0. For draw and gendraw only, if
         mask is nil, a mask of all ones is used. These
         restrictions may weaken in later implementations.

display
         Tells on which display the image resides.

screen
> If the image is a window on a Screen (see draw-screen (2)), this field refers to that screen; otherwise it is nil.

dst.gendraw(r, src, p0, mask, p1)
> Similar to draw() except that it aligns the source and mask differently: src is aligned so p0 corresponds to r .min and mask is aligned so p1 corresponds to r.min. For most purposes with simple masks and source images, draw is sufficient, but gendraw is the general operator and the one the other drawing primitives are built upon.

dst.line(p0, p1, end0, end1, thick, src, sp)
> Line draws in dst a line of width 1+2*thick pixels joining points p0 and p1. The line is drawn using pixels from the src image aligned so sp in the source corresponds to p0 in the destination. The line touches both p0 and p1, and end0 and end1 specify how the ends of the line are drawn. Draw->Endsquare terminates the line perpendicularly to the direction of the line; a thick line with Endsquare on both ends will be a rectangle. Draw->Enddisc terminates the line by drawing a disc of diameter 1+2*thick centered on the end point. Draw->Endarrow terminates the line with an arrowhead whose tip touches the endpoint. See the description of arrow for more information.
>
> Line and the other geometrical operators are equivalent to calls to gendraw using a mask produced by the geometric procedure.

dst.poly(p, end0, end1, thick, src, sp)
> Poly draws a general polygon; it is equivalent to a series of calls to line joining adjacent points in the array of Points p. The ends of the polygon are specified as in line; interior lines are terminated with Enddisc to make smooth joins. The source is aligned so sp corresponds to p[0].

dst.bezspline(p, end0, end1, thick, src, sp)
> Bezspline takes the same arguments as poly but draws a quadratic B-spline (despite its name) rather than a polygon. If the first and last points in p are equal, the spline has periodic end conditions.

dst.fillpoly(p, wind, src, sp)
> Fillpoly is like poly but fills in the resulting polygon rather than outlining it. The source is aligned so sp corresponds to p[0]. The winding rule parameter wind resolves ambiguities about what to fill if the polygon is self-intersecting. If wind is ~0, a pixel is inside the polygon if the polygon's winding number about the point is non-zero. If wind is 1, a pixel is inside if the winding number is odd. Complementary values (0 or ~1) cause outside pixels to be filled. The meaning of other values is undefined. The polygon is closed with a line if necessary.

dst.fillbezspline(p, wind, src, sp)
> Fillbezspline is like fillpoly but fills the quadratic B-spline rather than the polygon outlined by p. The spline is closed with a line if necessary.

dst.ellipse(c, a, b, thick, src, sp)
>   Ellipse draws in dst an ellipse centered on c with
>   horizontal and vertical semiaxes a and b. The source is
>   aligned so sp in src corresponds to c in dst. The
>   ellipse is drawn with thickness 1+2*thick.

dst.fillellipse(c, a, b, src, sp)
>   Fillellipse is like ellipse but fills the ellipse
>   rather than outlining it.

dst.bezier(a, b, c, d, end0, end1, thick, src, sp)
>   Bezier draws the cubic Bezier curve defined by Points a,
>   b, c and d. The end styles are determined by end0
>   and end1; the thickness of the curve is 1+2*thick. The
>   source is aligned so sp in src corresponds to a in dst.

dst.fillbezier(a, b, c, d, wind, src, sp)
>   Fillbezier is to bezier as fillpoly is to poly.

arrow(a, b, c)
>   Arrow is a function to describe general arrowheads; its
>   result is passed as end parameters to line, poly, etc.
>   If all three parameters are zero, it produces the
>   default arrowhead, otherwise, a sets the distance along
>   line from end of the regular line to tip, b sets the
>   distance along line from the barb to the tip, and c
>   sets the distance perpendicular to the line from edge
>   of line to the tip of the barb, all in pixels.

dst.text(p, src, sp, font, str)
>   Text draws in dst characters specified by the string
>   str and font font; it is equivalent to a series of
>   calls to gendraw using source src and masks determined
>   by the character shapes. The text is positioned with
>   the left of the first character at p.x and the top of
>   the line of text at p.y. The source is positioned so sp
>   in src corresponds to p in dst. Text returns a Point
>   that is the position of the next character that would
>   be drawn if the string were longer.
>
>   For characters with undefined or zero-width images in
>   the font, the character at font position 0 (NUL) is
>   drawn.

src.readpixels(r, data)
>   Readpixels fills the data array with pixels from the
>   specified rectangle of the src image. The pixels are
>   presented one horizontal line at a time, starting with
>   the top-left pixel of r. Each scan line starts with a
>   new byte in the array, leaving the last byte of the
>   previous line partially empty, if necessary. Pixels are
>   packed as tightly as possible within data, regardless
>   of the rectangle being extracted. Bytes are filled from
>   most to least significant bit order, as the x
>   coordinate increases, aligned so x=0 would appear as
>   the leftmost pixel of its byte. Thus, for ldepth 0, the
>   pixel at x offset 165 within the rectangle will be in a
>   data byte with mask value 16r04 regardless of the
>   overall rectangle: 165 mod 8 equals 5, and 16r80 >> 5
>   equals 16r04. It is an error to call readpixels with an
>   array that is too small to hold the rectangle's pixels.
>   The return value is the number of bytes copied.

dst.writepixels(r, data)
>   Writepixels copies pixel values from the data array to
>   the specified rectangle in the dst image. The format of
>   the data is that produced by readpixels. The return

value is the number of bytes copied. It is an error to
call writepixels with an array that is too small to
fill the rectangle.

win.top()

If the image win is a window, top pulls it to the
''top'' of the stack of windows on its Screen, perhaps
obscuring other images. If win is not a window, top has
no effect.

win.bottom()

If the image win is a window, bottom pulls it to the
''bottom'' of the stack of windows on its Screen,
perhaps obscuring it. If win is not a window, bottom
has no effect.

image.flush(flag)

The connection to a display has a buffer used to gather
graphics requests generated by calls to the draw
library. By default, the library flushes the buffer at
the conclusion of any call that affects the visible
display image itself. The flush routine allows finer
control of buffer management. The flag has three
possible values: Flushoff turns off all automatic
flushing caused by writes to image, typically a window
or the display image itself (buffers may still be
written when they fill or when other objects on the
display are modified); Flushnow causes the buffer to be
flushed immediately; and Flushon restores the default
behaviour.

win.origin(log, scr)

When a window is created (see draw-screen(2)), the
coordinate system within the window is identical to
that of the screen: the upper left corner of the window
rectangle is its physical location on the display, not
for example (0, 0). This symmetry may be broken,
however: origin allows control of the location of the
window on the display and the coordinate system used by
programs drawing on the window. The first argument, log,
sets the upper left corner of the logical (in-window)
coordinate system without changing the position of the
window on the screen. The second argument, scr, sets
the upper left corner of physical (on-screen)
coordinate system, that is, the window's location on
the display, without changing the internal coordinate
system. Therefore, changing scr without changing log
moves the window without requiring the client using it
to be notified of the change; changing log without
changing scr allows the client to set up a private
coordinate system regardless of the window's location.
It is permissible for values of scr to move some or all
of the window off screen. Origin returns -1 if the
image is not a window or, in the case of changes to scr,
if there are insufficient resources available to move
the window; otherwise it returns 1.

Inferno Manual

C.8 Fonts

NAME
      Font - character images for Unicode text

SYNOPSIS
      include   "draw.m";
      draw := load Draw Draw->PATH;

      Font: adt
      {
          name: string;
          height: int;
          ascent: int;
          display: ref Display;

          open: fn(d: ref Display, file: string):   ref Font;
          build: fn(d: ref Display, name, desc: string):   ref Font;
          width: fn(f: self ref Font, str: string):   int;
      };

DESCRIPTION
      The Font type defines the appearance of characters drawn
      with the Image.text primitive (see draw-image(2)). Fonts are
      usually read from files and are selected based on their
      size, their style, the portion of Unicode space they
      represent, and so on.

      Fonts are built from a series of subfonts that define
      contiguous portions of the Unicode character space, such as
      the ASCII or the Greek alphabet. Font files are textual
      descriptions of the allocation of characters in the various
      regions of the Unicode space; see font(6) for the format.
      Subfonts are not visible from Limbo.

      A default font, named *default*, is always available.

      The type incorporates:

      ascent, height
                  These define the vertical sizes of the font, in
                  pixels. The ascent is the distance from the font
                  baseline to the top of a line of text; height
                  gives the interline spacing, that is, the distance
                  from one baseline to the next.

      name   This field identifies the font, either the name of
                  the file from which the font was read, or
                  "*default*" for the default font.

      display   Tells on which display the font resides.

      open(d, file)
                  The open method creates a Font by reading the
                  contents of the named file. Fonts are cached, so
                  an open request may return a pointer to an
                  existing Font, without rereading the file. The
                  name "*default*" always describes a defined font.
                  Fonts are created for an instance of a Display
                  object, even though the creation functions are in
                  type Font.

      build(d, name, desc)
                  Build creates a Font object by reading the

description from the string desc rather than a
file. Name specifies the name of the font to be
created.

f.width(str)

The width method returns the width in pixels that
str would occupy if drawn by Image.text in the
Font f.

Inferno Manual

FONT(6)   FONT(6)

NAME
       font, subfont - external format for character fonts and
       subfonts

DESCRIPTION
       Fonts are constructed as a list defining a range of Unicode
       characters and a subfont containing the character images for
       that range. Subfonts are not directly accessible from Limbo.

       External fonts are described by a plain text file that can
       be read using Font.open; Font.build reads the same format
       from a string rather than a file (see draw-font(2)).

       The format is a header followed by any number of subfont
       range specifications. The header contains two numbers: the
       height and the ascent, both in pixels. The height is the
       inter-line spacing and the ascent is the distance from the
       top of the line to the baseline. These numbers should be
       chosen to display consistently all the subfonts of the font.
       A subfont range specification contains two or three numbers
       and a file name. The numbers are the inclusive range of
       characters covered by the subfont, with an optional starting
       position within the subfont, and the file name names an
       external file holding the subfont data. The minimum number
       of a covered range is mapped to the specified starting
       position (default zero) of the corresponding subfont. If the
       subfont file name does not begin with a slash, it is taken
       relative to the directory containing the font file. Each
       field must be followed by some white space. Each numeric
       field may be C-format decimal, octal, or hexadecimal.

       External subfonts are represented in a more rigid format: an
       image containing character images, followed by a subfont
       header, followed by character information. The image has the
       format for external image files described in image(6). The
       subfont header has 3 decimal strings: n, height, and ascent.
       Each number is right-justified and blank padded in 11
       characters, followed by a blank. The character info consists
       of n+1 6-byte entries, each giving values called x (2 bytes,
       low order byte first), top, bottom, left, and width for the
       successive characters from left to right (in increasing
       Unicode order) in the subfont. The rectangle holding the
       character is (x, top, xn, bottom), where xn is the x field
       of the next character. When the character is to be drawn in
       an image at point p, the rectangle is placed at (p.x+left,
       p.y) and the next character to be drawn is placed at
       (p.x+width, p.y). The x field of the last entry is used to
       calculate the image width of the previous character; the
       other fields in the last entry are irrelevant.

       Note that the convention of using the character with value
       zero (NUL) to represent characters of zero width (see the
       description of Image.text in draw-image(2)) means that fonts
       should have, as their zeroth character, one with non-zero
       width.

FILES
       /fonts/* font directories
SEE ALSO
       draw-intro(2), draw-font(2), draw(3)

                         Inferno Manual

C.9 Tk

NAME
     Tk - graphics toolkit

SYNOPSIS
     include "tk.m";
     tk := load Tk Tk->PATH;

     Tki: type ref Draw->Image;

     Toplevel: adt
     {
         id: int;
         image: ref Draw->Image;
     };

     toplevel: fn(screen: ref Draw->Screen, arg: string): ref Toplevel;
     namechan: fn(t: ref Toplevel, c: chan of string, n: string): string;
     cmd: fn(t: ref Toplevel, arg: string): string;
     mouse: fn(screen: ref Draw->Screen, x, y, button: int);
     keyboard: fn(screen: ref Draw->Screen, key: int);
     windows: fn(screen: ref Draw->Screen): list of ref Toplevel;
     intop: fn(screen: ref Draw->Screen, x, y: int): ref Toplevel;
     imageget: fn(t: ref Toplevel, name: string): (Tki, Tki, string);
     imageput: fn(t: ref Toplevel, name: string, i: Tki, m: Tki): string;

DESCRIPTION
     The Tk module provides primitives for building user
     interfaces, based on Ousterhout's Tcl/TK. The interface to
     the toolkit itself is primarily the passing of strings to
     and from the elements of the toolkit using the cmd function;
     see section 9 of this manual for more information about the
     syntax of those strings.

     Toplevel creates a new window called a Toplevel, which is
     under the control of the Tk toolkit, on an existing screen,
     usually one inherited from the graphics Context (see
     draw-context(2)). The Toplevel is passed to cmd and namechan
     (q.v.) to drive the widgets in the window. Arg is a string
     containing creation options (such as -borderwidth 2) that
     are applied when creating the toplevel window.

     Cmd passes command strings to the widgets in the Toplevel t
     and returns the string resulting from their execution. For
     example, given a canvas .c in the Toplevel t,
         x := int tk->cmd(t, ".c cget -actx");
     returns the integer x coordinate of the canvas.

     Bindings can be created in a Toplevel that trigger strings
     to be sent on Limbo channels. Such channels must be declared
     to the Tk module using namechan. For example, to create a
     button that sends the word Ouch when it is pressed:
         hitchannel := chan of string;
         tk->namechan(t, hitchannel, "channel");
         tk->cmd(t,
             "button .b.Hit -text Hit -command {send channel Ouch}");
         expl := <-hitchannel; # will see Ouch when button pressed

     Mouse and keyboard pass mouse and keyboard events to Tk, for
     delivery to widgets; they are usually called only by a
     window manager.

     Windows returns a list of windows on the given screen. Intop

returns a reference to the window under point (x,y) on the
given screen, returning nil if none is found.

Imageget returns copies of the image and mask of the Tk
bitmap or Tk widget with the given name associated with
Toplevel t; either Image could be nil. Imageput replaces the
image (i) and mask (m) of the Tk bitmap image name in t.
Both functions return strings that are nil if the operation
was successful, but contain a diagnostic on error (e.g.
invalid top level or name).

SOURCE
        /interp/tk.c
        /tk/*.c

SEE ALSO
        intro(9), tkcmd(1), sh-tk(1), draw-context(2), wmlib(2),
        'An Overview of Limbo/Tk', this manual, Volume 2.

BUGS
        Because Tk input is handled globally per Screen, there can
        be only one instance of a Tk implementation on a given
        machine, a restriction that will be lifted.

NAME
> intro - introduction to Inferno Tk

DESCRIPTION
> This section of the manual provides a reference for the
> Inferno Tk implementation, which is accessed by Limbo
> programs via tk(2), and from sh(1) via sh-tk(1).
>
> The following pages were derived by Vita Nuova from
> documentation that is
>
>> Copyright © 1990 The Regents of the University of
>> California
>> Copyright © 1994-1996 Sun Microsystems, Inc.
>> See copyright(9) for the full copyright notice.
>
> The format of the pages has changed to follow the format of
> the rest of this manual, but more important, the content has
> been changed (typically in small ways) to reflect the
> variant of Tk implemented by Inferno.

Programming Interface
> The interface to Inferno Tk is exclusively through the tk(2)
> module; all the Tk commands described in this section of the
> manual are excecuted by passing them as strings to the cmd
> function in that module. The Inferno Tk implementation is
> based on the Tk 4.0 documentation, but there are many
> differences, probably the greatest of which is that there is
> no associated Tcl implementation, so almost every Inferno
> application using Tk will need to have some Limbo code
> associated with it (the sh-tk(1) shell module can also
> fulful this role). See ''An Overview of Limbo/Tk'' in Volume
> 2 for a tutorial-style introduction to the use of Inferno Tk
> which summarises the differences from Tk 4.0.

Tk Commands
> The command string passed to tk->cmd may contain one or more
> Tk commands, separated by semicolons. A semicolon is not a
> command separator when it is nested in braces ({}) or
> brackets ([]) or it is escaped by a backslash (\). Each
> command is divided into words: sequences of characters
> separated by one or more blanks and tabs.
>
> There is also a 'super quote' convention: at any point in
> the command string a single quote mark (') means that the
> entire rest of the string should be treated as one word.
>
> A word beginning with an opening brace ({) continues until
> the balancing closing brace (}) is reached. The outer brace
> characters are stripped. A backslash can be used to escape a
> brace in this context. Backslash characters not used to
> escape braces are left unchanged.
>
> A word beginning with an opening bracket ([) continues until
> the balancing closing bracket (]) is reached. The enclosed
> string is then evaluated as if it were a command string, and
> the resulting value is used as the contents of the word.
>
> Single commands are executed in order until they are all
> done or an error is encountered. By convention, an error is
> signaled by a return value starting with an exclamation mark
> (!). The return value from tk->cmd is the return value of
> the first error-producing command or else the return value
> of the final single command.

To execute a single command, the first word is examined. It must either begin with dot (.) in which case it must name an existing widget, which will interpret the rest of the command according to its type, or one of the following words, each of which is documented in a manual page of that name in this section:

button	entry	listbox	destroy
menu	scale	pack	image
canvas	frame	bind	update
menubutton	scrollbar	focus	send
checkbutton	label	grab	variable
radiobutton	text	cursor	

Widget Options
Each manual page in this section documents the options that a particular command will accept. A number of options are common to several of the widgets and are named as ''standard options'' near the beginning of the manual page for each widget. These options are documented in options(9). The types of value required as arguments to options within Inferno Tk are documented under types(9).

SEE ALSO
options(9), types(9), tk(2), sh-tk(1), tkcmd(1), wmlib(2), draw-intro(2), ''An Overview of Limbo/Tk'' in Volume 2.

BUGS
The bracket ([]) command interpretation is not applied consistently throughout the Inferno Tk commands (notably, the argument to the send(9) command will not interpret this correctly). Moreover, if the string to be substituted is significantly bigger than the command it was substituting, then it will be truncated.

NAME
>   types - Standard types required by widget options.

DESCRIPTION
>   This manual entry describes the the standard types that can
>   be given as arguments to Inferno Tk widget options. When an
>   option is documented, the type of argument that it accepts
>   is either documented there, or the name of the argument
>   refers to one of the names documented below.

>   anchorPos
>>   One of the values n, ne, e, se, s, sw, w, nw, or center.
>>   See -anchor in options(9).

>   boolean
>>   A true or false value, one of the following: 0, no, off,
>>   false (false), 1, yes, on, true (true).

>   bitmap
>>   Identifies an image which can be drawn, or used as a
>>   mask through which something else is drawn. If bitmap
>>   begins with a '@', the remaining characters must be the
>>   path name of an Inferno image file. If bitmap begins
>>   with the character '<', the remaining characters must
>>   be a decimal integer giving the file descriptor number
>>   of an open file (see sys-open(2)) from which the bitmap
>>   can be loaded. Otherwise, bitmap should be the name of
>>   a bitmap file in the directory /icons/tk.

>   color
>>   A color parameter can be a color name or an RGB (red,
>>   green and blue luminance) value. The color names
>>   recognized are:

>> | aqua | yellow | red | teal | white |
>> |------|--------|-----|------|-------|
>> | fuchsia | black | blue | darkblue | |
>> | maroon | gray | green | lime | |
>> | purple | navy | olive | orange | |

>>   For RGB values, either #rgb or #rrggbb can be used,
>>   where r, rr, etc. are hexadecimal values for the
>>   corresponding color components.

>   dist
>>   Dist specifies a distance on the screen, in the
>>   following form: an optional minus sign (-), then one or
>>   more decimal digits (with possible embedded decimal
>>   point), then an optional units specifier. The unit
>>   specifiers are the following:

>>   c   centimeters

>>   m   millimeters

>>   i   inches

>>   p   points (1/72nd inch)

>>   h   height of widget's font (only applicable if the
>>   widget has an associated font, and if the font has
>>   previously been set).

>>   w   width of the zero (0) character in widget's font
>>   (see above).

>>   Measurements are converted into pixels assuming 100
>>   dots per inch on an average CRT display.

font
     A font parameter gives the full path name of an Inferno
     font file; for example, /fonts/pelm/unicode.9.font.

frac
     A numeric, possibly fractional, value.

relief
     One of raised, sunken, flat, ridge, or groove. See
     -relief in options(9).

SEE ALSO
     intro(9), options(9)

                      Inferno Manual

NAME
    options - Standard options supported by widgets.

DESCRIPTION
    This manual entry describes the common configuration options
    supported by widgets in the Tk toolkit. Every widget does
    not necessarily support every option (see the manual entries
    for individual widgets for a list of the standard options
    supported by that widget), but if a widget does support an
    option with one of the names listed below, then the option
    has exactly the effect described below. For a description of
    kinds of values that can passed to the various options, see
    types(9).

    In the descriptions below, the name refers to the switch
    used in class commands and configure widget commands to set
    this value. For example, if an option's command-line switch
    is set to -foreground and there exists a widget .a.b.c, then
    the command may be used to specify the value black for the
    option in the the widget .a.b.c.

    -activebackground color
        Specifies background color to use when drawing active
        elements. An element (a widget or portion of a widget)
        is active if the mouse cursor is positioned over the
        element and pressing a mouse button will cause some
        action to occur.

    -activeborderwidth dist
        Specifies a non-negative value indicating the width of
        the 3-D border drawn around active elements. See above
        for definition of active elements. This option is
        typically only available in widgets displaying more
        than one element at a time (e.g. menus but not
        buttons).

    -activeforeground color
        Specifies foreground color to use when drawing active
        elements. See above for definition of active elements.

    -actx
        Returns the current x position of the widget relative
        to the origin of its top-level window.

    -acty
        Returns the current y position of the widget relative
        to the origin of its top-level window.

    -actwidth
        Returns the current allocated width of the widget.

    -actheight
        Returns the current allocated height of the widget.

    -anchor val
        Specifies how the information in a widget (e.g. text or
        a bitmap) is to be displayed in the widget. Val must be
        one of the values n, ne, e, se, s, sw, w, nw, or center.
        rFor example, nw means display the information such
        that its top-left corner is at the top-left corner of
        the widget.

    -background color or -bg color
        Specifies the normal background color to use when
        displaying the widget.

-bitmap bitmap
>   Specifies a bitmap to display in the widget. The exact
>   way in which the bitmap is displayed may be affected by
>   other options such as anchor or justify. Typically, if
>   this option is specified then it overrides other
>   options that specify a textual value to display in the
>   widget; the bitmap option may be reset to an empty
>   string to re-enable a text display. In widgets that
>   support both bitmap and image options, image will
>   usually override bitmap.

-borderwidth dist or -bd dist
>   Specifies a non-negative value indicating the width of
>   the 3-D border to draw around the outside of the widget
>   (if such a border is being drawn; the relief option
>   typically determines this). The value may also be used
>   when drawing 3-D effects in the interior of the widget.

-font font
>   Specifies the font to use when drawing text inside the
>   widget.

-foreground color or -fg color
>   Specifies the normal foreground color to use when
>   displaying the widget.

-image image
>   Specifies an image to display in the widget, which must
>   have been created with the image create command.
>   Typically, if the image option is specified then it
>   overrides other options that specify a bitmap or
>   textual value to display in the widget; the image
>   option may be reset to an empty string to re-enable a
>   bitmap or text display.

-jump boolean
>   For widgets with a slider that can be dragged to adjust
>   a value, such as scrollbars, this option determines
>   when notifications are made about changes in the value.
>   If the value is false, updates are made continuously as
>   the slider is dragged. If the value is true, updates
>   are delayed until the mouse button is released to end
>   the drag; at that point a single notification is made
>   (the value ''jumps'' rather than changing smoothly).

-justify val
>   When there are multiple lines of text displayed in a
>   widget, this option determines how the lines line up
>   with each other. Val must be one of left, center, or
>   right. Left means that the lines' left edges all line
>   up, center means that the lines' centers are aligned,
>   and right means that the lines' right edges line up.

-orient orientation
>   For widgets that can lay themselves out with either a
>   horizontal or vertical orientation, such as scrollbars,
>   this option specifies which orientation should be used.
>   Orientation must be either horizontal or vertical.

-padx dist
>   Specifies a non-negative value indicating how much
>   extra space to request for the widget in the
>   X-direction. When computing how large a window it
>   needs, the widget will add this amount to the width it
>   would normally need (as determined by the width of the
>   things displayed in the widget); if the geometry

manager can satisfy this request, the widget will end
up with extra internal space to the left and/or right
of what it displays inside. Most widgets only use this
option for padding text: if they are displaying a
bitmap or image, then they usually ignore padding
options.

-pady dist
      Specifies a non-negative value indicating how much
      extra space to request for the widget in the
      Y-direction. When computing how large a window it
      needs, the widget will add this amount to the height it
      would normally need (as determined by the height of the
      things displayed in the widget); if the geometry
      manager can satisfy this request, the widget will end
      up with extra internal space above and/or below what it
      displays inside. Most widgets only use this option for
      padding text: if they are displaying a bitmap or
      image, then they usually ignore padding options.

-relief val
      Specifies the 3-D effect desired for the widget.
      Acceptable values for val are raised, sunken, flat,
      ridge and groove. The value indicates how the
      interior of the widget should appear relative to its
      exterior; for example, raised means the interior of
      the widget should appear to protrude from the screen,
      relative to the exterior of the widget.

-selectbackground color
      Specifies the background color to use when displaying
      selected items.

-selectborderwidth dist
      Specifies a non-negative value indicating the width of
      the 3-D border to draw around selected items.

-selectforeground color
      Specifies the foreground color to use when displaying
      selected items.

-text val
      Specifies a string, val, to be displayed inside the
      widget. The way in which the string is displayed
      depends on the particular widget and may be determined
      by other options, such as anchor or justify.

-underline integer
      Specifies the integer index of a character to underline
      in the widget. This option is used by the default
      bindings to implement keyboard traversal for menu
      buttons and menu entries. 0 corresponds to the first
      character of the text displayed in the widget, 1 to the
      next character, and so on.

-xscrollcommand command
      Specifies the prefix for a command used to communicate
      with horizontal scrollbars. When the view in the
      widget's window changes (or whenever anything else
      occurs that could change the display in a scrollbar,
      such as a change in the total size of the widget's
      contents), the widget will generate a Tk command by
      concatenating command and two numbers. Each of the
      numbers is a fraction between 0 and 1, which indicates
      a position in the document. 0 indicates the beginning
      of the document, 1 indicates the end, .333 indicates a
      position one third the way through the document, and so

on. The first fraction indicates the first information
in the document that is visible in the window, and the
second fraction indicates the information just after
the last portion that is visible. The command is then
passed to the Tk interpreter for execution. Typically
the -xscrollcommand option consists of the path name of
a scrollbar widget followed by ''set'', e.g.
''.x.scrollbarset'': this will cause the scrollbar to be
updated whenever the view in the window changes. If
this option is not specified, then no command will be
executed.

-yscrollcommand command
    Specifies the prefix for a command used to communicate
    with vertical scrollbars. This option is treated in
    the same way as the -xscrollcommand option, except that
    it is used for vertical scrollbars and is provided by
    widgets that support vertical scrolling. See the
    description of -xscrollcommand for details on how this
    option is used.

Bibliography

1. 1990 *Understanding Computers: Computer Languages*. Time-Life Books, Alexandria, VA.

2. H. Abelson, G. J. Sussman and J. Sussman, 1996 *Structure and Interpretation of Computer Programs*. MIT Press, Cambridge, MA, 2nd edn.

3. R. H. Baer, W. T. Rusch and W. L. Harrison, 1972 Television gaming apparatus and method. US Patent number 3 659 285, Sanders Associates, Inc., Nashua, NH.

4. E. R. Berlekamp, J. H. Conway and R. K. Guy, 1982 What is life? *Winning Ways for Your Mathematical Plays* **2**.

5. M. Blaze, 1993 A cryptographic file system for Unix. In *Proceedings of the First ACM Conference on Computer and Communications Security*, pp. 9–16. Fairfax, VA.

6. M. Blaze, 1994 Key management in an encrypting file system. In *USENIX Summer 1994 Technical Conference, Boston, MA*.

7. R. E. Bryant and D. R. O'Hallaron, 2003 *Computer Systems: A Programmer's Perspective*. Prentice-Hall.

8. N. Bushnell, 1974 Video image positioning control system for amusement device. US Patent number 3 793 483.

9. D. R. Butenhof, 1997 *Programming with POSIX Threads*. Addison-Wesley.

10. D. E. Comer, 2000 *Internetworking With TCP/IP*, Vol. I: *Principles Protocols, and Architecture*, 4th edn. Prentice-Hall.

11. D. E. Comer and D. L. Stevens, 1999 *Internetworking With TCP/IP*, Vol. II: *Design, Implementation and Internals*. Prentice-Hall, 3rd edn.

12. D. E. Comer and D. L. Stevens, 2000 *Internetworking With TCP/IP*, Vol. III: *Client–Server Programming and Applications, Linux/POSIX Socket Version*. Prentice-Hall.

13. R. Cox, E. Grosse, R. Pike, D. L. Presotto and S. Quinlan, 2002 Security in Plan 9. In *Proceedings of the 11th USENIX Security Symposium*, pp. 3–16. San Francisco, CA.

14. W. Diffie and M. E. Hellman, 1976 New directions in cryptography. *IEEE Transactions on Information Theory* **IT-22**, 644–654.

15. S. M. Dorward, R. Pike, D. L. Presotto, D. M. Ritchie, H. Trickey and P. Winterbottom, 1997 The Inferno operating system. *Bell Labs Technical Journal* **2**, 5–18.

16. T. ElGamal, 1984 A public-key cryptosystem and a signature scheme based on discrete logarithms. *Advances in Cryptology: Proceedings of CRYPTO 84* **196**, 10–18.

17. J. Foley, A. van Dam, S. Feiner and J. Hughes, 1996 *Computer Graphics: Principles and Practice in C*, 2nd edn. Addison-Wesley.

18. J. M. Fossaceca, J. D. Sandoz and P. Winterbottom, 1998 The PathStar access server: facilitating carrier-grade packet telephony. *Bell Labs Technical Journal* **3**, 86–102.

19. M. Fratto, 2001 Lucent Brick 1000 and LSMS 6.0 (BETA): Hotter than a Haitian sunset. *Network Computing* 1219 (September).

20. M. Fratto, 2002 Improvements tighten Lucent's security management server. *Network Computing* 1316 (August).

21. W. K. Giloi, 1978 *Interactive Computer Graphics. Data Structures, Algorithms, Languages*. Prentice-Hall.

22. D. Goldberg, 1991 What every computer scientist should know about floating-point arithmetic. *ACM Computing Surveys* **23**, 5–48.

23. E. Grosse, 1997 Real Inferno. In *Proceedings of the IFIPTC2/WG2.5 Working Conference on the Quality of Numerical Software, Assessment and Enhancement* (ed. R. F. Boisvert), pp. 270–279. Oxford.

24. J. Gutknecht, 1984 Tutorial on Modula-2. *BYTE* **9**(8), 157–176.

25. C. A. R. Hoare, 1978 Communicating sequential processes. *Communications of the ACM* **21**, 666–677.

26. L. Huelsbergen and P. Winterbottom, 1998 Very concurrent mark-&-sweep garbage collection without fine-grain synchronization. In *Proceedings of the First International Symposium on Memory Management*, pp. 166–175. Vancouver.

27. B. W. Kernighan, 1996 A descent into Limbo. Unpublished document, available on the WWW.

28. B. W. Kernighan and C. J. Van Wyk, 1998 Timing trials, or the trials of timing: experiments with scripting and user-interface languages. *Software—Practice and Experience* **28**, 819–843.

29. T. J. Killian, 1984 Processes as files. In *Proceedings of the 1984 Usenix Summer Conference*, pp. 203–207. Salt Lake City, UT.

30. B. Liskov, 1993 A history of CLU. *ACM SIGPLAN Notices* **28**, 133–147.

31. Lucent Technologies, 2000 Dis virtual machine specification. In *Inferno 3rd Edition Programmer's Manual, vol. 2*. Vita Nuova Holdings Ltd.

32. Lucent Technologies, 2000 An overview of Limbo/Tk. In *Inferno 3rd Edition Programmer's Manual, vol. 2*. Vita Nuova Holdings Ltd.

33. M. D. McIlroy, 1990 Squinting at power series. *Software—Practice and Experience* **20**, 661–683.

34. M. K. McKusick and K. Bostic and M. J. Karels and J. S. Quarterman, 1996 *The Design and Implementation of the 4.4BSD Operating System*. Addison-Wesley.

35. N. H. Margolus, 1999 Crystalline computation. In *Feynman and Computation* (ed. A. Hey), pp. 267–305. Perseus Books.

36. P. Mattos, 1984 The transputer. *IEE Colloquium on New Microprocessors, London*, vol. 97, pp. 1–3.

37. D. May, 1984 Occam. In *IFIP Conference on System Implementation Languages: Experience and Assessment*. Canterbury.

38. D. May and R. Shepherd, 1984 The transputer implementation of Occam. In *Proceedings of the International Conference on Fifth Generation Computer Systems*, pp. 533–541. Tokyo.

39. R. Milner, 1980 *A calculus of communicating systems*. Lecture Notes in Computer Science, vol. 92.

40. R. Milner, 1993 Elements of interaction. *Communications of the ACM* **36**, 78–89.

41. R. Milner, 1999 *Communicating and Mobile Systems: The π Calculus*. Cambridge University Press.

42. R. Milner, M. Tofte and R. W. Harper, 1990 *The Definition of Standard ML*. MIT Press, Cambridge, Massachusetts.

43. P. Morrissey, 2001 Follow the mellow brick road. *Network Computing*, 1223 (November).

44. National Institute of Standards and Technology 1993 *FIPS PUB 180: Secure Hash Standard (SHS)*. National Institute of Standards and Technology, Gaithersburg, MD.

45. National Institute of Standards and Technology 1995 *FIPS PUB 180-1: Secure Hash Standard*. National Institute for Standards and Technology, Gaithersburg, MD, USA. Supersedes FIPS PUB 180 1993 May 11.

46. J. von Neumann, 1966 *Theory of Self-Reproducing Automata*. University of Illinois Press, Urbana. Edited and completed by A. W. Burks.

47. B. Nichols, D. Buttlar and J. Proulx Farrell, 1996 *Pthreads Programming, A POSIX Standard for Better Multiprocessing*, 1st edn. O'Reilly & Associates.

48. J. K. Ousterhout, 1994 *Tcl and the Tk Toolkit*. Addison-Wesley.

49. B. C. Pierce, 2002 *Types and Programming Languages*. MIT Press, Cambridge, MA.

50. R. Pike, 1990 The implementation of Newsqueak. *Software—Practice and Experience* **20**, 649–659.

51. R. Pike, 1994 Acme: a user interface for programmers. In *Proceedings of the Winter 1994 USENIX Conference*, pp. 223–234. San Francisco.

52. R. Pike, 2000 Lexical file names in Plan 9, or getting dot-dot right. In *USENIX Annual Technical Conference* pp. 85–92, San Diego, CA.

53. R. Pike, D. Presotto, S. Dorward, B. Flandrena, K. Thompson, H. Trickey and P. Winterbottom, 1995 Plan 9 from Bell Labs. *Computing Systems* **8**, 221–254.

54. R. Pike, D. Presotto, K. Thompson and H. Trickey, 1991 Designing Plan 9. *Dr. Dobb's Journal of Software Tools* **16**, 49–50, 52, 54, 56–60.

55. Plan 9 Distribution. http://www.cs.bell-labs.com/plan9dist/.

56. Plan 9 File Protocol, 9P, 2002 *Plan 9 4th Edition Programmers Manual, Section 5*. Lucent Technologies, Murray Hill, NJ.

57. T. Porter and T. Duff, 1984 Compositing digital images. *Computer Graphics* **18**, 253–259.

58. D. L. Presotto, 1997 Inferno security. In *Proceedings of IEEE Compcon '97*, pp. 251–253.

59. D. Presotto and P. Winterbottom, 1993 The organization of networks in Plan 9. In *Proceedings of the Usenix Winter 1993 Technical Conference*, pp. 271–280.

60. R. Peppé, 2000 Program development under Inferno. In *Inferno 3rd Edition Programmer's Manual, vol. 2*. Vita Nuova Holdings Ltd.

61. L. Rau, 1997 Programming in Limbo. *BYTE* **22**, 53–54.

62. M. Reiser, 1991 *The Oberon System—User Guide and Programmer's Manual*. Addison-Wesley.

63. E. Rescorla, 2000 *SSL and TLS: Designing and Building Secure Systems*, 1st edn. Addison Wesley Professional.

64. D. Ritchie, 1998 Invited talk. In *MASPLAS*, New Brunswick, NJ.

65. D. Ritchie and R. Pike, 1999 The Styx architecture for distributed systems. *Bell Labs Technical Journal* **4**, 146–152.

66. D. M. Ritchie, 2000 The Limbo programming language. In *Inferno 3rd Edition Programmer's Manual, vol. 2*. Vita Nuova Holdings Ltd.

67. W. T. Rusch, 1972 Television gaming apparatus. US Patent number 3 659 284. Sanders Associates, Inc., Nashua, NH.

68. P. H. Salus, 1994 *A Quarter Century of Unix*, 1st edn. Addison-Wesley.

69. R. Sandberg, D. Goldberg, S. Kleiman, D. Walsh and B. Lyon, 1985 Design and implementation of the Sun network filesystem. In *Proceedings of the Summer USENIX Conference*, pp. 119–130. Portland, OR.

70. D. Sangiorgi and D. Walker, 2001 *The π Calculus. A Theory of Mobile Processes*, 1st edn. Cambridge University Press.

71. B. Schneier, 1994 *Applied Cryptography: Protocols, Algorithms and Source Code in C*. John Wiley & Sons, Inc., New York.

72. R. Sharma, 1999 Distributed application development with Inferno. In *Proceedings of the 36th Design Automation Conference (DAC'99)*, pp. 146–150.

73. P. Shirley, 2002 *Fundamentals of Computer Graphics*. A K Peters Ltd, 1st edn.

74. W. Stallings, 1998 *Cryptography and Network Security: Principles and Practice*, 2nd edn. Prentice-Hall International.

75. P. Stanley-Marbell, 2000 Inferno application development with Limbo. *Dr. Dobb's Journal of Software Tools* **25**, 113–114, 116, 118, 120.

76. A. S. Tanenbaum, 1992 *Modern Operating Systems*. Prentice-Hall, Englewood Cliffs, NJ.

77. A. S. Tanenbaum and A. S. Woodhull, 1997 *Operating Systems—Design and Implementation*, 2nd edn. Prentice-Hall, Upper Saddle River, NJ.

78. T. Toffoli and N. Margolus, 1987 *Cellular Automata Machines: A New Environment for Modeling*. MIT Press, Cambridge, MA.

79. Vita Nuova Holdings Limited, 2000 *Inferno 3rd Edition Programmer's Manual*, Vol. 1.

80. Vita Nuova Holdings Ltd.2000 Installation of the Inferno software. In *Inferno 3rd Edition Programmer's Manual, vol. 2*. Vita Nuova Holdings Ltd.

81. P. Winterbottom, 1992 Alef Language Reference Manual. In *Plan 9 Programmer's Manual*. AT&T Bell Laboratories, Murray Hill, NJ.

82. P. Winterbottom and R. Pike, 1997 The design of the Inferno virtual machine. In *Hot Chips IX*. IEEE Computer Society Press.

83. N. Wirth, 1982 *Programming in Modula-2*. Springer.

84. N. Wirth, 1988 The programming language Oberon. *Software—Practice and Experience* **18**, 671–690.

85. C. F. Yurkoski, L. R. Rau and B. K. Ellis, 1998 *Using Inferno to execute Java on small devices*. Lecture Notes in Computer Science, vol. 1474, pp. 108–118.

86. E. Zadok, I. Badulescu and A. Shender, 1998 Cryptfs: a stackable Vnode level encryption file system. Technical Report CUCS-021-98, Computer Science Department, Columbia University.

Index